Peter Winch

Philosophy Now

Series Editor: John Shand

This is a fresh and vital series of new introductions to today's most important and exciting philosophers. Combining rigorous analysis with authoritative exposition, each book gives clear, comprehensive and enthralling access to the ideas of those who have made a defining and original contribution to the discipline. Together the volumes comprise a remarkable gallery of the thinkers who have been at the forefront of philosophical ideas.

Published:

Peter Winch
Colin Lyas

Forthcoming titles include:

Donald Davidson
Marc Joseph

Michael Dummett
Bernhard Weiss

Nelson Goodman
Gabriela Sakamoto

Thomas Kuhn
Alexander Bird

Thomas Nagel
Alan Thomas

Robert Nozick
Alan Lacey

John Rawls
Catherine Audard

John Searle
Nicholas Fotion

Peter Strawson
Julian Dodd

Charles Taylor
Ruth Abbey

Peter Winch

Colin Lyas

*For Cyril George Lyas and
Margaret Elizabeth Lyas*

My parents and my friends

© Colin Lyas, 1999

This book is copyright under the Berne Convention.
No reproduction without permission.
All rights reserved.

First published in 1999 by Acumen

Acumen Publishing Limited
17 Fairfax Road
Teddington
TW11 9DJ

ISBN: 1-902683-01-3 (hardcover)
ISBN: 1-902683-02-1 (paperback)

British Library Cataloguing-in-Publication Data
A catalogue record for this book is available
from the British Library.

Excerpt from "Little Gidding" in Four Quartets, © 1943 by T. S. Eliot and
renewed 1971 by Esme Valerie Eliot, reprinted by permission of Harcourt
Brace & Company.

Designed and typeset in Century Schoolbook
by Kate Williams, Abergavenny.
Printed and bound by Biddles Ltd., Guildford and King's Lynn.

Contents

	Preface	vi
	Introduction: Peter Winch, a glimpse of a life	1
1	"Such understanding as I have": The influence of Wittgenstein	9
2	"I was investigating the notion of the social": The idea of a social science	39
3	"Seriously to study another way of life": Understanding another society	69
4	"Good examples are indispensable": The ethical life	101
5	"The concept of God is used": The religious forms of life	129
6	"The interval of hesitation": Peter Winch's Simone Weil	155
7	"Someone willing to die for truth": Peter Winch's legacy	181
	Envoi	205
	References	207
	Index	211

Preface

There is a form of philosophical perplexity that arises out of knowledge and that is an essential precondition for philosophizing. I found myself in that condition when I first encountered Bishop Berkeley's apparent demonstration of the "impossibility that the objects around me should have any existence out of the minds or thinking things that perceive them".

But there is another kind of perplexity, which I often felt as a beginning student, and which I often still feel: a perplexity that arises out of a *lack* of knowledge, that must be remedied if philosophy is to be done at all. Often I hear names mentioned, with a certain reverence, by those who purport to be insiders; mentioned, moreover, with the implication that anyone interested in philosophy will be on easy nodding terms with the deliberations of the bearers of those names. And of those names and their associated deliberations I am quite ignorant. Sometimes, of course, the names aren't that important, being instances of that law of propinquity by which graduate students are fated to overestimate their supervisors. More often the names *are* important, and knowledge of the deliberations of their bearers is a prerequisite for engaging in philosophy.

Where such names are rooted in the history of the subject, overcoming ignorance is easy. Histories of philosophy abound. When we come to contemporary philosophy, and to its influential figures, matters become more difficult. The student hears such names as Quine, Kripke, Davidson, Dummett and Goodman mentioned by philosophers in the kinds of tones reserved, in other contexts, for

Preface

Michael Jordan, Radiohead or Jennifer Aniston, and has no idea what contribution has been made to philosophy by this or that name, nor how that contribution fits into the overall map of philosophy. This volume seeks to elucidate the work of one such name: Peter Winch. My aims are threefold. My first aim is to tell the reader why Winch is an important philosopher, a task that requires only that I tell the reader what Winch actually said and why he said it. My second aim is to describe for that reader the main kinds of objections that have been offered to Winch's work. My third aim is to bring the reader to see where Winch's work fits into the overall map of philosophy and, so, to bring the reader some understanding of the present state of that subject. Of course, Winch's work provides only one window through which to survey the scene, each of the philosophers in the present series providing another. I have been acutely aware that the constraints imposed by a short general introduction have led me to terminate discussions just at the point where further work needs to be done. But I shall be contented if that stimulates the reader to some necessary further work.

My interest in the kind of philosophy to be found in Peter Winch's work, a philosophy much indebted to the work of Wittgenstein, was first cultivated under the very different influences of Norman Malcolm and Max Black when I had the extraordinary good fortune to be at Cornell University. I owe a very great debt to them both. I have also been very much helped by the work of many other philosophers, some friends, and some who I have, to my loss, never met. They include Cyril Barrett, Dick Beardsmore, Stanley Cavell, Ted Cohen, Ilham Dilham, Rai Gaita, Peter Hacker, Ossie Hanfling, Roy Holland, Hild Leslie, Peter Lewis, Graham Mcfee, Michael McGhee, Marie McGinn, Stephen Mulhall, Dewi Phillips, Bob Sharpe, Tim Tessin and Ben Tilghman. My understanding of sociology has been aided by the extensive library and the equally extensive knowledge of Dr John Leslie.

Various institutions have been an inspiration to me. One is the University of Swansea, where Peter Winch had his first lectureship, and which has, without always receiving its proper due, kept alive an important way of approaching philosophy. On that score, I must also mention the University of Bergen, from whose philosophers I have often received help and friendship.

A culture is emerging in the higher education system of this country that is forcing apart teaching (which is increasingly

Peter Winch

becoming a form of meagrely rewarded indoor relief for the postgraduate poor) from something called "research", where only published research is counted (scholarship being beneath notice). It was with enormous relief, therefore, that I discovered that there are, particularly in the USA, institutions resistant to this ethos. I had the singular good fortune to teach at one of them, Carleton College in Minnesota, where I found living proof of my unyielding conviction that it is possible to combine the very highest standards of research and scholarship with an unwavering devotion to the intellectual and humane development of one's students. Indeed, the two are inseparable. The influence of the life of that institution on me has been very great and I am happy to acknowledge again my debt to it.

Edinburgh, March 1998

> It hath been usual, with the honest and well-meaning host, to provide a bill of fare, which all persons may peruse at their first entry into the house: and having thence acquainted themselves with the entertainment they may expect, may enter, stay and regale with what is provided for them or may depart to some ordinary better accommodated to their taste. . . . The provision then which we have made here is no other than HUMAN NATURE.
> (Henry Fielding, Tom Jones, Book 1, Preface)

Introduction
Peter Winch, a glimpse of a life

This is not a biography of Peter Winch. In particular it does not discuss Winch's private life, intrusions into which he resisted. It is no more than an attempt to give my reader some sense of a rather special human being. Peter Winch was born in London in 1926. Towards the end of the Second World War he served on a naval destroyer. In this there is a peculiar connection with Norman Malcolm, who was later to become his close friend, and with whom he shared the inheritance of Wittgenstein's manner of philosophizing. Malcolm, too, served on destroyers, his comments on the boredom of war in the navy drawing a typical rejoinder from Wittgenstein, whose own record in the First World War was quite extraordinary (Malcolm 1958; Monk 1990: Ch. 6). Winch served as sonar operator and perfected his German during shore patrols in various German ports in the immediate aftermath of the war. It is reported that his interest in philosophy was aroused by conversations with an officer on his destroyer, but I am unable to identify that officer. Whoever he was, his influence set Winch on a distinguished career. After the war he completed his BA at Oxford University and followed this with a BPhil, during the course of studies for which he was influenced by Ryle; an influence that is clearly perceivable in an early paper (Winch 1953). In 1951 he was appointed to his first academic position as assistant lecturer in philosophy at University College, Swansea in the University of Wales. He thus became one of that extraordinarily impressive list of postwar philosophers who have held positions at Swansea, a list that includes such talents as Dick

Beardsmore, Karl Britton, Cora Diamond, W. B. Gallie, Roy Holland, O. R. Jones and Rush Rhees. (I spare the blushes of its active and living members by leaving them in undeserved anonymity.)

The Swansea in which Winch arrived was one of those distinctive provincial communities that are rapidly being eroded in the homogenization produced by the rapid growth of communications. (The Bradford of J. B. Priestly, the Manchester of the still lamented *Manchester Guardian* and the Free Trade Hall, the Nottingham of D. H. Lawrence, and the Stoke-on-Trent of John Wain, also come to mind in this connection.) It was a Swansea where Dylan Thomas could be met in pubs, although he was but one representative of a local culture. A more wicked glimpse of that provincial life can, however, be had from Kingsley Amis's *Take a girl like you* (not well filmed as *That uncertain feeling*). (A further glimpse of the penury to which assistant lecturers were subjected can be had from *Lucky Jim,* Amis's immortal exposé of academic life as viewed, looking upward, from its nether regions.) The younger Kingsley Amis was a colleague and a friend to, and, on at least one occasion, a co-author with Peter Winch (Amis *et al.* 1961).

At Swansea, Winch quickly made his mark. In 1953 he produced a striking paper in which he discussed the philosopher Reid from the new perspective that Ryle had given his contemporaries (Winch 1953). The same commitment to a different way of doing philosophy, but now with a reference to Wittgenstein, was also evidenced in an article for *Universities Quarterly* defending that new perspective against charges that this approach, always too loosely called "linguistic" philosophy, trivialized the subject. I rather cherish the following passage as capturing some of Winch's distinctive combination of trenchant and perceptive judgement economically achieved:

> The whole orientation is towards the understanding of the significance of various forms of human activity. The majority of its practitioners, no doubt, have little of permanent value to contribute to such an understanding; but that defect lies in the calibre of the individuals concerned, not in the method of philosophising developed by Wittgenstein.
>
> (Winch 1955–6: p. 37)

Also to be remarked on, and dating from this time, if only for the accuracy of its forecasts, is a remarkable article on the

Introduction

dangers confronting universities (Winch 1957–8). This begins with the typically pugnacious remark that "universities have no purpose whatsoever: they belong to a category which does not logically permit of a purpose" (Winch 1957–8: p. 14), and continues that "only by seeing that university education has no purpose can we see that it has a point" (1957: p. 15). The mistake is to look for that point as lying "outside academic work in itself" (1957: p. 15), a remark he also applies in his later writings to ethics (Winch 1972: pp. 173ff.). Hence, "what makes sense to a university worker is internal to the context of his work. It may not make sense to the different life of a businessman, but that is no reflection on its validity" (1972: p. 15). That passionate concern with the value of, and the need for integrity in, academic life never left Winch. It showed itself, too, in more practical ways, in his influence on the conduct of academic affairs at Swansea. Roy Holland kindly made available to me unpublished internal memoranda that have a bearing on this, including proposals that would have made courses with a philosophical orientation central to the general education of students. Winch also produced in that unpublished material a striking intervention in a dispute over the censorship of an undergraduate journal called *Dawn*, which deliciously begins:

> I am told that there are some undergraduates who cannot see why *Dawn* should be published at all. I am sorry for them on account of the state of their souls. I am also sorry for myself on account of belonging to a college where such views are allowed influence when it comes to allocating student funds. (Word has even got out that the acquisition of a television set in the Student's Union was not unconnected with the non-appearance of *Dawn* that year. But to believe this would be to contemplate depths of depravity that I should be unwilling to face).

The article stresses something that was integral to Winch's philosophy. This was a commitment to the notion that there must be a place (and where else, if not in academic life) for "uninhibited discussion", for "it is through critical discussion that standards of good work arise. And standards which an individual develops in this way will have the inestimable advantage of being his own". Would that lesson could be learned by the lunatics who now propagate the gospel of self-instruction by packaged learning. To them I offer Winch's reply that, without proper opportunities for

3

discussion, opportunities, I add, not granted in packed "seminars":

> We have a danger that students' standards will be a mere superficial varnish applied from without. How real a danger this is can perhaps only appear to those who have, in checking essays and examination scripts, to plough through garbled regurgitation of imperfectly understood material which they have disseminated in their own lectures.

Two things came together for Winch at Swansea. One was the beginning of a deeper understanding of Wittgenstein. Wittgenstein had had close associations with Swansea through his friend and executor Rush Rhees. Winch continually acknowledges a debt to Rhees for the influence of his thinking, including his thinking about Wittgenstein. Very much later, at King's College in London, Winch, Rees and Malcolm were to come together in a formidable triumvirate; sharing a deepening understanding of Wittgenstein with each other and with those fortunate to study with them. Second, Winch took over the teaching of a course in which students of social administration did some philosophy. That brought a tradition of thinking inherited from Wittgenstein face to face with things that were being said in social studies. This produced an article, published in 1956, which stands as the prolegomena to Winch's more extended work on the social sciences; and which is a useful short introduction to that work (Winch 1956). That in turn led Roy Holland, a colleague at Swansea and the editor for Routledge and Kegan Paul of a distinguished series entitled "Studies in philosophical psychology", to commission what was published in 1958 as *The idea of a social science*. That work had what Tony Palmer calls, a "succès de scandale" (Palmer 1992) and took an important section of the world of philosophy by storm. It certainly had a deep effect on the development of hermeneutic thought in Germany as developed by Apel and Habermas. It still attracts wide attention today, some forty years after its publication. That is a remarkable testimony to the interest and power of the ideas that it contains. One has to add that the reaction was not without vitriol. Some social scientists were, although this was a misunderstanding of Winch's intention, vexed that a philosopher should wish to lay the law down to them. Gellner, for example, wrote that

> Mr Winch believes he can establish significant conclusions for the benefit of the practitioners of the social sciences ... a

Introduction

philosophical superman flying in from outside and setting things right for earthbound social scientists.
(Gellner 1973: pp. 47–8)

The issues dealt with in his first book were, in 1964, enlarged upon in an article, which has also become legendary, entitled "Understanding a primitive society" (Winch 1972). This article was first read at a conference in upstate New York and, Winch reports, was greeted with responses ranging from derision to contempt. However, one response stood out as different, for Norman Malcolm, then still at Cornell, showed understanding and sympathy for what Winch was saying. That led to a deep friendship that was to become, especially after Malcolm moved to London, a delight to Winch. He spoke with affection of their walks on Hampstead Heath, their dinners and, above all, their discussions. What he found in Malcolm was something at which he had always aimed. This was "a patient honesty", which, he remarked, was "not just a moral adjunct to intellectual ability, but a moral quality that is an intellectual power in itself, without which the peculiar clarity that philosophy seeks cannot be achieved" (Winch 1992a: p. 223). How robust their discussions must have been can be gleaned from Winch's last published piece; a review of a posthumous collection of Malcolm's work (Winch 1997b).

Winch's many books and essays are dealt with in the body of this work, so it would be otiose to summarize them here. But mention must be made of his contributions to the understanding and transmission of Wittgenstein's legacy. Winch made various contributions here. One, as we shall see, and which is evidenced in *The idea of a social science* (1958), was to apply that legacy in areas that Wittgenstein at best only touched upon; areas, for example, such as ethics. Another was to devote himself to the exegesis of Wittgenstein's writings. Those exegeses showed a mastery of the full range of Wittgenstein's work. He stressed, in particular, the continuities between the *Tractatus* and the *Philosophical investigations* (Winch 1969; and see Rashid 1970). He was to become, in 1989, an executor of Wittgenstein's literary estate after the death of Rhees, and as such was required to attend to the complex task of editing and issuing the extraordinarily complex collection of notes and other writings left behind by Wittgenstein (referred to as the "*Nachlass*"). I strongly advise the reader to visit the website at the University of Bergen, where the *Nachlass* is being edited, for a fascinating insight into what that task involves (http//www. hd. uib. no. wab). And then, too, Winch was a sensitive translator of Wittgenstein's work, most notably of the collection of remarks published in English as *Culture and value* (Wittgenstein 1984; see also Wittgenstein 1976).

In 1964 Winch left Swansea for a readership at Birkbeck College in London and from there was elected, in 1967, to the chair in philosophy at King's College, London, where he developed a department of great and lasting distinction. He was a distinguished editor of *Analysis* and a president of the Aristotelian Society. On his retirement from his professorship in 1984 he took a senior appointment in the department of philosophy at the University of Illinois at Urbana-Champaign. During that period, which lasted for twelve highly productive years, he served a term as president of the central division of the American Philosophical Association. It was on returning from a meeting of that body that he died suddenly in 1997.

Winch had a fierce passion for philosophy that led him to spare no careless thinking and no attitude that took philosophy anything less than seriously. He had, incidentally, a distinctive mannerism: he would grind his teeth when agitated by folly. That was usually a signal that one ought to reconsider some remark. Some never took the hint. The late and deeply lamented Dick Beardsmore alleges that, after a Winch paper at Swansea, a somewhat demented amateur ontologist asked him whether he knew *how many different kinds of things there were*. Winch, teeth grinding, began to reply to the effect that it depended on the kind of investigation on which one was engaged, only to be interrupted by the proud revelation that his interlocutor had definitively determined the answer to be twenty-seven.

Winch inspired in his students and colleagues a deep loyalty and affection. He certainly demanded that they think for themselves, whatever the cost. Tim Tessin, who studied with Winch, makes the penetrating comment that "you were never simply a *student* but a *partner in philosophical enquiry*". We should all aspire to that! As we shall see, he loved literature and brought it to bear with remarkable effect on philosophical problems. Tessin tells me that Winch spoke highly of the diaries of Samuel Pepys and *Middlemarch*. He would often mention Kafka, Celan and Mann (remarking that *Doktor Faustus* would be his choice in a philosophy and literature course). It was Tessin, however, who introduced Winch to the luminous Primo Levi, *The periodic table*

Introduction

becoming (rightly) a particular favourite. Winch also loved opera. It is a matter of sadness that he did not live to write the book on Benjamin Britten that he projected.

After *Maurice* was published Bernard Levin lamented that he would now have no other Forster novel to read. Indeed, when one loves a novelist, one sometimes puts off reading the last novel, knowing there to be no more to come. But there is a Winch *Nachlass*, in the hands of his former student and colleague, D. Z. Phillips, so we may yet have more of the demanding delights that his work provides.

Chapter 1
"Such understanding as I have": The influence of Wittgenstein

> Anything I have had to say ... is grounded in such understanding as I have of Wittgenstein's philosophy.... My attitude to Wittgenstein's work has always been one of gratitude for the help it has given me in seeing what are the important questions and what kind of questions they are.
> (Winch 1987: p. 1)

Influences

No active philosophers come innocent to their enquiries. Even a philosopher as apocalyptic in rejecting the past as Nietzsche aspired to be, comes to that task equipped with a knowledge of the problems that have constituted the subject matter of philosophical enquiries, of the methods by which these problems have been approached and of the kinds of solutions that have been proposed for them. The beginning of wisdom in understanding this or that contemporary philosopher is, therefore, the discovery of the relation of that philosopher to the history, both recent and more distant, of the subject.

With Peter Winch the question of influence is easy to determine. Wittgenstein was the philosopher to whom Winch gave his categorical allegiance, to the extent of believing anything he had to say to be "grounded in an understanding" of that philosopher.

Some of Winch's writings sought to give exegeses of various aspects of the work of Wittgenstein and to correct what he thought to be mistaken accounts of that work. Others, which constitute Winch's own distinctive contribution to philosophy, sought to apply what he learned from Wittgenstein to questions not always explicitly or fully dealt with in Wittgenstein's work; questions, for example, about ethics, the nature of social science and religion.

To say that Winch endorsed and sought to apply the philosophy of Wittgenstein, however, simply defers illumination until one is told to what beliefs Winch was committed by that endorsement.

Winch was, to begin with, committed to *a view of philosophy*, a view that can best be understood by first seeing how philosophy became a challenged subject, and, then, by contrasting the view of philosophy that Winch derived from Wittgenstein with a popular alternative.

Philosophy challenged

We are now used to the notion of a *subject* for study; a notion invoked when, on meeting a fellow student, the polite equivalent of the dog-sniffing ritual is the question "What's your subject?", where the reply "Physics" is greeted with respect, "Psychoanalysis" with alarm and "Philosophy" with the fixed smile of baffled incomprehension.

A distinct subject, it is thought, must have some distinct subject matter to study and some distinct way of going about it. Philosophy becomes challenged when we ask "What is its distinct subject matter?" For puzzlement about philosophy is almost certainly due to the fact that people do not know *what* philosophers study. They think that there must be some distinctive objects in the world that are studied by philosophy as atoms are studied by physics and feet by chiropody.

The trouble is that all the high quality goods seem already to have been appropriated by other flourishing enterprises. Physics has sub-atomic particles; chemistry, molecular structures; biology, the fauna and flora; astronomy, the stars; religion, the gods; psychology, our minds; mathematics, the numbers; linguistics, the languages; criticism, the objects of art; and history, the past. What is left over, such things as, say, the divination of lottery numbers and the distillation of sunbeams from cucumbers, seem not to offer philosophy ready or attractive substitutes.

The influence of Wittgenstein

The underlabouring philosophers

Faced with this challenge there emerged, with Locke as a notable early proponent, the notion of the philosopher as an "underlabourer". Winch quotes the following vivid expression of this view, where for Boyle and Sydenham, Newton and Huygenius we may substitute Hawkins, Einstein, Dorothy Hodgkin and Marie Curie. Locke wrote that:

> The commonwealth of learning is not at this time without its masterbuilders, whose mighty designs, in advancing the sciences, will leave lasting monuments to the admiration of posterity: but everyone must not hope to be a Boyle or a Sydenham; and in an age which produces such masters as the great Huygenius and the incomparable Mr Newton ... it is ambition enough to be employed as an underlabourer in clearing the ground a little, and removing some of the rubbish that lies in the way of knowledge. (quoted in Winch 1958: pp. 3–4)

Suppose, using the underlabourer account of philosophy, we find a term used unclearly in one of the special disciplines, the term "cause", say, in psychology, and that problems arise in that discipline from that unclarity. The philosopher will analyse this term, clarify its meaning and then psychology can get on with its job of giving us understanding of its special area of the universe. Philosophy is not, according to this view, in competition with, say, the natural sciences. It is, rather, parasitic on the special disciplines. In performing its cleaning up role, it will be tolerated by the special disciplines of the intellectual community, much as other sharks tolerate the parasitic fish that clean the debris from their teeth.

But now suppose someone *wonders about the very existence of things*. Suppose, that is, people ask, as Berkeley did, not whether *particular things*, dolphins, say, exist but whether *things as such* really exist, independently of any perception of them. These are metaphysical and epistemological questions. They are metaphysical because we are asking not whether this or that particular thing exists, but what it is for something of whatever sort really to exist. They are epistemological because we are now concerned not to acquire knowledge but to comprehend under what conditions, if any, knowledge is possible at all.

Simply to raise these questions is already to damage the underlabourer view. For, according to that view, philosophy has problems only because, for example, psychology or literary criticism have problems. But the metaphysical and epistemological questions I have instanced are not questions we have only because we have the special disciplines. When Hamlet asked whether he had seen a ghost, he might have been asking a straightforward question about whether there was present an object answering a certain description. But he could, equally, have been puzzled as to the criteria for ghostly reality. He did not have to wait for the development of science to ask that question. These epistemological and metaphysical questions are not questions about existents, which might well be answerable by empirical observation, but are questions about what it is to exist and what it is to know that something exists.

Philosophy and reality

We can see the ultimate shortcomings of the underlabourer view by more closely considering questions about real existence. Suppose I ask "Are there really people who believe that Tiger Woods will achieve what Jack Nicklaus has achieved?" You can answer that question simply by producing some people who testify to that conviction. But suppose I ask "Are there really human beings?" There are circumstances in which this question might well be answered in the same sort of way as the previous one, for example, during a discussion between aliens in the kind of intergalactic trucker stop portrayed in *Star Wars*. But if I ask the question here and now, it is unlikely that my question will be answered to my satisfaction by your producing the population of Paris, Texas. For my questions will be "Are these *really* people?", and "How do I know that there are minds behind those movements?" And this shows my puzzlement not to be about the existence of a certain kind of fauna on this planet, but, rather, as Winch puts it at the beginning of his *The idea of a social science*, about the *concept* of reality; about *what it is* for something to be real.

The claim for science

Suppose the answer were given that for something to be real is for it to be available to the kinds of empirical observational methods

The influence of Wittgenstein

used in the natural sciences and in everyday life. What exists is what, in some sense, observably exists. Here Winch takes a fundamental step, deriving from a reading of Wittgenstein, from which the remainder of his own philosophy unfolds.

To begin with, suppose we have the assertion that what *really* exists is decided by reference to what is available to the observational methods of the natural sciences. We then need to distinguish two questions. First we might ask whether that assertion gives a correct account of what it is for something to have the *kind* of reality in which *natural science* is interested. Is science only interested in the observable? Even if that were so, there is the further question of whether that assertion gives a correct account of what it is for something to be real *in any sense whatsoever*. Even if we know what it is for something to be "observably", "empirically" ("scientifically") real, we may still ask whether that is the only way something can be real. Here Winch simply points out that we need an argument for the assertion that science provides the only viable notion of reality. That assertion is *about* science, and whether or not it is true is not for science to decide. So, Winch asserts, "it is evident that the expression . . . 'independent reality' . . . cannot . . . be explained by reference to the scientific universe of discourse", as this would "beg the question" whether science does provide the only measure of reality (Winch 1972: p. 13). Hence, the assertion that whether or not something is real is decided by whether or not it is available to the empirically observational methods of science, is *not* itself an observationally based scientific assertion. Rather it is a statement about the meaning of the term "real".

I do not think that Wittgenstein or Winch would have been in the least inclined to deny that the reality of the rabbits at the bottom of my garden is a matter to be determined in some way observationally. What they resisted was the inclination to make the observational methods thought characteristic of the natural sciences the *only* yardstick by which to determine whether something is or is not real. Certainly, it is not the method by which one determines whether there really is a prime number between 9987 and 15667.

When one does make these scientific methods the yardstick by which to test claims about reality, then, of course, religion, aesthetics and ethics are in trouble. What observations underpin claims about the reality of an eternal creator who transcends the observational world? What empirical means are used to detect the value of a picture or the wrongness of murder? And in the absence of this observational evidence, then, were science to give us our only understanding of what is for something to be real and our only access to that reality, it would follow that values and religious entities do not really exist. That follows, however, only if one has established that empirical verifiability *is* the *only* criterion for reality, and one doesn't automatically establish that by establishing that empirical verifiability is the criterion of *scientific* reality.

Winch doubts that our notion of reality is to be confined to what science admits as existent. He writes:

> science is wrapped up in its own way of making things intelligible to the exclusion of all others. . . . This non-philosophical unselfconsciousness is for the most part right and proper in the investigation of nature . . . but it is disastrous in the investigation of a human society, whose very nature is to consist in different and competing ways of life, each offering a different account of the intelligibility of things.   (Winch 1958: p. 103)

And he writes that "science is one . . . mode . . . [of social life] . . . and religion is another; and each has criteria of intelligibility peculiar to itself" (1958: p. 100).

It does not follow from this that Winch is, as some who cannot have read him carefully supposed, anti-science. "Philosophy has no business to be anti-scientific: if it tries to, it will succeed only in making itself look ridiculous" (Winch 1958: p. 2). One must not confuse queries about the pretensions of science to be the *only* way to knowledge, with queries about whether science offers *any* way to knowledge.

The empirical and the conceptual

So far, then, we have the claim that, although whether there really are still Tasmanian tigers may be a scientific question, what is meant by attributing reality to something is a philosophical question. Further if a scientist were to say that what is real is a matter of what can be determined by the methods, whatever they are, of the empirical sciences, this is not a statement from *within* science but a statement *about* science, and, so, is an assertion the truth of which science itself cannot decide. We have also seen that Winch is inclined to query the truth of that assertion. That,

The influence of Wittgenstein

however, leaves a number of things unclear, including the question "What kind of statements are *philosophical* statements about the meaning of terms like 'real'?" and the question "How is the truth of such statements to be determined?"

The empirical study of language?

Let us begin by noting that claims about what is meant by the term "real" are claims about what we in fact mean by a word. Some then claim that as the term "real" is in fact used, to say that something is real is simply to say that its existence is determinable by the observational methods of the natural sciences. Winch, let us suppose, denies that. How is that dispute to be resolved?

It has been claimed that assertions about how we use words are themselves ordinary empirical claims, to be tested by the methods of the empirical science of linguistics. That yields this striking conclusion: philosophy, which undertakes to tell us the meaning of terms like "real", is itself an empirical science (and one due to be superseded by the empirical science of linguistics). It is this claim, which strikes at the roots of Winch's position, and a certain conception of philosophy embodied in it, that I now wish to examine. Winch was, I think, clearly aware of this challenge. He remarked in a very early paper that certain comments he makes about the use of the word "suggests" are, as he put it "made with reference to the current uses of words" (Winch 1953: p. 335). That he supposes, might lead to questions about whether he has properly and scientifically investigated those uses. To that he replies, not entirely perspicuously, that "philosophical questions about the use of language are not the same type as grammatical, etymological or philological questions" (1953: p. 336). The difference, he tells us, is that philosophers analyse *concepts*. So, this puts them on "a different level from analyses of language" (1953: p. 336), But then he adds that concepts are best analysed by analysing the *actual* use of language. That seems to put us back with the original question; why are these enquiries into how language is actually used not empirical enquiries?

It is not just strawmen who have said that philosophy, if it studies the actual meaning of terms, simply is, Winch's objections to the contrary, an empirical science. Just this has been widely asserted by those critical of the approach of which Winch is a

15

prominent representative. C. G. New says that "facts about the use of language must be studied empirically" (New 1971: p. 571). Fodor and Katz assert that the truth of such statements "must be established by the usual empirical means" (Fodor & Katz 1963: p. 70). Benson Mates says that such statements have a "factual basis" and are "refutable by observation of ordinary folk, magistrates, parents and teachers" (Mates 1958: p. 164). Ernest Gellner says that if philosophy is to investigate the actual uses of language, it will have to be "hard headed and empirical" (Gellner 1968: p. 166). C. K. Mundle writes of the "empirical linguistics that Wittgenstein recommended but did not practice" (Mundle 1970: p. 261) and David Pears has said of the characterizations offered by Wittgenstein that they "must of course be true empirical statements about language" (Pears 1971: p. 108).

Given the kinds of assertions that, according to Winch, philosophers make about the meaning of our words having been characterized as empirical statements, it is not surprising also to be told that the proper way to investigate them is by the methods of empirical linguistics. New tells us that this is "a study that belongs to descriptive linguistics"; a subject with its own "disciplines and techniques" (New 1971: p. 377). Fodor and Katz tells us that such linguistic characterizations "should be subject to the same modes of confirmation and disconfirmation that linguists accept" (Fodor & Katz 1963: p. 71). Mundle writes that "when answers to philosopher's questions can, and only can adequately be verified by systematic observation and experiment, it is time for philosophers to leave it to specialists" (Mundle 1970: p. 262).

Here, then, is the first substantial challenge to Winch's position. He tells us that it is the *philosopher's* (and not the scientist's) job to tell us about the meaning of the term "real". But on the objection we are examining, that philosopher's job, involving as it does the examination of the way words are "actually used", is one that empirical science alone can perform. Hence Winch's distinction between philosophy and empirical science collapses. I wish now to defend Winch against this line of attack.

What techniques?

Although philosophers like Winch are often advised to utilize the distinctive techniques of empirical linguistics it is not easy to

The influence of Wittgenstein

discover what those who advise this have in mind. Since we are dealing with enquiries into meaning let us turn to the relevant part of linguistics, namely "semantic theory". In a work that makes a special study of empirical methods of testing linguistic characterizations, we are told of ways in which the intuitions of informants are to be invoked by the empirical linguistic scientist in search of semantic information (Leech 1969, 1974). The informants of empirical linguistic scientists are invited to use their powers of intuition on questions like these:

Is "I am an orphan" *synonymous* with "I am a child with no father and mother"?
Does "I am an orphan" *entail* "I have no father"?
Is "I am an orphan" *inconsistent* with "I have a father"?
Is "This orphan has no father" a *tautology*?
Is "This orphan has a father" a *contradiction*?
Is "This orphan's father drinks heavily" *semantically anomolous*? (Leech 1974: p. 94)

These questions, we are told, issue in statements that report intuitions. This being so, we have not found anything philosophers haven't been doing for millennia. When Socrates, in Plato's *Republic,* asked "Would it be called 'just' to return weapons to someone who, since lending them, has gone mad?", he was asking whether the sentence "It is just to return weapons to a madman" went against our intuitions; whether it is, to use the jargon, semantically anomalous.

Since the questions *asked* in semantics seem no different from those asked by philosophers, talk of the superiority of empirical linguistics must boil down to the claim that *new and improved methods* have been devised in that discipline for *answering* these questions. Here the clear implication of the quotations I have given is that *empirical informant testing* should supersede traditional philosophy. First, what are the methods of traditional philosophy?

Here I note that one of the complaints against philosophers, like Winch, who have made claims about what we actually mean by terms like "real", is that they have *no adequate test procedures* for what are usually characterized as "armchair intuitions". This is not true.

Suppose, I conclude that the term "real" is used in a certain way. As every philosopher has ever done, I will try my conclusion out on my students and colleagues. I might even, if sufficiently panicked by research selectivity exercises, publish my view and reply to any comments. I may, after all this, amend or withdraw my original assertion. I bring my characterization to the bar of disconfirmation by offering it to a sample, which is, particularly if I publish, open-ended. It is simply absurd then to say, as New did, that philosophers rely on "unsupported intuition and introspection" (New 1971: p. 376) or as Mates put it, eschew "laborious questioning of other people" (Mates 1958: p. 165).

It is not necessary to offer any great detail about what the sample called "the philosophical audience" might do in testing a claim about how a term like "real" is used. It will do, for my present purposes, to suppose that those offering such claims are interested in exploring relationships of entailment between expressions in which that word is used and other expressions, as when it is claimed that expressions involving the word "real" entail expressions like "determinable by observation". To falsify a philosopher's characterization of a use of language is to show that the entailment relations do not hold. In those discussions we ask questions like "*Would* you use 'real' in such and such a case?" or aren't there cases (talking about prime numbers, for example) where we use 'real' without implying observational confirmation?" These procedures of questioning, imagining and storytelling, all of which, as we will see, are strikingly exemplified throughout Winch's work, form an activity not improperly called "dialectic", by which the philosophical audience tests the claims that are offered to it. A powerful and compelling picture is given of this procedure by Winch:

> It is very common in philosophical discussion to find that a way of speaking and thinking which seems perfectly clear and acceptable to oneself is met with incomprehension by other people. . . . In such circumstances one is bound to ask whether what one wants to say really does make sense or not. Discussion with other people will often be very important in one's attempt to settle this question – it was, after all, the incredulous, uncomprehending reactions of others which prompted the doubt in the first place. . . . Discussion will take the form of raising difficulties and trying to see one's way round them. . . . If one recognises the possibility of being mistaken in one's initial belief that one had understood what was being said . . . one can equally, after discussion, recognise that one may have over or underestimated the difficulties which have emerged. But that does not mean that one's views are subjected to some

ultimate criterion. .... It means only that new difficulties, and perhaps new ways of meeting the difficulties, are always lurking below the horizon and that discussion continues. Sometimes if one is lucky, the discussion clarifies or extends one's concept of what is possible for human beings.
(Winch 1972: p. 88)

It is asserted, however, that empirical linguistic science has better confirmation procedures than traditional dialectic. So, we are told,

the introspections of the linguist as his own informant are accorded a provisional measure of evidential validity but are held answerable ultimately to more objective confirmation provided by corpus evidence and informant tests.
(Leech 1974: p. 8)

The starting point here, to which I assent, is that, since intuition can err, *some* check is necessary. The further claim must be that informant testing by corpus evidence and questionnaire is a better check than the dialectical activities of the philosophical audience. This is simply not so, and the case is best illustrated by an example.

Suppose I assert that a meaning relationship exists between the terms "killing" and "death". I claim that, as we usually employ the terms, "killed" is used only of people who are dead. I try this out on what Austin once called my "cantankerous colleagues", and publish it in the *Journal of Thanatology*. Various objections are raised, as the result of which I refine my claim, or even withdraw it. This, I claim, constitutes an adequate, although not infallible, test procedure.

What am I now offered as an alternative from empirical linguistics? Examination of the literature turned up only one example. Geoffrey Leech has investigated, and once advocated, "objective correlation" by questionnaire sampling.

Suppose, says Leech (1974), that we wish to test the claim that when we say that someone was killed we imply that he or she is dead. To do so one offers a range of informants the following: "Assuming it is true that someone killed the Madrid chief of police last night, must it be true that the Madrid chief of police died last night?" One then gives the following instruction: "If you think that it must be true, write 'yes' in the box provided. If you think that it must be false that he died, put 'no'. If you think that it might be

true or false, put 'yes/no'. If you don't know what to put, put a '?'".
The results of this test were as follows: 96 per cent of the sample said that if it is true that someone killed the Madrid chief of police last night, then it must be true that he died last night; 0 per cent thought it must be false that he died; 3 per cent thought he might or might not have died on being killed and 1 per cent couldn't or wouldn't say.

The chief difficulty about these tests as an alternative to dialectic is an obvious one. The results of these tests would not, *by themselves* confirm *anyone's* intuitions about the use of words. To know whether or not they confirm my intuitions I need to know what my informants *meant* by their answers. Take the 96 per cent who (I think wrongly) agree that the killing of a Madrid police chief last night entails his or her death last night. Can't I be held to have killed someone even if he or she dies some time later. Is that what the 3 per cent thought, who might then be right, even if out of line with the vast majority? How am I to discover this without talking to them dialectically?

Informant tests do not bear their confirmatory or disconfirmatory status upon their faces. They need to be accompanied by enquiries that elicit their significance. These, however, can be none other than those kinds of enquiries that my philosophical audience makes into claims about meaning. Hence far from replacing dialectic, the methods of informant sampling, if they are to have a disconfirmatory role, presupposes it.

Intermediate summary

Winch, then, offers a distinction between the kinds of questions answered in the enquiries of the special disciplines, including the natural sciences, and epistemological and metaphysical questions, where the latter have to do with what we are saying when we claim to know that something is real. Here two points have emerged. First, it is open to someone to say that whether or not something really exists is a matter of whether it is available to empirical observation. That, though, is a philosophical statement *about* science and its access to reality, and not one for science to adjudicate. Second, I have denied that philosophical assertions about what we mean when we use the word "real" are the province of the empirical science of linguistics.

But now Wittgenstein writes:

> These are not, of course, empirical problems; they are solved by looking into the workings of our language, and that in such a way as to make us recognise those workings; in despite of an urge to misunderstand them. These problems are solved not by giving new information, but by arranging what we have always known. (Wittgenstein 1953, s. 109)

Winch clearly endorses this: "Philosophy is crippled ... by mistaking conceptual enquiries into what it makes sense to say for empirical enquiries which must wait upon experience for their solution" (Winch 1958: p. 17). Yet Wittgenstein also writes that "philosophy may in no way interfere with the actual use of language; it can in the end only describe it (Wittgenstein 1953: ss. 124).

That raises the question why, if our task *is* to describe the actual use of language, albeit by the methods of philosophical dialectic, this is not an empirical enquiry. What is meant by saying, as both Wittgenstein and Winch do, that the enquiry is not empirical but *conceptual*?

"It is there, like our lives"

Let us begin with this thought: language was not invented. (In what language would any would-be inventors form their ideas of a language?) Our language developed as we developed and fits the capacities that we have acquired. Because we evolved as creatures making certain sorts of visual sortings of things with a need to communicate those sortings, so, too there evolved a colour language. Because the phenomenon of error was part of our development, so we evolved a language in which we could talk about knowledge, belief, doubt and error.

We are born into linguistic communities and we learn the language of those communities because we have certain capacities and, no less than dogs that can learn to retrieve sticks, can respond to training in various ways. As a result of that training, we use, without strain, the words of our language. Our language is there, like our lives, and it reflects the forms that our lives take. To imagine a language must be to imagine the kind of life into which it is woven and to which it gives expression.

From this picture come the characteristic features of Wittgenstein's and Winch's philosophy. In particular comes the exhortation that when we wish to understand an expression we should trace it back to its home in its use within the practices into which it is woven, just as, if we wish to know what it means to call a piece of metal a coin, we have to ask how that piece of metal is used.

Three things can now be said, all of which throw light on Peter Winch's many projects. First, it is easy to forget how subtle the distinctions are that we can make. (Consider here the difference between saying that something is a delusion and saying that something is an illusion, or between saying that one likes something and saying that it is beautiful.) Austin remarked rightly that:

> Our common stock of words embodies all the distinctions men have found worth drawing, and the connections they have found worth marking, in the lifetimes of many generations: these surely are likely to be more numerous, more sound, since they have stood up to the long test of the survival of the fittest, and more subtle, at least in all ordinary and reasonably practical matters, than any that you and I are likely to think up in our armchairs of an afternoon. . . . Certainly . . . ordinary language is *not* the last word. Only remember, it is the *first* word.
> (Austin 1961: pp. 130, 132)

Second, when we theorize, there is a temptation to overlook the varieties of our various modes of expression and to take one of them as central. This can produce distorted accounts, as happened when it was assumed that aesthetics was solely to do with the word "beautiful" or that morality was solely a matter of using the term "good". Then we need to be reminded of the subtlety of our language. Winch, as we shall see, was a master at such reminders.

Third, certain features of our languages can, when we are not using our words but thinking about them, suggest the wrong things to us. We hear someone profess not to know what is "in" someone else's head, and think of the mind as place to which only its possessor can obtain access. So we come to wonder how we can know of the mind of another at all.

On the account we have given, we use words with no sense of strain in what Wittgenstein called "the traffic of life". Our problems arise when we stop using the terms and start to think about them. Hence Wittgenstein's remark that philosophical problems arise "when language goes on holiday" (Wittgenstein 1953: ss. 38). When that happens the task is to call us back to our actual uses. Philosophy assembles "reminders for particular purposes" (1953: ss. 127). We have, then, a view of language that roots language in the life forms of those who use it. Words are to be understood in terms of their use in the lives of those who deploy them. That picture is one to which Winch unreservedly subscribes. Thus, suppose the question is "What is a fact?" Then, Winch writes:

> The concept of factuality is not given; it arises out of the way men live. We have to consider the conditions which make it possible for us to have a concept of "the facts", which involves taking into account the modes of human behaviour, together with the kinds of decisions involved in them, in which the concept of "the facts" plays a part and from which it receives its sense. (Winch 1972: p. 57)

No less than Wittgenstein he was aware that we could mischaracterize these practices. For there is a "standing danger that when not actually involved in the practice, we shall misconstrue the relation of our use of such expressions to it" (Winch 1987b: p. 57).

How does this bear on the issue whether philosophical questions are empirical ones, which Winch denied in arguing that philosophy is conceptual rather than empirical?

As he uses the expression, an empirical enquiry is one that *finds out* some *new* fact, such as for example, the fact, if it is a fact, that a certain language has seventeen words for snow. "Genuine, new knowledge", he writes, "is acquired by scientists by experimental and observational methods" (Winch 1958: p. 5). But, by that token, philosophical assertions about the use of terms are not empirical. For we already know the truth of those assertions in knowing the language that we speak. We are *reminded* of what we know, not provided with new knowledge. Thus, in discussing Kripke's famous discussion of Wittgenstein's views on rules (Winch 1987b: pp. 54–63), Winch takes his task to be to point out things that are "overlooked" (1987b: p. 59) in this discussion of our words, where reminders rather than new information are required.

That these assertions are verifiable and falsifiable does nothing to support the contention that they are empirical. For if someone, apprised of mathematics, says that $798 - 567 = 1368$, what he or she says is falsifiable (and is indeed false). But that does not show that it is empirical. When we falsify it, we do not do so by supplying new information to the person who asserted it, but by reminding that person that he or she already has the means of knowing that the assertion is false. So, too, when Socrates reminded someone of the case in which weapons were returned to a lender who had subsequently gone mad, the counter-example worked by *reminding* the person of something he had overlooked. The characteristic reaction to such reminders is not "Whoever would have thought it!" but "Of course! I should have thought of that!"

However, the real force of the distinction between empirical and conceptual enquiries emerges when we note that it is typical of an empirical statement of the kind we encounter in the natural sciences that, even if true, it could have been false. If I say truly that there are dolphins, then it is equally intelligible that there might not have been. That contrasts with the case in which we truly say that 6 × 8 = 48. This could not be false, which is why it is not an empirical statement. Wittgenstein and Winch would maintain that true philosophical statements are not empirical either.

Here it is instructive to consider Wittgenstein's view of the relationship between language and reality as expressed in the *Philosophical investigations*. For Wittgenstein, the question "What is real?" can only be asked if terms like "real" have been given a use in our language. Thus, Winch writes, "Our idea of what belongs to the realm of reality is given for us in the language that we use. The concepts we have settle for us the form of experience we have of the world" (Winch 1958: p. 15).

Let us suppose, then, that we have discovered how we actually use the word "real". Let it even be supposed that, as we use the term "real", it is true that we only say that something really exists if its existence is determinable by observational evidence. Then let us ask whether that true assertion about the use of the term "real" could have been false, whether, that is, in using the term "real" as we do, *we could have got reality wrong*. And the answer is "No". That is not an empirical discovery. We cannot look at reality and see whether our use of the term "reality" captures its true nature. For the use of that word in our human practices tells us what it is to look at reality. (Although, as we shall see in Chapter 7, Winch denies that this means that reality depends on language.) It will follow that to investigate the *concept* of reality, as opposed to investigating which flora and fauna exist, is not *empirically* to investigate the living language in which we talk of reality.

Strikingly anticipating Wittgenstein, Kant also seemed to suggest that we cannot ask whether the forms of our language get reality right, because our very concept of right and wrong is given in that language. Hence:

The influence of Wittgenstein

To seek out from ordinary knowledge the concepts which are not grounded in any particular experience and nonetheless occur in all knowledge by experience ... presupposes no greater reflection or more insight than to seek out from a language rules of the real use of words in general and thus to collect the elements for a grammar (in fact both enquiries are very closely related to one another), without being able to state the ground, why any language has exactly this and no other formal nature. (Kant 1953: p. 85)

Reality as "systematically ambiguous"

In Wittgenstein's view, what we can say is real and what we can say is not real will depend on how the term "real" is used. There is, however, simply no guarantee, within any culture, that there will be one concept of "reality", one use of the term "real". The characteristic feature of Winch's philosophy is his wholehearted endorsement of this view. Having asserted that to make a distinction between what is real and what is not is to make the world intelligible, Winch writes,

> The scientist, for instance, tries to make the world more intelligible; but so too do the historian, the religious prophet and the artist; so does the philosopher. ... It is clear that the objectives of each of them differ from the objectives of any of the others. (Winch 1958: pp. 18–19)

As we shall see in Chapter 5, this is why Winch thinks that criteria that are relevant when reality is attributed by religious people to God are not necessarily the criteria relevant to the determination of the kind of reality with which the scientist is concerned. Hence religion is not necessarily undermined by advances in scientific understanding. Moreover, as we shall see in Chapter 3, the matter is also central to what Winch controversially has to say in the legendary paper "Understanding a primitive society" (Winch 1972). In his account, there is no guarantee that the understanding of reality operative in the natural sciences as they are practised in the USA and Europe, will necessarily help us to understand what is happening when people in other cultures talk of the reality of witches. Whether that entails any form of cultural relativism is a matter to which we will continually return.

Peter Winch

The charge of conservatism

Wittgenstein had said that "philosophy must in no way interfere with the actual use of language. It can in the end only describe it". It leaves "everything as it is" (Wittgenstein 1953: ss. 124). Winch, too, enjoins a neutrality on the philosopher:

> Philosophy is an *uncommitted* enquiry.... Philosophy is concerned with elucidating and comparing the ways in which the world is made intelligible in different intellectual disciplines; and how this leads on to the elucidation and comparison of different forms of life.... It is equally concerned to elucidate its own account of things.... In performing this task the philosopher will be particularly alert to deflate the pretensions of any form of enquiry to enshrine the essence of intelligibility as such, to possess the key to reality.... To take an uncommitted view of such competing conceptions is peculiarly the task of philosophy; it is not its business to award prizes to science, religion, or anything else. It is not its business to advocate any *Weltanschauung*.... In Wittgenstein's words, "Philosophy leaves everything as it was [sic]".
>
> (Winch 1958: p. 103)

Some have objected that this is simply an unsavoury form of totalitarian conservatism, a construction that Winch vehemently, and rightly, denied: "am I setting the status quo in concrete as is well known to be the sneaky practice of Wittgensteinian conservatives? No" (Winch 1991: p. 236).

I shall deal with versions of the accusation of conservatism, notably those made by Gellner and MacIntyre, in Chapter 2. Here I deal with Marcuse's instructive version of the charge that Wittgenstein's (and Winch's) view of philosophy is an unsavoury form of reactionary totalitarianism. Marcuse writes:

> The contemporary effort to reduce the scope and truth of philosophy is tremendous, and philosophers themselves proclaim the modesty and inefficacy of philosophy. It leaves established reality untouched; it abhors transgression.... Wittgenstein's assurance that philosophy "leaves everything as it is" – such statements exhibit, to my mind, academic sado-masochism, self-humiliation and self-denunciation of the intellectual whose labour does not issue in scientific, technical or like achievements.
> (Marcuse 1972: p. 141)

The influence of Wittgenstein

The present world order *is* unjust, mutilating and deforming. There *are* better and different possible worlds. Yet, Marcuse believes, here is a philosophy that seems to tell us that everything is all right as it is. Isn't that just damagingly reactionary? Here there is a massive misunderstanding.

First, in his writings Marcuse offers a description of society as it is, using such terms as "distorting", and "unjust", in a *reminding* way, in order to get us to *see* our defective social reality. That procedure must assume the truth of Wittgenstein's assertion that philosophy may in no way interfere with the actual use of our language. Marcuse must assume a shared use with us of the descriptive and evaluative terms that are used to characterize our societies. He is not at liberty to invent terms. As he says in terms straight out of Wittgenstein: "language is nothing private and personal, or rather the private and personal is mediated by the available linguistic material, which is societal material" (Marcuse 1972: p. 157). Hence, he, too, must assume that language is all right as it is. (It might, of course, be asked whether a language itself might be conceptually conservative, as some have argued that forms of expression in English grammatically embody a retrograde conception of the male as superior to the female. I return to that question and to the question how one might determine that a language is conceptually conservative in Chapter 7.)

Next, Marcuse's basic assumption is that a human being is in essence a being whose fulfilment lies in its happiness. We evaluate possible societies according to whether they enable or frustrate this flourishing.

There are problems in the definition of "happiness" of which Marcuse is well aware (Marcuse 1968). For my present purposes the interesting question is about the status of Marcuse's assertion that "human being" means "happiness seeker".

Marcuse does not argue this claim. It is put before us, in the spirit in which Wittgenstein says that the philosopher must proceed, in a way intended to make us see its truth. Marcuse writes,

> The desideratum is to make the existing language itself speak what it conceals or excludes, for what is to be revealed and denounced is operative within the universe of ordinary discourse and action. (Marcuse 1972: p. 158)

Just so, Wittgenstein wrote:

> Philosophy simply puts everything before us and neither

explains nor deduces anything. . . . The aspects of things that are most important to us are hidden because of their simplicity and familiarity. (One is unable to notice something – because it is always before one's eyes . . . – and this means that we fail to be struck by what once seen is most striking and most powerful. (Wittgenstein 1953: ss. 6, 129)

Marcuse does not offer us a discovery. We are invited to think about the concept of a human being *as we already have it* and are invited to see that we mean by "human being" what Marcuse says we mean. If I do not see that "human being" means what Marcuse says it means, he cannot simply stipulate that meaning for the term. What force would that stipulation have? For there to be communication between us, I have to see him as reporting my use of language as well as his own. If there is disagreement, then Marcuse must try to get me to see that as *I* use the term "human being" I speak the language as he does. If we don't agree, the best we can be offered, in the process that I have called "dialectic", is further reminders.

In the end I think Marcuse's accusations of conservatism rest upon a confusion between two claims. One is that *the existing structure of society* is all right as it is. The other is that *language* is all right as it is. Marcuse attributes the former to Wittgenstein. That is absurd. It was Wittgenstein who wrote, "It is not impossible that it should fall to the lot of this work, in its poverty and in the darkness of this time, to bring light into one brain or other – but of course it is not likely" (Wittgenstein 1953: p. viii). What Wittgenstein said was not that *society* is all right as it is, but that *language* is all right as it is. Marcuse must subscribe to that if he is to speak to us at all. Even if I think that the language embodies, say, a defective view of females, I am going to have to use the agreed language to say that.

Rules

I come, now, to the central piece in the jigsaw puzzle of Winch's inheritance from Wittgenstein, the notion of rules. This needs attention, if only because Winch himself placed the analysis of rule-following at the centre of his account of philosophy and, as a consequence, at the centre of his account of the notion of a society. For Winch the social is the *meaningful* and the meaningful is the

The influence of Wittgenstein

rule-governed. From that it follows that any understanding of society requires an understanding of rule-governed behaviour.

The intelligible

Winch claims that the notion of reality is related to the notion of making something *intelligible*. That looks right. When we know what sort of reality is possessed by this or that object, a mountain, say, or God, then what there is, and how it is, become *intelligible* to us. Thus Winch begins with the assumption that the task of philosophy is "to throw light on the question how far reality is intelligible and what difference would the fact that he could have a grasp of reality make to the life of man" (Winch 1958: p. 9).

What it is to make the world intelligible varies according to the context:

> The scientist, for instance, tries to make the world more intelligible; but so too do the historian, the religious prophet and the artist; so does the philosopher. And although we may describe the activities of all of these kinds of thinker in terms of the concepts of understanding and intelligibility, it is clear that in very many ways, the objectives of each of them differ from the objectives of any of the others . . . It would be foolish . . . to suppose that the results of all these activities should add up to one grand theory of reality.   (Winch 1958: pp. 18–19)

The next step is to ascertain for each discipline what kind of reality is possessed by the objects it studies. That will determine the kinds of questions that can meaningfully be asked. It is indeed this thought that underlies Winch's criticisms of certain social scientists, Pareto, for example, who, Winch thought, wrongly assumed that the object of the study of social science, namely social life, has the kind of reality that is possessed by the objects studied by the natural sciences.

Winch next asserts that when we investigate the related notions of intelligibility and reality we are investigating the connection between language and reality.

> To ask whether reality is intelligible is to ask about the relation between thought and reality. In considering the nature of thought one is led also to consider the nature of language. Inseparably bound up with the question of whether

reality is intelligible, therefore, is the question of how language is connected with reality, of what it is to say something.
(Winch 1958: p. 12)

And:

Everything I have so far said has been based on the assumption that what is really fundamental to philosophy is the question regarding the nature of and intelligibility of reality. It is easy to see that this question must lead on to a consideration of what we mean by intelligibility in the first place. What is it to understand something, to grasp the sense of something? What then makes it possible to say something and to be understood? What makes language possible? (Winch 1958: p. 18)

At this point, the answers given by Winch in *The idea of a social science* and by Wittgenstein in *Philosophical investigations* come together.

Philosophical investigations deals adversely with the view that a word gets meaning attached to it by an act of pointing – so that a child is taught "mountain" by its parent pointing at a mountain and uttering a sound. Here we may ask, first, how is the meaning of that pointing gesture to be explained? By a further act of pointing? Second, we need to ask how the child knows that the parent is teaching it the *general notion of a mountain* rather than simply *naming a particular mountain*, or teaching it the word "mountain" rather than the word "high"? Third, a child has learned the word "mountain" if it goes on to apply the word correctly on future occasions, if, that is, it has learned the *rule* for the use of the term "mountain". But how can *one* act of pointing to a *particular* object generate a *general* competence, one which will show itself in indefinite numbers of future cases? No rote learned formula can guarantee this. Even if I say "a mountain is anything *like this*", still, on each future occasion of use, the learner will have to decide if *this* new case *is* like that earlier one. The problem is exacerbated when we consider that any rule we might be given to guide us in our decision making in cases of perplexity will *itself* have to be interpreted in each new case. Following a rule is not helpfuly analysed by talk of being "guided" by rules.

Here is an instructive example. We learn "vivid" of certain *colours* and, with no feeling of difficulty, apply it in that way. One day we hear someone say "he was so wet, you could shoot seagulls off him". You say to me, "That was a vivid turn of phrase". Here you

The influence of Wittgenstein

use, of *expressions*, a term that was learned in order to talk of *colours*. And, strikingly, I understand *exactly* what you are saying. I apply that term in the new context as a natural continuation of its use in the previous context. Further I did not deliberate before following your extended application. As Wittgenstein put it, I obey the rule "blindly" (Wittgenstein 1953: ss. 219) or, in another phrase that Winch quotes, "as a matter of course" (Winch 1958: p. 31). If I did not just do this, no formula, no stressing that the cases were the same or similar, could be guaranteed to help me.

The social vision of language

These examples show that the possibility of communication rests on the brute fact that we *agree* in the projections we make in the use of our terms. *Every* term that we use functions as "vivid" does in my example. A child learns "dog" for *this* dog, yet goes on to call indefinite numbers of new examples of dogs by that term. And we can talk because, as a matter of fact, we agree in those projections. Our language is thus *socially* founded. A *language*, then, cannot be private. With a language I *speak*, that is, engage with others, but I can speak only if we agree in the projections we make. If you are the only person who makes a projection, then you cannot speak. Stanley Cavell memorably put it thus:

> We learn and teach words in certain contexts, and then we are expected, and expect others, to be able to project then into further contexts. Nothing ensures that this projection will take place (in particular not the grasping of universals nor the grasping of books of rules), just as nothing ensures that we make, and understand, the same projections. That on the whole we do is a matter of our sharing routes of interest and feeling, modes of response, senses of humour and of significance and of fulfilment, of what is outrageous, of what is similar to what else, what a rebuke, what forgiveness, of when an utterance is an assertion, when an appeal, when an explanation – all that whirl of activity that Wittgenstein calls "forms of life". Human speech and activity, sanity and community, rest upon nothing more, but nothing less, than this. It is a vision as simple as it is difficult, and as difficult as it is (and because it is) terrifying. (Cavell 1968: pp. 160–1)

Here the word "terrifying" is appropriate because we are on our own with language. No authority coming from outside us can give our communal life the sense it has. That sense rests on a brute, and possibly fragile, agreement in the forms of our lives.

Now, we can begin to see emerging a central thought about the social. For social behaviour is meaningful behaviour and meaningful behaviour is behaviour that accords with rules. An outsider who cannot understand what is going on in a football match or a marriage lacks that understanding because he or she has not grasped the rules being followed by those who participate in those rule-governed activities. In this, understanding a marriage is not like understanding the appearance of an icicle. Understanding the latter is a matter of understanding regularities, the investigation of which are the province of the natural sciences, rather than of understanding rules that give meaning to behaviour. The notion of rules, Winch stresses, unlike the notion of regularities, involves the possibility of *going wrong*. If, counter to regularities hitherto noted, a low pressure area does not bring rain, I can't *blame* the weather, save in Basil Fawlty hyperbole, for not playing by the rules. But if you point to a penguin and say "That's a canary", that option is open to me. Rules are normative.

"An enigma to another"

The remark, "That was a vivid turn of phrase", was, in fact, transparent to me. But I might have replied, "What do you mean? 'Vivid' applies to *colours*. How can a *phrase* be vivid?" You then seem to be reduced to saying, "Can't you *see* the similarity?" Suppose I can't? What we might do in such cases is a matter to which I shall return when discussing Winch's views about what we might do in cases of misunderstandings, such as between societies and in ethics. We are not without resources, but, whatever those resources might be, they can come to an end in our not seeing what another sees. Then we learn that

> One human being can be an enigma to another. We learn this when we come into a strange country with entirely strange traditions: and what is more even given a mastery of the country's language. We do not understand the people . . . . We cannot find ourselves in them. (Wittgenstein 1953: p. 223)

The influence of Wittgenstein

That gives us, as we shall see, a way of grasping, and correcting mischaracterizations of, what Winch wished to argue about the problem of understanding another society. For the language of that society will be rooted in the forms of its life, which may be different from ours. And the projections that they make may be as enigmatic to us as they are transparent to them. This may be so even if we learnt their language and could speak to them. I might learn enough to ask "Is this a case of witchcraft?" in a society permeated by that notion, and I could elicit the appropriate answer without understanding the *point* of that practice. For learning a language is not merely a matter of learning rules that allow me to say a word at an appropriate time, but of seeing "the point which following those rules" has in a particular society (Winch 1972: pp. 27–8).

Conservatism again

I discussed earlier the allegation that Wittgenstein and his followers are conservatives, who simply accept the status quo, who, as Marcuse put it, "abhor transgression". We can now see, first, that if "transgression" entails using words in ways that pay no heed to the underpinning of communication by agreement, then "transgression" is not liberating but a short cut to unintelligibility.

Second, far from Wittgenstein's notion of language as something used in the traffic of our lives being confining, that notion celebrates our freedom. To use a language is necessarily to be creative in projecting what we have learned into ever new contexts. This is something *we* have to *do* and not something, as some structuralists believed, that language does to us. The child who, having learned that to use the term "dog" of *this* object, can project the term into new contexts, is kindred to the poets. Hence Croce's remark that

> Rather than saying *poeta nascitur* [a poet is born a poet] we should say *homo nascitur poeta* [man is born a poet]. . . . Inspiration is not something descended from heaven but is the essence of humanity itself. (Croce 1992: p. 16)

Language is not conservative, although its users often are. Those, discussed in Winch's "Who is my neighbour?" (Winch 1987b), who on grasping the parable of the good Samaritan, were then able to project their use of the term "neighbour" to cover new cases, were no conservatives, although they followed the rules of their language. Although they followed what was "already implicit in ways of acting and talking", they creatively projected those ways.

Kripke

Since Wittgenstein's analysis of rule following is so central to Winch's work, I conclude this preliminary chapter with a much discussed difficulty that Kripke has raised about it.

Suppose someone learns to count, one at a time, up to a thousand, at which point he or she continues 1002, 1004, 1006 . . . . Someone else, however continues 1001, 1002, 1003 . . . . The latter is likely to say to the former, "But you didn't go on the same way. You were supposed to add one each time". But in learning 1, 2, 3, 4 . . . nothing was said about what one was to do on reaching 1000. All that was said, if anything, was that on reaching 1000 (or whatever number you like) *we were to go on in the same way*. As with any projection, what actually happens on reaching that number depends on what it seems natural for someone to do *then* in order to carry out the instruction "add one". So someone who added two each time on reaching a thousand could, incomprehensibly as it would seem to us, sincerely say, "I *am* going on in the same way". That person could learn that we proceeded differently and even try to accommodate to our inclinations: but if he or she saw no point in so doing, he or she would not really understand us. But then the person who says that adding one is the correct continuation *and* the person who says that adding two is the correct continuation *and*, indeed, anyone who says that *anything* is the correct continuation seem equally right. And then, it would seem, there can't be a wrong continuation. And since, Winch claims, for him, and for Wittgenstein, the notion of rules is a *normative* notion, one that is "inseparable from the possibility of making a mistake", the notion of rules is called into question.

Kripke therefore concludes that on this account it might seem that

> There can be no such thing as meaning anything by any word. Each new application we make is a leap in the dark; any present intention could be interpreted so as to accord with

The idea of a social science

anything we may choose to do. So there can be neither accord, nor conflict. (Kripke 1982: p. 55)

That is then attributed also to Wittgenstein on the strength of his remark that "This was our paradox: no course of action could be determined by a rule because every course of action can be made out to accord with the rule" (Wittgenstein 1953: ss. 201).

Winch discusses this "sceptical argument" in "Facts and superfacts" (Winch 1987b: pp. 54–63). One of a number of problems on which he focuses is the word "interpreted" in the passage that I have just quoted from Kripke. For that suggests that following a rule is learning a formula and then interpreting it at each step. Suppose I learn the rule "The word 'mountain' is used to refer to this thing and anything *like* this". If interpretation is made central to rule following, then, for each new case, I have to look at the rule and ask whether it could be so interpreted as to permit me to call this new case a mountain. Well, since everything is, I suppose, like something else in some respect and different in some other, I suppose that I could always so interpret the rule as always to say that something is a mountain or never to say this. (A mountain is like an apple in being a spatio-temporal object; Everest is not like K2 in height.) That would undermine the whole notion of projectibility, upon which the notion of rules is founded, by leaving me to make a decision in every new case, but with no grounds upon which to make it.

To that Winch replies that Kripke simply overlooks the passages in which Wittgenstein insists that "there is a way of grasping a rule which is *not* an *interpretation*" (Wittgenstein 1953: ss. 201). He writes, further, "When I obey a rule, I do not choose. I obey the rule blindly" (1953: ss. 219). I might be brought to see things differently, and how that happens will concern us when we come to the discussion of ethical disputes. But then I am brought to *see* something, not to be *given the option of interpreting something as something*. Those who understood the parable of the good Samaritan came to see in the injured man a neighbour and projected the term "neighbour" on to him. But they did not *interpret something* (what?) *as* a neighbour.

Where, though, does the possibility of being *mistaken* in applying rules then come from? For that is integral to Winch's account and, he says, to Wittgenstein's also. Why isn't what *seems* to me a right projection is right simply *because* it seems right to me?

Here it is necessary to remember that *language* exists because we *agree* in the projections that we make. Language is social and bound up with practices. Within those practices we can say that someone, in deviating from us, has made an error. But there follow from that two things that are at the heart of the applications that Winch makes of Wittgenstein's philosophy. First, getting someone to see that he has made a mistake and has deviated from our agreements, is not a matter of *saying* that the person is in error, but of *getting that person to see* what *we* agree in seeing. That, as we shall see, has striking implications for moral argument. Second, *mere* deviation from our practices does not *entail* error. For those who differ from us in projections that they make may agree in making them. By our standards they make no sense, but neither might we by theirs. That insight underlay much that Winch had to say about the difficulties and the possibilities of understanding what used to be called "primitive" societies.

Transition

Winch had learned from Wittgenstein that philosophy is not concerned with discovering what there is, nor is it the handmaiden of those disciplines that have that concern. It deals with questions about what it is for something to be real. He drew as a corollary of that the conclusion that, for an enquiry to be well founded, it must operate with a proper understanding of the kind of reality possessed by the objects that it studies. For example, he thought it essential to an understanding of sociology to grasp what it is that sociality involves. Understanding the kind of reality that the social has will tell us to what any study of the social must attend, and how it might attend to it. Here, having learned, also from Wittgenstein, that rule following is essentially a social activity, he thought it true also that social activities were necessarily rule-following activities. That the "science of the social" had often got this wrong was the burden of what was possibly Winch's most famous work, *The idea of a social science*. It is to that application, in that work, of his inheritance from Wittgenstein that we must now turn.

Further reading

Since his influence on Winch was so great the reader may wish to look further into the work of Wittgenstein. Quite apart from the essays by Winch himself, collected in Winch (1972, 1987b), great pleasure will be derived from reading Ray Monk's biography *Ludwig Wittgenstein: The duty of genius* (London: Cape, 1990). Shorter, but equally compelling, is Norman Malcom's *Ludwig Wittgenstein: A memoir* (Oxford: Oxford University Press, 1958). Andy Hamilton tells me that Hans Sluga's introduction to H. Sluga & D. Stern (eds), *The Cambridge companion to Wittgenstein* (Cambridge: Cambridge University Press, 1996) is the best short presentation of Wittgenstein's life and thought that he has read. Absolute beginners will learn something useful from J. Heaton & J. Groves, *Wittgenstein for beginners* (Cambridge: Icon, 1994). Three accessible intermediate books on Wittgenstein's philosophy are O. Hanfling, *Wittgenstein's later philosophy* (London: Macmillan, 1989), N. Malcolm, *Nothing is hidden* (Oxford: Blackwell, 1986) and M. McGinn, *Wittgenstein: The philosophical investigations* (London: Routledge, 1997). Eventually you should aspire to graduate to reading the *Philosophical investigations* in company with G. P. Baker's and P. M. S. Hacker's monumental exegetical work, for example, the *Analytical commentary* (Oxford: Blackwell, 1983).

The influence of Wittgenstein on Winch was mediated, at least in part, through Rush Rhees. Winch particularly draws attention to the paper "Art and philosophy" reprinted in the collection of Rhees' articles entitled *Without answers* (London: Routledge and Kegan Paul, 1969), pp. 133–54. Much of that book has remarks cognate to those made by Winch, for example, the remarks about science as only one form of rationality. See also, in this connection, the light thrown on the relations between Rhees and Winch by the recently published collection of papers by Rhees on religion in D. Z. Phillips (ed), *Rush Rhees on religion and philosophy* (Cambridge: Cambridge University Press, 1997).

This first chapter has talked much about the difference between empirical and conceptual studies. That distinction, and a whole tradition of philosophy) has been called into question by an alternative tradition in part initiated by Quine's "Two dogmas of empiricism", in his *From a logical point of view*, 2nd edn (Cambridge, Mass.: Harvard University Press, 1964), pp. 20–46, on which see H. P. Grice & P. F. Strawson, "In defence of a dogma", in *Studies in the way of words*, H. P. Grice (Cambridge, Mass.: Harvard University Press, 1989), Chapter 13 and G. Hunter, "Quine's 'Two dogmas of empiricism: Or the power of bad logic'", *Philosophical Investigations* **18**, pp. 305–28, 1995. For a discussion of the debate over philosophy as an empirical science see Essay XIII in G. P. Baker & P. M. S. Hacker, *Essays on the philosophical investigations, volume one* (Oxford: Blackwell, 1980). The chronicle of scientific influences on philosophy, and their effect on the waning of the influence of Wittgenstein's philosophy, is compellingly told in P. M. S. Baker, *Wittgenstein's place in twentieth-century analytic philosophy* (Oxford: Blackwell, 1996).

The literature on Wittgenstein's discussion of rules is lengthy. There is a good introduction to Wittgenstein's analysis of rules in D. Bloor, *Wittgenstein, rules and institutions* (London: Routledge, 1997). In addition to the work of Kripke that is discussed in the text there is also a useful collection, S. H. Holtzmann, & C. M. Leich (eds), *Wittgenstein: To follow a rule* (London: Routledge and Kegan Paul, 1981), which includes Crispin Wright's important "Rule following, objectivity and the theory of meaning". Also useful are M. Budd, "Wittgenstein on meaning, interpretation and rules", *Synthese* **58**, pp. 303–23, 1984, and H. Glock, *A Wittgenstein dictionary* (Oxford: Blackwell, 1996), pp. 323–9.

Winch argues that rules and meaning go together so that "the analysis of meaningful behaviour must allot a central role to the notion of a rule" (Winch 1958: pp. 51–2). That has been queried in C. Williamson, "Following a rule", *Philosophy* **64**, pp. 487–504, 1989. Margaret Gilbert has discussed Winch's notion of rules as social in her paper, "On whether language has a social nature: Some aspects of Winch and others on Wittgenstein", *Synthese* **56**, pp. 301–18, 1983. Like many others she thinks that the possibility of Robinson Crusoes shows the possibility of private rule following, on which see Winch (1958: pp. 33–9; 1997b: p. 53).

Chapter 2
"I was investigating the notion of the social": The idea of a social science

> That the social sciences are in their infancy has become something of a platitude amongst writers of text books on the subject. They argue that this is because the social sciences have been slow to emulate the natural sciences. . . . I propose, in this monograph, to attack such a conception.
>
> (Winch 1958: p. 1)

Sociology

The academic senates, which once governed the academic life of British universities, were often rocked to nightmare by contentious issues. These ranged from the important, for example, whether women should be admitted to a university, to the trivial, for example, whether students should be allowed to write with ball-point pens. Rarely, however, in my long experience, did senates address themselves to questions about the purposes of a university education and to questions about the inclusion of which subjects of study might or might not serve that purpose.

About thirty years ago, not long after the publication of Peter Winch's controversial book, *The idea of a social science*, the university of which I am a member, being then a new foundation in the diastole of its development, addressed itself to just that sort of question. For the question arose whether sociology should be added to the list of subjects appearing on the academic menu. The debates that ensued were, for our present purposes, enormously instructive. (A delicious glimpse of them is to be found in Malcolm Bradbury's novel *The history man.*)

In the 1960s sociology was a glamorous subject, attempts to refurbish the glamour of which are regularly made by the applications of such elixirs as Bauldrillacqeur. Part of the explanation of that glamour was doubtless that the tides of fashion, which, in their flow raise such ephemera as Oasis, Kate Moss and stiletto heels to iconic status had, in a kind of exceptional tidal surge, washed sociology, with its associated hippy images and fashion accessories, particularly high up on the beach of public consciousness. A more serious part of the explanation, however, was that sociology seemed to be not purely theoretical, but to offer a hope that anyone practicing it might come to understand the working of the levers of social change and to a consequent ability to operate them in such a way as to institute a golden era of social improvement. This was not unconnected with the fact that possibly the most important sociologist of them all, Marx, seemed to promise just that. Philosophy, which had merely tried to understand the world, might properly be asked to step aside for those who addressed the question of how to change it.

In the light of what we have just discovered about Wittgenstein and Winch we can understand an even deeper reason why the study of social phenomena rightly struck its advocates as profound; for one of the lessons we have learned is that to study the social is to study ourselves. We are the kinds of beings that we are by virtue of being social beings, and, in particular, language-using beings, so that to study social life is to study what is constitutive of our identity. As the next chapter will show, even if we study a society very different from our own, we would still be studying ourselves. Hence Winch's remark, which has impressed many of my students, that, "seriously to study another way of life is necessarily to seek to extend our own" (Winch 1972: p. 33).

Those attracted to sociology were right, therefore, if they were attracted by the intuition that the study of sociality, properly conducted would take them towards a deeper understanding of what it is to be human. Winch's claim, is, as we shall see, that this study has not always been properly conducted.

The science of society

If there were those who were dazzled by the prospect of bringing sociology into the university, there were also those who had severe reservations. The motivations varied. Some, like aging film stars, clearly did not want to stand next to anything too young and glamorous. Many honestly expressed their belief that sociology necessarily involved a leftish trend, so that taking it on as cargo would entail a severe list to port, a belief, *post hoc ergo propter hoc*, they thought to be immediately confirmed by the student insurrections in the university in the early 1970s.

But there were those who seriously debated the issue whether sociology was a genuine subject, that is to say, a discipline with its own distinctive subject matter and a proper method of studying it. Often the debaters were natural scientists (practitioners of certain of the humanities and business school subjects, themselves open to methodological challenges, keeping well below the parapet). I suspect the natural scientists little knew that they were repeating an allegation, which Winch quotes from Mill (Winch 1958: pp. 66–7), that the state of social sciences *as sciences*, is a scandal. I suspect that they equally thought, with Mill, that this scandal could be remedied only if social science adopted the methods of the natural sciences.

We can now target more precisely what it is that Winch was after in his critical work on social science. For those natural scientists who had reservations about sociology as a science could see only two alternatives. Either sociology remade itself in the image of a successful natural science like physics, or nothing properly to be called an attempt to understand the social could be made. Winch's criticism is now two-fold. First, he argues, too many philosophically maladroit sociologists, notably Mill, *did* try to remodel sociology in the prescribed way. And he wished to show why social science could not be like a natural science. Second, he wished to show that even though social science was not a natural science, there is, none the less, something properly to be called the study of the forms of sociality, and he wished to indicate what form that study might take.

It is convenient, now, to divide the discussion into two chapters. In this chapter I deal with three things. First I deal with Winch's generalization of his account of language as a social phenomenon

into a general account of social behaviour as meaningful behaviour. Second I show how this leads to a criticism of any attempt to reform sociology as a natural science. Third, I discuss some common misunderstandings of Winch's project.
In this chapter I draw largely negative conclusions; those in Chapter 3 are more positive. In Chapter 3 I reiterate, first, the way in which Winch depicts the study of the social as the attempt to *understand* a society or a social practice, marriage, say, within a society. Second, I discuss Winch's claim that understanding might run up against limits, particularly when we seek to understand a different society. Third, I discuss Winch's views on the resources available to us when these limits were reached. That will require us to take on the fascinating charge of relativism, where that amounts to the claim that it is impossible to understand or to criticize societies very different from our own.

I Social behaviour as meaningful behaviour

We naturally associate the notion of meaning with the meaning that *words* have in a language. But the kind of meaning that we attribute to words is also possessed by other things. A gesture may have a meaning, as Wittgenstein realized, to the deteriment of his earlier views on language, when he asked what the two-fingered gesture, central to the vernacular of certain cab drivers, meant. Crossing oneself is a similarly meaningful gesture, although rendered somewhat ambiguous when prefixed to episodes of professional fisticuffs. Objects, too, can have a meaning. In the remarkable film *The gods must be crazy*, a Coca-Cola bottle, jettisoned from an aircraft, falls among a remote tribe in Africa. The tribe attributes a meaning to it, not in the sense in which it might have been thought to mean that hail might now take a different form, but in the sense that it was thought that someone was trying to convey something meaningful by sending it.

To explain the notion of meaning operative in these cases, Winch generalizes the account he has already given of linguistic meaning as a social, rule-governed practice. A number of things about that generalization deserve emphasis.

Reasons

First, Winch introduces (Winch 1958: Ch. 3, ss. 1 and 2) the notion of a *reason for acting*. If someone who does not know that praying involves kneeling asks why people are kneeling, the answer, "They are praying", gives the reason. To give that reason is to give the meaning of the act, although that will only be fully illuminating to someone who knows what praying is and who is not, additionally, confused as to why these people are praying here and now.

A corollary of this is that we have only correctly understood and characterized the meaning of an action, kneeling, say, if *we* understand what it is to pray and we correctly believe that the person concerned knows what praying is. We also have to believe that the person not only knows what prayer is but is kneeling *in order to pray*. (This is not necessarily to assume that the person concerned thought about praying while praying.)

Reasons and causes

On Winch's account (Winch 1958: Ch. 3, s. 3; 1976) an agent's reason for an action, although it explains an action, is not the cause of the action. "Because" is ambiguous. If asked why I smeared jam on the vice-chancellor I reply, "Because my arm was jogged", I give a cause of my action. If I reply, "In order to effect an aesthetic improvement", I give my reason for acting. Here we are pitchforked into a passionate contemporary debate about whether reasons *can* be distinguished from causes, a distinction denied by, for example, Donald Davidson (Davidson 1963: pp. 685–99).

Humean causation

I begin by noting that Winch is operating with the notion of causation as it is found in Hume and later adopted, for the social sciences, by Mill. That notion of Humean causation and its irrelevance in explaining human action is more specifically discussed in Winch 1976. It is necessary, incidentally, to observe that the proof Winch goes on to offer for the assertion that a reason for acting is not a Humean cause leaves it open that it is a cause in some other sense. One of the problems here is that we lack an adequate analysis of the notion of causation (see Sosa and Tooley 1993).

If we take as our example the claim to know that the varying positions of the moon cause alterations of the tides, then, it seemed to Hume, we could not experience (see, touch, and so on) any connecting link between the moon up there and the tidal movements down here. All we have is the facts: first, that the moon appears in a certain place; then (temporal succession) that the tides move a certain way; third, that the two events occur reasonably together (contiguity); and, fourth, that this keeps on happening (constant conjunction).

According to this view cause and effect are *separate occurrences*. From what we know of one thing we can deduce nothing about how it will affect anything else. The most we have is the evidence of past conjunctions. Hume writes,

> Suppose two objects be presented to us. . . . It is plain that, from the simple consideration of one or both of these objects, we shall never . . . be able certainly to pronounce that there is any connection between them. (Hume 1911: p. 139)

Whatever the truth of this as an analysis of causation, it does not seem adequately to characterize the relationship between a person's actions and the reasons in terms of which we understand those actions. Many arguments have been given for saying this, of which I mention one.

If my reason for an action were its cause, then, on the Humean account of causation, there must be *two* things. There would be, on the one hand, an action; kneeling down, say. On the other, there would be some entirely distinct existent, a state of mind perhaps, which is the reason (cause) for the action. In this case the cause would be wanting to kneel in prayer. On Hume's account the two things just happen to go together. But, then, the reason/cause (in our example, wanting to kneel in prayer) might equally well, on a future occasion, be succeeded by a quite different event, say scratching one's nose. Suppose that happened. Then, if the reason is the cause, we would have to say, in answer to the question "Why is she scratching her nose?", "Because she wants to kneel in prayer". But that is *not* the reason why she is scratching her nose. The reason she is scratching her nose is that something has gone haywire in her control of her body, so that when she wants to kneel she

The idea of a social science

finds herself scratching her nose. That behaviour may indeed have a cause, and when we have found it we can say why she scratches her nose whenever she wants to kneel. Winch, indeed, remarks that to accept a causal explanation of my action is to be inclined to withdraw the claim that *I* did it (Winch 1976: pp. 132–3).

In the odd cases we are describing, a gap opens up between what a person wants and what the person involuntarily does, and that opens also the way to a causal explanation. This is the subject of two remarkable papers by Winch, one on Wittgenstein's treatment of the will and one on trying (Winch 1972: pp. 110–50). For suppose someone who wants to pray simply kneels. Where is the gap? The intention is at one with the action. To know that intention is to know the reason for the action and so to know its meaning. In that sense scratching one's nose involuntarily when one wants to pray has no meaning because it does not manifest my intentions or reasons for acting.

If we can distinguish reasons from Humean causes we have a knock-down disproof of any attempt, such as, Winch alleges, Mill's, to recast social science as a natural science, *where that is conceived as the investigation of causes as Hume conceives them* (Winch 1958: Ch. 3). Since reasons are not Humean causes, nothing in any science that investigates such causes can help with what Winch takes to be the foundational task of social study, namely to understand social action in terms of the reasons of social agents.

Rules again

Social activities, such as playing chess, have meaning because agreed and shared rule-governed social practices have emerged that are called "playing chess". It doesn't particularly matter what shade of white the pieces might be, or what they are made of, or how large the board is, or whether one actually has to touch the pieces in order to move them, or what time of day one plays. But if someone moved the bishop now diagonally, now laterally, and claimed to be going on the same way, then we could not play chess with him.

These institutions that give meaning to social actions ground the forms our lives have taken. In the particular culture in which we live, various forms that this development has taken have led to such institutions as marriage and to other notions such as fatherhood. In other cultures life has taken different forms.

As we saw, on the notion of linguistic rules to which Winch subscribes, the notion of a rule is open-ended. It is open-ended in two ways. First, we have no complete control over the way in which things might change and, having changed, occasion changes in the forms our lives might take. Cloning might so change the father–child relationship that what we now express by fatherhood, including its Freudian trappings, might become as odd to us as Winch claims they might even now seem, given different kinship relations, to the Trobrianders (Winch 1958: p. 90).

Second, even without those radical changes, we continually have to apply what we have learned in new circumstances. We project our rules into new contexts, share the routes of projection made by others and expect them to share ours. But we have no algorithms, no books of rules, no laws, that tell us how to make these projections. Winch writes, therefore,

> Questions of interpretation and consistency . . . are bound to arise for anyone who has to deal with a situation foreign to his previous experience. In a rapidly changing social environment such problems will arise frequently, not just because traditional customary modes of behaviour have broken down, but because of the novelty of the situations in which those modes of behaviour have to be carried on. Of course the resulting strain may *lead* to a breakdown in the traditions. . . . Human history . . . is the story of how men have tried to carry over what they regard as important in their modes of behaviour into the new situations which they have had to face. (Winch 1958: pp. 64–5)

Winch, then, has generalized his account of the way in which words get meaning into an account of the way in which the meaningful actions get their meaning from institutions, where those institutions themselves are meaningful by virtue of agreements in human practices as these have evolved to meet the exigencies, varying from society to society, of human situations. Those who live within those practices have open to them the possibilities of meaningful behaviour. They exploit these possibilities by engaging in rule-governed behaviour; that is, by applying rules in ever novel situations, rules that alone make behaviour meaningful. It is not enough to learn what marriage is: that notion has to be applied in ever changing circumstances, so that to some it will seem quite natural to say that same sex marriages are marriages; to others it will not seem so.

The idea of a social science

The possibility of social life is nothing other than the possibility of meaningful behaviour; the behaviour of those who manifest an understanding, however intuitive, of the meaning giving forms of life that define a culture.

In giving this account Winch is the heir to a tradition. For Weber, too, as Winch observes, sociology is concerned with behaviour "if and insofar as the agent or agents associate a subjective sense with it" (Winch 1958: p. 45). Weber explains behaviour in terms of meaning. Croce, too, defined "sociality" as the expressive activities found in human beings and not, because detachment from the causality of nature is not possible for them, in stones or plants (Croce 1992: pp. 6–7). Croce, incidentally, avers that if animals should be shown to have capacities for social life, this will be because they display, in ways appropriate to their modes of existence, those norm-governed activities definitive of social life. He left it open whether this could be shown (1992: pp. 25–6). In this Croce is more generous to the animals than is Winch, who (Winch 1958: p. 60) speaks as if dogs, for example, can simply acquire habits rather than act socially (see also Bloor 1983: p. 172).

II Consequences: sociology, philosophy and science

Two conclusions follow from Winch's account of sociality. First, there are conclusions about the relationships between sociology and philosophy. Second there are conclusions about the possibility of casting sociology as a natural science.

The first conclusion: sociology and philosophy

Winch claims that natural science, religion and art are activities that seek to make sense of the world. The ways in which they make sense of the world will tell us what, for each activity, is considered real. What those who participate in each of these activities is saying, when she or he says that, say, atoms are real, or that God is real, will be a function of the criteria used for determining what is real that are used by participants in that activity.

The philosophy of art, of natural science and of religion will have the task of ascertaining what, for the activity in question, reality amounts to; ascertaining, as Winch puts it, "the peculiar forms which understanding takes in particular kinds of context" (Winch 1958: p. 41).

Over and above these activities, however, there stands, for Winch, the activity of *philosophy as such*. Whereas particular forms of philosophy will seek to elucidate the religious form of life, or the scientific form of life, philosophy, as Winch puts it, seeks to "elucidate what is involved in the notion of a form of life as such" (1958: p. 41). Wittgenstein's answer, as we have seen, involves the "analysis of the concept of following a rule and his account of the peculiar kind of interpersonal agreement which this involves" (1958: p. 41). This, however, strikingly entails that the relationship between sociology and philosophy is quite unlike the relationship between, say, natural science and philosophy.

The argument runs that each subject must have some conception of what its proper subject matter is. The *theory* of that subject will tell us this. Presumably, the subject matter of sociology is the social. We are owed, then, by the theory of sociology, an account of what the social is. As Winch puts it,

> one can hardly in the end avoid including in sociology a discussion of the nature of social phenomena in general; and this is bound to occupy a special place amongst the various disciplines devoted to the study of society. (1958: p. 41)

But, so the argument continues, to elucidate the social is to elucidate the notion of a meaning-giving form of life. However, this, as we saw, is nothing other than the task set itself by philosophy, which, as we have just said, seeks to elucidate "what is involved in the notion of a form of life as such" (1958: p. 41). Hence "the relations between sociology and epistemology must be . . . very much closer than is usually imagined to be the case" (1958: p. 42).

Winch remarks that subjects, like physics, often throw up philosophical difficulties as they progress. In physics one such difficulty, about the meaning of the term "simultaneous", confronted Einstein and led to the formulation of the special theory of relativity. That *temporary* stage of philosophical puzzlement ("philosophical" because about the *meaning* of a term used by physicists) having been lived through, physics put philosophy aside and continued on its way. This is not, however, the way it is with sociology and philosophy. Sociology is not, like physics, a discipline in which the occasional philosophical problem needs to be solved in

The idea of a social science

the course of its progress. An *inescapable* part of theoretical sociology, the determination of the nature of social phenomena, always will be the central issue in sociology, and it simply *is* philosophy. Winch therefore writes:

> The central problem of sociology, that of giving an account of the nature of social phenomena in general, itself belongs to philosophy. In fact, not to put too fine a point on it, this part of sociology is really misbegotten epistemology. I say 'misbegotten' because its problems have been largely misconstrued, and therefore mishandled, as a species of scientific problem.
> (Winch 1958: p. 43)

For Winch, then, as far as theory goes, sociology and philosophy are one. But that is not the end of the matter. For, so far, what we have is the assertion that there is the task of demarcating the subject matter of sociology. That this task puts philosophy at the core of sociology does not entail, once the subject matter has been demarcated, that there is nothing else left for sociology to study. Winch, indeed, never denied that, for example, empirical generalizations or other kinds of sociological explanations are possible. He writes that, although the special sciences could not answer philosophical questions, yet:

> This does nothing to show that explanations may not be found by such sciences which provide perfectly good answers to other kinds of questions. For instance, there are many cases in which historians, anthropologists or linguists give well founded explanations of the existence of this or that practice. Why ever not? (Winch 1993: p. 106)

And:

> [compare] . . . two children, one of whom does learn the language of his or her community while the other does not. Why the difference? The answer might be in terms, for instance, of the development of one child's brain, as contrasted with that of the other; it might be answered in terms of differences in sociological or psychological circumstances in the two cases.
> (1993: p. 107)

However, he remarks, "The important question *for us* to ask is this: what relevance would such explanations have to the resolution of *philosophical* difficulties" (1993: p. 106).

Anyone who is in doubt as to what that means, might consider the way in which, no matter how many discoveries are made about the brain and the way in which changes in the brain occasion changes in behaviour, we are still left with the philosophical question of whether mind and brain are one.

The second conclusion: the rejection of an empirical science of sociology

Is the door, then, left open to saying that once we have established, philosophically, what the nature of subject matter of sociology is, this subject matter is then to be investigated using the kinds of methods typical of the natural sciences? For this is precisely the step that Winch wishes to prevent. He writes, "I want to show that the notion of a human society involves a scheme of concepts which is logically incompatible with the kind of explanations offered in the natural sciences" (Winch 1958: p. 72). Why does Winch say this? Isn't there a contradiction between saying, in the passages just cited, that *explanations* of behaviour *are* possible, whilst yet denying that the subject is an empirical science? How, then, does Winch get from his analysis of what it is for something to be social, to the conclusion that the social is not apt, as nature is, for scientific study?

Winch on Mill

Chapter 3 of *The idea of a social science* takes Mill as its example of someone who wrongly tries to reform sociology along the lines of the natural sciences. Winch's discussion is perplexing, not least because of its extreme brevity. Let us see what clarity we can bring.

Central to the account is the claim that Mill's conception of scientific investigation rests on Hume's ideas about the nature of causation, where to assert that A caused B is to say that the temporal succession of A and then B is an instance of a *generalization* to the effect that events like A are always found, in our experience, to be followed by events like B. According to Winch, this view represents science as "establishing causal sequences". We have an example of this when, after observing correlations, we assert generally that (A) movements of the moon cause (B) tidal changes. An instance of this in the case of social behaviour might be the generalization that if (A) perpetrators of crimes are brought into face-to-face discussion with their victims then (B) they will be less likely to reoffend. Winch claims that this commits Mill to the conclusion that a scientific investigation of any subject matter is possible only if the subject matter is one between the members of which it is possible to establish such causal sequences. His strategy is then to argue that, since this can't be done for social phenomena, they cannot be dealt with scientifically.

In the case of social actions, questions about regularities and irregularities (why, for example, some people do and some don't reoffend on meeting their victims), will be explained, for Mill, by coming to understand their motives, where that is to come to understand the deeper laws of human nature, the "Laws of Mind" as Mill calls them. These too are simply generalizations based on observable regularities; what Winch describes (Winch 1958: p. 75) as "high level causal generalisations". That allows him to represent Mill's view as ultimately standing or falling on the claim that Mill makes "motive explanations a species of causal explanation" (1958: p. 78). Since, as I have argued in discussing reasons and causes, Winch thinks they aren't, the claim on which Mill's account of sociological explanation is founded is false. As we have seen already, whatever the relation is between a mental state and the action that a person does, the relation is not, for Winch, one of Humean causation.

Science

It will be noted that even if Mill's view is ultimately incoherent, this only counts as an argument against the possibility of using the methods of natural science in sociology, if Mill's version of a Humean account is the only one available as a model of how sociology might be modelled on the natural sciences. It is not clear that it is.

The problem in dealing with Winch's discussion of the difference between sociology and the natural sciences is that he is somewhat unforthcoming about what he takes the natural sciences to be. We are given rough characterizations: "the scientist investigates the nature, causes and effects of particular real things and processes" (Winch 1958: p. 8) by "experimental methods" (1958: p. 9); its questions are "empirical" (1958: pp. 9, 16); he "generalises from particular instances" (1958: p. 9) to form "empirical generalisations" (1958: p. 83); he "tries to make the world more intelligible" (1958: p. 19); in its Humean form at least science seeks laws that record regularities observed between distinct events (1958: p. 67–9). (It is interesting to note in this connection a story, which the untimely death of Martin Hollis has made it impossible for me directly to confirm, to the effect that, when asked why he did not produce a new edition of *The idea of a social science*, Winch expressed to Professor Hollis the view that a major weakness of the book was its inadequate conception of natural science.)

Had Winch dealt more fully with these matters it would have been easy for him to show that *if science is about explanation*, it needs no digression through the nature of social phenomena to see off *Mill's* view of science. On the Mill/Hume account the scientist simply notes more and more regularities. But *noting* a regularity is not *explaining* that regularity. The scientist's job is not to note that typhoid follows the drinking of certain kinds of water, but to *explain* why typhoid follows the drinking of certain sorts of water. So, too, to revert to my example, the task of scientific sociological explanation is not to note that those who meet their victims do not so often reoffend, which might be a useful thing to know, but to *explain* why this is so.

Seeing off Mill in this way, however, is not enough to see off explanatory social science, given that there are accounts of scientific enterprise that *do* treat it as explanatory. These seem better fitted as models for sociology as a science.

Realist science

One such model is what might be called "realist" science. That view begins by rejecting the Humean account of causation, thereby also bypassing any criticism, such as Winch's, of any science based on that account. Keat and Urry, who are proponents of realist science, quote the following two instructive passages. The first is from Hume:

> We say, for instance that the vibration of this string is the cause of this particular sound. But what do we mean by that

The idea of a social science

affirmation? We . . . mean *that this vibration is followed by this sound and that all similar vibrations have been followed by similar sounds.* (Keat & Urry 1975: p. 29)

In reply they quote Rom Harré, a realist philosopher of science:

> This, Hume contends, must be the correct analysis, since we can form no idea of the connection between the vibration and the sound. But the theory and the experiments of sonic physics and neuro-physiology give us a very good idea of the connection between the vibration and the sound. We all know nowadays of the train of pressures in the air, the operation of the ear drum, the cochlea, and so on, and we know something of the train of electro-chemical happenings between the inner ear and that part of the brain identified as the seat of audition. . . . To explain what we mean by "the vibration causes the sound", rather than something else, typically involves . . . reference to the intervening mechanism which links the vibration in the string to the sound we hear. The vibration in the string stimulates a mechanism which then acts in such a way that we are stimulated and hear a sound. (Keat & Urry 1975: p. 29)

In saying that *A* causes *B*, then, we are not, contrary to Hume, merely noting a regularity. We are, in addition, positing some intervening, actually existing and potentially observable mechanism that links them together, and which it is the task of the scientist to discover.

Why then should we not, as Keat and Urry do, take this as our model for social science? Here their model is Marx, and they argue that Marx gives an exemplary case of social theory as a realist science. For Marx, as Keat and Urry put it:

> takes the more apparent and observable features of social life to be explicable in terms of . . . underlying structures. They can be characterised by the discovery of causal mechanisms central to each structure; these mechanisms are characterised in terms of relations between a small number of theoretical entities. Marx's advocacy here of analysing the nature of these mechanisms implies a non-Humean view of causal relationships. He does, however, believe in the possibility of an objective science of social formations. He is both a naturalist and a realist. (Keat & Urry 1975: p. 96)

Peter Winch

Comments

Keat and Urry offer Marx as their model of a realist social scientist, but they do so not as finished business, and, indeed, canvas a number of *very* powerful possible objections to that construction of Marx's project (Keat & Urry 1975: pp. 116–18), to which I commend the reader. For my part I offer these initial comments.

1 A lacuna

Since Winch directed his fire only at Humean accounts, of which Mill's was an exemplar, it is quite unclear what we should say about his possible reaction to realist views about sociology as an empirical science. (One thing he could have said, which is hinted at by Keat and Urry themselves, is that the intervening mechanisms that are posited by realist science, examples of which are mentioned in the quotation from Harré above, are themselves reducible to Humean concomitant regularities.)

That he did not discuss the realist view of science is explained by the fact that a writer can only take as a target what is around at the time. At the time that Winch wrote *The idea of a social science,* what might be called "positivist" views about the nature of social science, views that took the task of the sociologist to be to establish observable regularities in behaviour and nothing more, were predominant. In 1964, six years after the publication of Winch's book, the flavour of American sociology was positivistic. Thus Lundberg wrote of a sociology in which "numerical units and manipulating devices can be utilised in accurate and objective description of qualities and relationships" (Lundberg 1964: pp. 81–2). Timasheff was even more strongly of the opinion that "the school dominating present day sociology at least in America is the neopositivist one", with a convergence "in the direction of the theory and methods of natural science" (quoted in Keat and Urry 1975: p. 92). That view, if it is based on Humean notions of causality, is the kind of view put to rout in Winch's book, a rout confirmed by the rough ride that positivist views of science have received in recent years (Keat & Urry 1975: Ch. 1).

2 Prediction

Keat and Urry allow that one of the reasons that one might think of Marxism as a science is that it has predictive power. I leave aside the allegation that none of the predictions made by Marx seem to have been much good. Winch would, I suspect, be more worried about two aspects of any account of a social science that (like Mill's) had the need for predictability *of a certain sort,* what he calls "scientific" prediction, built into it (Winch 1958: pp. 93–4).

First, any representation of the meaning-giving structures of a society that entails that these structures deterministically and in predictable ways extrude actions from human beings, so that we are the passive playthings of social forces, is at odds with Winch's analysis. (Keat and Urry themselves suggest that there is an unclarity, which must infect their own account, about whether Marx's account is meant to cite things that "determine what happens" (Keat & Urry 1975: p. 117).) In Winch's account (and, indeed, in the accounts given by Derrida and Merleau-Ponty, to take but two examples (Lyas 1997: pp. 170–84)), this cannot be so. There *are* structures that give meaning, but they have to be *applied* in *particular cases* by *particular human beings.* General structures are refracted through individual psychologies. Each of those applications, as we have seen, is a free creative act, in which the individual projects his or her understanding in new circumstances. We could not predict that someone who had learned "vivid" with respect to colours would find a use for it with respect to turns of phrase. Thus Merleau-Ponty spoke of the difference between the meaning-giving structures of the language and the actual speaking of that language as the gap that each person who speaks and writes must leap (Merleau-Ponty 1960: p. 30).

Second, it is not clear that one can predict, in the way in which Marx may have thought he could, a direction of change in social institutions. For that would suggest only certain ways of going onwards lie open at particular junctures. But whether, given that human cloning were operative, we would still want to say that someone was a father, would depend on whether we see some similarity between fathers now and fathers then. Nothing in our past practice gives us any obvious grounds on which to make assumptions about what *will* seem the same to us in changed circumstances (Winch 1958: pp. 64ff.).

In fact, introducing talk about prediction may be a red herring, since it is unclear that one needs to make prediction necessary to science. It is not essential to science that one be able to predict in advance what is going to happen; it may be enough to be able to give some account after the event. The difficulties with realist social science are, as we shall see, more basic than problems about prediction.

3 Vacuous explanations

Winch says things that might suggest little sympathy for certain realist attempts to explain by positing, as Keat and Urry suggest, mechanisms or entities underlying human actions, as when in, Chapter 3, section 3 of *The idea of a social science*, he discusses accounts that posit *motives* as lying behind and explaining overt behaviour.

Let us suppose that we wish to explain why, in a certain set of circumstances, an agent does an action. Let us assume, even, that we have a statistical regularity that tells us that whenever circumstances of a certain sort occur, an agent tends to do a particular thing (as when the inimitable Basil Fawlty invariably responds to the stimulus of frustration with the fist waving expostulation of "Thank you, God!"). Now, a realist scientist will want to say that this is only explained, if we posit some mechanism that intervenes between the action and stimulus.

Take now, as Winch does, those who introduce here the notion of an intervening inner motive that connects stimulus and response. In Newcomb's account this is "a state of the organism in which bodily energy is directed towards a part of the environment" (quoted in Winch 1958: p. 76). We also have talk of "drives", which are "bodily states felt as restlessness, which initiate tendencies to activity" (Winch 1958: p. 76). Winch writes, "clearly a mechanical model is at work here: it is as if the actions of a man were like the behaviour of a watch where the energy contained in the tensed spring is transmitted *via* the mechanism in such a way as to bring about the regular revolution of the hands" (1958: p. 76).

Newcomb admits that nothing like a motive thus described has ever been seen by a psychologist. So much for this as a realist science, since, as we saw, in that science one hopes eventually to get empirical confirmation of the real existence of the intervening mechanism. However, he certainly claims to have circumstantial evidence of the existence of such mechanisms. Thus, in 1927 Zeigarnik gave a set of people twenty tasks with a strict, but unspecified time limit for each task. Each subject was stopped on completing half the tasks, irrespective of time taken, and told that the allowed time had elapsed. It was discovered that the subjects remembered the tasks they had to complete more readily than those they had completed and expressed a wish to be allowed to complete them. Newcomb concluded:

> Such evidence suggests that motivation involves a mobilisation of energy earmarked, as it were, for achieving a specified goal. The experimental data do not provide final "proof" for such a theory, but they are consistent with it and are difficult to explain in any other way.
> (cited in Winch 1958: p. 78)

Winch remarks that the behaviour reported by Zeigarnik is perfectly intelligible without all this palaver about drives and motives. We could simply have said that the subjects' interests were aroused by the tasks and they were irritated because they had not been allowed to finish them. Nothing is added to that understanding by talk of drives and motives. We don't invoke these when we come to understand why someone acted in a certain way. There is, in fact, nothing for a realist science to work on. When Basil Fawlty acts as he does, the explanation is that he overreacts, and the reason why he regularly does so is that he is of a nervous disposition. The reason for that, if we want one, will have to do with common-sense facts about his life experiences. As Winch remarks:

> To discover the motives of puzzling action *is* to increase our understanding of that action; that is what "understanding" means as applied to human behaviour. But this is something that we in fact discover without any significant knowledge of other people's physiological states; therefore our accounts of their motives can have nothing to do with their physiological states. (Winch 1958: p. 78)

The challenge to a realist science, which posits explanatory undermechanisms for actions, is to show that it does something more than what could be done by describing our social conditions in terms that seem not part of science, as when Simone Weil (1955) simply draws to our attention the kinds of oppression possible in a factory system.

Here it needs to be remarked that the points Winch made in 1958 have an immediate relevance to 1998, the year in which I write. There is something now called the "theory-theory", which attempts to represent our ability to attribute a mind to another as a matter of our possessing a theory. As Bob Sharpe put it, "the suggestion is that whenever we talk of beliefs or wants we engage in a process similar to talking about quarks" (Sharpe 1997: p. 7). Here is a choice expression of the theory-theory:

> The child's early understanding of the mind is an implicit theory analogous to scientific theories, and changes in that understanding may be understood as theory changes. . . . such theories should involve appeals to abstract theoretical entities, with coherent relations among them. Theories should invoke characteristic explanations phrased in terms of these abstract entities and laws . . . recent evidence suggests that during the period from three to four many children are in a state of transition between two . . . theories.
> (cited in Sharpe 1997: p. 7)

The detailed discussion of this can be found in Sharpe's reply. I note one point relevant to our present discussion. Sharpe correctly observes that the account just cited is preposterous if the child is conceived as an infant Galileo conjuring ideas of belief, desire, motive and emotion out of thin air in order to account for the movements of other children and adults. To repeat Winch's question, what more do these speculations tell us than that children learn these concepts as they learn to talk? Loose chat to the effect that the concepts are "hard-wired in" simply veil lucidity in metaphor.

The intimacy of the relationship between the explainer and the explained

But there is a more fundamental reason why, even if we admit that a realist account of science *is* correct as an account of the workings of empirical natural science, we might think that there is still a difference between that science and the study and explanation of social behaviour.

The idea of a social science

Winch notes that enquiries in a special discipline, say physics, are intelligible relative only to that mode of enquiry as constituted by its regulative rules. So:

> In a physical science the rules are those governing the procedures of the investigators in the science in question. For instance, someone with no understanding of the problems and procedures of nuclear physics would gain nothing from being present at an experiment like the Cockcroft-Walton bombardment of lithium by hydrogen. (Winch 1958: p. 84)

The rules of a discipline being based on "the social context of common activity", it follows that:

> to understand the activities of an individual scientific investigator we must take account of two sets of relations: first, his relation to the phenomena which he investigates; second his relation to his fellow scientists. . . . That they belong to different types is evident from the following considerations. The phenomena being investigated present themselves to the scientist as an *object* of study; he observes them and notices certain facts about them. But to say of a man that he does this presupposes that he already has a mode of communication in the use of which rules are already being observed. For to notice something is to identify the relevant characteristics, which mean that the noticer must have some *concept* of such characteristics. . . . So we come back to his relation to his fellow scientists. . . . In the course of his investigations the scientist applies and develops the concepts germane to his particular field of study. This application and modification are "influenced" both *by* the phenomena to which they are applied and also by the fellow-workers *in participation with* whom they are applied. But the two kinds of "influence" are different.
> (Winch 1958: p. 85–6)

And now, in a section entitled, significantly, "Understanding social institutions", Winch produces this remarkable passage, which takes us to the heart of his views on the social and much else:

> Mill's view is that understanding a social institution consists in observing regularities in the behaviour of its participants and expressing these regularities in the form of generalisations. Now if the position of the sociological investigator (in a

59

broad sense) can be regarded as comparable, in its main logical outlines, with that of the natural scientist, the following must be the case. The concepts and criteria according to which the sociologist judges that, in two situations, the same thing has happened, or the same action has been performed, must be understood in relation to the rules governing sociological investigation. But here we run against a difficulty; for whereas in the case of the natural scientist we have to deal with only one set of rules, namely those governing the scientist's investigation itself, here what the sociologist is studying, as well as his study of it, is a human activity, and is therefore carried on according to rules. And it is these rules which govern the sociologist's investigation, which specify what is to count as "doing the same sort of thing" in relation to that kind of activity . . . [for example] . . . The sociologist of religion will be confronted with an answer to the question: Do these two acts belong to the same kind of activity?; and this answer is given according to criteria which are taken not from sociology, but from religion itself. But if the judgments of identity – and hence the generalisations – of the sociologist of religion rest on criteria taken from religion, then his relation to religion cannot be just that of the observer to the observed. It must rather be analogous to the participation of the natural scientist with his fellow workers in the activities of scientific investigation. Putting the point generally, even if it is legitimate to speak of one's understanding of a mode of social activity as consisting in a knowledge of regularities, the nature of this knowledge must be very different from the knowledge of physical regularities. . . . The point is reflected in such commonsense considerations as the following: that a historian or sociologist of religion must have some religious feeling if he is to make sense of the religious movement he is studying. A historian of art must have some aesthetic sense if he is to understand the problems confronting the artists of his period; and without this he will have left out of his account precisely what would have made it a history of art, as opposed to a rather puzzling external account of certain motions which certain people of a certain period have been perceived to go through. (Winch 1958: p. 86–8)

Part of this is obvious. No account of social phenomena that

The idea of a social science

attempts to abstract from the meaning of what it studies can be any good. If one tried to give an account of prayer in terms of the movements of the bodies of those who pray conceived as the movements of physical masses through spatio-temporal coordinates, that would not be an account of prayer but a puzzling account of certain motions. One must have some idea of the meaning of what one studies in order to study it at all, which immediately brings to the forefront the related questions of what it is to understand that meaning and whether it can always be guaranteed when studying another culture.

Even if technical terms are introduced into the study of social phenomena, they have to be related back to non-technical social activities that give them sense, so that, to use Winch's example (1958: p. 89), if the term "liquidity preference" is to *explain* anything to us, its logical tie must be shown to such notions as money, profit, cost and risk as they display themselves in pre-theoretic economic practices.

That, then, introduces something that explains why Winch's work had so substantial an impact on what is called the "hermeneutic" tradition, notably in Germany. When I understand something about atoms, I do not have to understand their meaning in the sense of empathizing with them. Nor, when I understand them, do they tell me anything about myself, although the task of studying them might. But an explanation of meaningful social actions and institutions is not like that. I cannot understand these unless I understand their meaning. If the social phenomenon which I wish to understand is not one in which I participate, that will raise problems about what explanation and understanding might be. If it is of an institution in which I participate, then in learning what I learn, I learn about myself.

That seems to me to be the central reason why Winch may have envisaged a difference between an explanation in the natural and an explanation in the social sciences. For an explanation in the natural sciences does not *remind* us of something. It tells us something we did not already know. That is why it is empirical, *a posteriori,* and all the other things that scientific discovery is traditionally said to be. We are not *reminded* about sub-atomic particles: we find things out about them.

If, however, we are dealing with meaningful social actions and with institutions of which we are practising members, the situation cannot be like that. Here I have to be *reminded* of how it is with me in the society that constitutes my identity and be brought to see what I am already committed to in belonging to it. The explanation only works if I *acknowledge* it. Two examples in Winch's work make this clear.

First, he points out (Winch 1958: pp. 89–90) that a psychoanalyst might explain a patient's neurotic behaviour in terms of factors unknown to the patient and of concepts that would be unintelligible to him. But not only do those concepts have to be related to terms that are in use in the society to which the patient belongs, terms like "family", "father", and the like, but in the end the explanation works as psychoanalysis only if the patient comes to see his or her life in a certain way *and* feels himself or herself to have acquired self-knowledge.

Second, I have no inclination to deny that Marx might have given an account of the surface features of my society in terms of such underlying notions as class, superstructure, base and the like. But if, in the end, I did not recognize what was offered to me as a characterization of *my* society, or, at the least, one with which I could empathize, what has been *explained* to me? Neilsen put it well:

> In catching ideological distortions . . . – in recognising appearances as mere appearances – we need to rely not only on our theoretical conceptions but also on a massive background of quite ordinary understanding without reference to which our iconoclastic interpretations . . . could not even be intelligibly formulated, let alone understood and confirmed or disconfirmed. (Neilsen 1981–2: pp. 478–9)

And that seems to suggest that confusion might be introduced if we think of *this* kind of understanding and of the understanding that is produced by empirical science as two forms of the same thing.

That brings us back full circle to what was said in Chapter 1. There I said that we might distinguish empirical and conceptual enquiries. An empirical enquiry teaches me something new. Natural sciences, in so far as they are empirical enquiries, do that. Conceptual enquiries bring us to see what is implicit in what we already know. Winch's arguments seem to me to suggest that the kind of insight brought by the best sociology is like that.

III Some possible misunderstandings

1 The structure of social institutions

David Bloor (1983) has argued that although the general approach evidenced in the work of Wittgenstein and Winch is right, more is needed if it is to help with an understanding of society. In particular he seeks an account of the ways in which the various institutions of a society can be perspicuously represented as hanging together. In this connection he offers the example of the work of Mary Douglas, who has given a systematic account of the ways in which societies react to "anomalies" in terms of a taxonomy of four basic kinds of society (Bloor 1983: Ch. 7).

Faced with this, my inclination is to say that I recognize what Douglas says as characterizing my society and, therefore, think that something has been illuminated for me. But that is not what is, at present at issue. Winch does not deny the possibility of systematic studies of practices, nor that these studies might illuminate our understanding. The question is whether the illumination received here is the kind we receive from empirical science or whether it is the kind we receive from being reminded of what we implicitly know. I am inclined to say that it is the latter for two reasons.

First, I do not merely feel that illumination has been shed. I feel that *I* have been illuminated. I can ask which kind of society *mine* is and, if I don't like what I find, I feel myself to have been in some way adversely judged. What comes is the sense of recognition, of the scales having fallen from the eyes, so that I have now a perspicuous view of myself and my society.

Second, what of the assessment of the truth of the view that is reported to us? It is not to be doubted that empirical evidence bears on it. But it bears on it in the sense in which reminding people of what they actually in fact say in certain situations bears on the truth of a claim about the meaning of a term like "real". That is to say, the discussion is dialectical. I might, for example, remind the speaker of facts that do not fit the picture that he or she offers as characterizing my society and that seem to require a revision in the account.

The same considerations seem to me to be confirmed when we look at the present state of sociology. In an important recent book,

Peter Winch

Scott Lash's *The sociology of post-modernism* (Lash 1990), I read:

> I shall offer a systematic and sociological description of postmodernism. Then I shall outline a very straightforward sociological explanation of this cultural "paradigm"... I shall draw on a great variety of concrete phenomena as illustrations in order to convince the reader of the validity of my schematic and explanatory models. (Lash 1990: p. 3)

This seems not be part of an empirical enquiry, typical of the natural sciences. Rather it seems to offer me a way of thinking about how my society is. The concrete phenomena that are offered as illustrations to convince the reader, will have that effect only if the reader acknowledges them as representing something that this reader is already in a position implicitly to recognize.

The hope is that I will recognize the fittingness of what I am told, and so see what was there to be recognized all along. Giddens, too, offers a characterization of contemporary society in terms of the concept of structuration. Again, however, that stands or falls by the sense of illumination that it brings. It does not seem to be offered in the spirit in which the discoveries about the behaviour of particles in nuclear accelerators is announced. For him, no less than for Winch, social theory is not *empirical work*, although it may suggest the place in which empirical work needs to be done. Thus Giddens writes:

> Social theory has the task of providing conceptions of the nature of human social activity and of the human agent which can be placed in the service of empirical work. The main concern of social theory is the same as that of the social sciences in general: the illumination of the concrete processes of social life. (Giddens 1984: p. xvii)

2 *Ideology and false consciousness*

MacIntyre (in Wilson 1970), Gellner (1973) and Milligan (1968–9) have stressed the centrality to accounts of the social of the phenomenon of false consciousness and the related phenomenon of ideology, where ideology hides from us how it really is with us. They take this to be a threat to Winch's account, which, they assume, stresses the knowledge the agent has of his or her reasons

The idea of a social science

for acting. A worker may believe that he or she is a free agent, freely bargaining his or her labour. When asked, this is how he or she describes his or her behaviour. But it is possible to be deluded about such things. MacIntyre, for example, writes:

> A distinction may be made between those rules which agents in a given society sincerely profess to follow and to which their actions in fact conform, but which do not in fact direct their actions, and those rules, which, whether they profess to follow them or not, do in fact guide their actions by providing them with reasons and motives. . . . The making of this distinction is essential to the notions of *ideology* and *false consciousness*.
> (MacIntyre in Wilson 1970: p. 118)

This is only a threat to anything that Winch says if he is taken to assert that whatever a person says about his or her motivation is authoritative and incorrigible. But he does not say that.

Here the question is not whether we can fail to see that our actions are guided by a reason other than the one that we explicitly profess, but what happens when we come to see that this is so, when, so to speak, the ideological blindfold is removed? When that blindfold is removed, we see *ourselves* and our real reasons. Without this reference to what we might admit to be our reasons, how could these be *our* reasons? There is, in this respect, a difference between believing that one has cancer and finding that one hasn't and between feeling that one is free and finding that one isn't. The former is a discovery, the latter a revelation.

When, therefore, Winch says that the correct description of an action is one that relates it to the agent's reasons, he is not obliged to say that the agent is always in the best position to say what his reasons are. On the contrary, it is the essence of Wittgenstein's work that we may need reminders of what we already implicitly know. That is so whether what we have forgotten is how we actually speak or what our motives really are. Thus he remarks:

> The aspects of things that are most important to us are hidden because of their simplicity and familiarity. (One is unable to notice something – because it is always before one's eyes) . . . – And this means that we fail to be struck by what once seen is most striking and most powerful . . .
> (Wittgenstein 1958: ss. 129)

Peter Winch

Transition

The study of social phenomena is, then, the study of meaningful behaviour. To study such phenomena we have to *understand* them, indeed, on Winch's account to study them *is* to seek understanding. That raises the question whether such an understanding is always possible, a question raised in vivid form when we encounter different cultures, cultures like the Azande who claim to have day-to-day dealings with witches. That naturally takes us to the consideration of Winch's views about social studies, ethics and religion to which I now turn.

Further reading

A thorough, authoritative and philosophically acute account of various conceptions of science, with a defence of realist science, is Keat and Urry (1975). See also the reference to Keat below for some updating.

One source of misunderstandings of Winch is the mistaken belief that he thought that his claim that theoretical sociology (the analysis of the concept of sociality) *is* philosophy entailed that sociology was nothing other than philosophy. I find some evidence of this in: Gellner (1973); A. Louch, "The very idea of a social science", *Inquiry* **8**, pp. 273–86, 1963; R. Bernstein, *The restructuring of social and political theory* (Oxford: Blackwell, 1973); D. Thomas, "Sociology and common sense", *Inquiry* **21**, pp. 1–32, 1978; D. Braybrooke, "Authority as a subject of social science", *Review of Metaphysics* **13**, pp. 476–85, 1959–60. Winch categorically denies this intention (see Winch 1964: p. 204). In this respect see the judicious paper by W. W. Sharrock, "Understanding Peter Winch", *Inquiry* **28**, pp. 119–22, 1985, which endorses Winch's claim (Winch 1964: p. 203) that he was investigating the concept of the social, and not telling sociology how to act in the light of that understanding. See also A. Levinson, "Knowledge and sociology", *Inquiry* **19**, pp. 132–45, 1966.

A quite different objection to Winch comes from Richard Rudner, who argues that Winch's claim that we must understand another society before we can engage in sociological explanations requires Winch to believe that the aim of science is to "duplicate reality", see his *Philosophy of social science* (Englewood Cliffs:

Prentice Hall, 1966), pp. 69–70, 82–83. On this odd claim see S. Harrison, "Rudner's reproductive fallacy", *Philosophy of Social Science* **11**, pp. 37–44, 1981.

For a penetrating defence of the claim that Winch's account of social science allows for ideology, see Neilsen (1981–2).

On Winch's discussion of the notion of prediction in the social sciences see M. Gilbert & F. Berger, "On an argument for the impossibility of prediction in social science", *American Philosophical Quarterly* **9**, pp. 99–111, 1975.

The Routledge encyclopedia of philosophy, Edward Craig's monumental editorial work, was published in 1998. It can be consulted on virtually every topic in this work. I draw attention to the articles on: reasons and causes, by Michael Smith; causation, by Nancy Cartwright; scientific realism and social science, by Russell Keat; and social science, philosophy of, by Alexander Rosenberg.

A telling recent defence of the conceptual rather than the empirical nature of philosophy is to be found in Jackson (1998), Chapters 2 and 3.

Chapter 3

"Seriously to study another way of life": Understanding another society

> Seriously to study another way of life is necessarily to seek to extend our own – not simply to bring the other way within the existing boundaries of our own. (Winch 1972: p. 33)

The paradox of tolerance

Those, and particularly those, living in nations that had colonial pretensions suffer conflicting intuitions. On the one hand, aware of the ways in which we imposed our own values and patterns of social life on others, we take it as axiomatic that we should respect differences in other cultures. That pushes us to tolerance. Then we note that a society embodies practices that we find repugnant, such as female circumcision, slavery or the selling of female children into marriage or labour. A moral hesitation occurs and we are immobilized between the impulse to tolerate and the impulse to condemn. That situation becomes more pressing when we find that there are apparently alternative cultures in our own territorial space, the matter being brought most prominently to our attention when the practices of a culture within a society come into conflict with the law, as when the wearing of turbans precludes obedience to the requirement that crash helmets be worn. As I shall show in this chapter and the next, the work of Peter Winch throws light, and optimistic light, on these vexing problems.

Peter Winch

Universal reason

Deep tides run through these issues. A pervasive feature of our culture is a strongly held commitment to rationality. One requirement thought to be imposed by that commitment is that, when there is some disagreement, in art, morality, science, there be procedures, binding on *everyone*, that are *guaranteed* to resolve it. Thus science and mathematics, are thought rational because they embody methods, deduction and induction, for conclusively resolving disputes. Lacking such decision procedures, ethics and aesthetics are thought irrational. Why else would there be continuing disagreements about such things as abortion?

What some call "modernism" is often said to inherit the Kantian, enlightenment, project of operating according to a set of rational principles, binding on all the endeavours of all humankind. That project seemed on the way to achievement in the advances produced in the natural sciences when they adopted rational principles of enquiry. It was reflected, also, in those forms of art which, unadorned by the superfluity of ornament, exemplify rationality. In ethics, utilitarianism offered the prospect of a rational calculus in terms of which ethical and social policies could be determined.

Then, so the story goes, the wheels came off the chariot of progress. Technical advances produced the mechanized catastrophes of the First World War and the mass exterminations of the Second World War. Rational social planning produced the tragedy of the Soviet farm collectivization programme and urban squalor.

When those wheels came off, various options presented themselves. One was a revival of religion, to return to the time when, before *human* rationality became the measure of all things, a *celestially* rooted order existed. Another (from which Winch explicitly distances himself), was a rejection of science.

But the most interesting reaction was to query the notion of universal rationality as the notion of the one way of making the world intelligible. Instead there was an inclination to allow a multiplicity of projects, each distinctive of a culture or sub-culture, each as rational, in terms of the needs and aspirations of those cultures, as any other.

Two related forms of this show themselves. One is the belief that the procedures by which we resolve disputes in science might be quite unlike the methods by which we come to terms with disagreements in, say, art, morality and religion. The other is the belief that different cultures may make sense of the world in different ways. These positions are evidenced in Peter Winch's work.

It is, I think, a mistake often made by those who write intellectual histories, to think that they are describing human history when they are describing only the history of the ideas about humanity that are held by a small subsection of the human race. My experience of life outside academies persuades me that, for most people, life is bound to such things as birth, marriage, work, leisure and death, into which thoughts about modernity and postmodernity rarely enter. Nor am I entirely convinced that the story of the rising crescendo and rapid diminuendo of an enlightenment project is accurate history, as if, long before 1914, Dickens, in *Hard times*, say, had not seen the problems of calculative rationality.

Yet it is possible to detect, if not along historically sequential lines, a difference between those, Apel for example (Apel 1990), who believe in universal rationality and those, like Wittgenstein and Winch, who appear not to do so. Those who ascribe to the latter view might *seem* committed to a tolerance of whatever other cultures do: those committed to the first view are not. The question of this chapter is whether this is true of Winch and Wittgenstein and whether they are, therefore, relativists.

Winch's difficult project

Consider, first, this remark by Winch:

> We start from the position that standards of rationality in different societies do not always coincide; from the possibility, therefore, that the standards of rationality current . . . [elsewhere] . . . are different from our own.   (Winch 1972: p. 31)

That immediately suggests a kind of relativism. What may seem irrational by our standards may well be rational by a different set of standards. That would seem to preclude any criticism, and, possibly, even any understanding, of the ideas and values of another culture.

But Winch also writes:

> We should not lose sight of the fact that the idea that men's ideas and beliefs must be checkable against something independent – some reality – is an important one. To abandon it is to plunge straight into a protagorean relativism, with all the paradoxes that this involves.   (Winch 1972: p. 11).

He adds

> [My argument was] ... not, absurdly, that ways men live together can never be criticized, nor even that a way of living can never be characterized as in any sense 'irrational'. Still less do I argue ... that men who belong to one culture can 'never understand' lives led in another culture.
>
> (Winch 1972: p. 3)

This emphasis on the possibility of cross cultural understanding and criticism is repeated at length in Winch's reply to Jarvie (Winch 1970).

That suggests that Winch may have found a way in which to acknowledge cultural difference without having to fall into relativism. If there is such a way, we will also have a way of reconciling the contrary pulls of tolerance and social conscience. That is what makes trying to understand and evaluate what Winch has to say of great contemporary relevance.

Roots

Peter Winch begins his justly famous paper "Understanding a primitive society" with the remark that "this essay will pursue further some questions raised in my book *The idea of a social science*" (Winch 1972: p. 8).

We should take this seriously. The key to understanding that paper is the earlier book. Indeed, everything said in the later paper is prefigured in the earlier book. Since the ideas in that work are an application of theses to be found in the later philosophy of Wittgenstein, the central ideas of the later essay can also be traced back to that foundation.

Here we need to recall the two central adoptions by Winch from Wittgenstein, namely the ideas of the dependence of language on forms of life, and the projectibility of rules.

To imagine a language means to imagine a form of life

First, human beings have emerged as a species not only through certain kinds of interactions with the natural world but also from interactions with recognized others. A thing that does not interact with recognized others needs no language and can do nothing

Understanding another society

meaningful. An iceberg certainly arises from the interaction of water and temperature and it may impinge upon passing vessels. But it does not recognize anything else, has no meaning to convey, and needs no language to achieve its effects.

Human beings (and possibly other animals) interact both with the world and also with each other, in such activities as hunting, farming, loving, procreation and dancing. The particular ways language evolves depend upon the forms that interactive lives can take. We have our forms of linguistic expression because we are the kinds of things that we are. Because we can go wrong, we have the words of knowledge, belief and doubt. Because we developed capacities of sight so, concomitantly, arose the language of visual perception.

If we wish to understand what a word means we have to see how it gets its sense from its use, from the activities of life that generate and sustain it. That is true for any word of any language, be it as humble as "pot" or "pan", or as elevated as "love", "real", "time" or "mind".

Projectibility

Having learned a word, by whatever means, we have to project it continually into new contexts. I might learn a word like "beer" in adolescence. I learn it with respect to *this or that instance* of beer. But I have only learned the word *as a part of language* if I can go on to use it in *new* contexts, and it is a condition for the existence of language at all that some others, at least, see the point in that projection and project as I do.

However, we also have this striking fact: I learn the word "deep" with respect to ponds. Then I hear someone say "his mind is deep". I can understand that projection, even though it has moved the application of "deep" from one range of things to another. That the use of the word in this projection functions as part of a *language* rests on the fact that others, too, find that a natural projection to make.

Failures to understand

The foundation stone of the discussion that unites *The idea of a social science* with "Understanding a primitive society" is a certain

73

Peter Winch

understanding of two possibilities of non-communication (Winch 1972: p. 61). One is the non-sharing of a form of life: the other is a deviation in projection.

Not sharing a form of life

Winch writes,

> An apparently very important part of European popular culture is a consuming interest in professional football. I do not merely not share this popular pastime; it is so alien to me that I do not feel I understand what most of my fellows feel for it. (Winch 1997a: p. 202)

I, however, grew up in a culture on to which soccer was even more closely grafted than now. My father, like the huge majority of his fellow men, worked for 10 hours a day, five days a week, and on Saturday morning. But Saturday afternoon, the myriad contemporary forms of recreation not having been opened by affluence, he went to the match. He went with millions of working men who stood, often exposed to the elements, and who identified with the heroes of the game, themselves not affluent. For a while he could be lifted into what even Winch recognized as "the beauties of skill" (Winch 1997a: p. 202) in the game and could be stirred by the shared passions of commitment and of victory or defeat. I grew from an early age into that culture and learned its vivid and often poetic vernacular. Here is a form of life and a language woven into it.

Consider some cases of not understanding that form of life. First, suppose I live with someone not brought up in the traditions of soccer supporting. He or she might understand the rules of the game, the names of the players and the remarks I make about them. But still, my love of the game might make me, as Wittgenstein says, an "enigma" to him or her. I have no doubt that many share that attitude.

Second, I might have a student who was brought up in the traditions of rugby league or baseball and could not see the appeal of *soccer* to me. However, he or she would understand something more than the person in my first example through realizing that I felt about that game as he or she felt about baseball. But he or she would not *fully* understand me because he or she did not share the form my life took.

Understanding another society

Take now an academic who in middle age goes to a match for the first time, becomes excited by it and becomes addicted to the game. He or she and I can share a language, but, for all that, I do not think he or she could claim to understand how it is with me. Strikingly he or she, like my next two cases, will not understand the difference that *standing* at a match makes.

Take next a child brought up in, and attracted to, the present soccer culture. One great difference is that this child will be unlikely to have a localized interest in a particular team. I *could* only watch my local team. It was woven into my locality and my sense of identity with it. Other players were heroes, but not my heroes. For a child today, all the heroes are his or her heroes. A supporter of a great team is as likely to come from Plymouth as from Manchester. Whereas it would have been thought presumption on my part to deck myself in the colours of my team, that will be commonplace now. And, again, I do not fully share a life with that person.

Finally, take someone for whom executive boxes were built. That person has as much understanding of my form of life as the business guests whose snores interrupt expensive performances of the Royal Opera.

It is important that we do not ignore the complex ways in which all the various forms of life might and might not overlap. From the overlap comes, as we shall see, the possibility of understanding another. I hope, too, that someone will feel that I have glamorized my past and misconstrued what was a degenerate and overrated male pastime. That, as we shall see, throws light on the possibility of criticizing a form of life. For the moment I wish only to illustrate how you might fail to understand *me* (even though we might understand the language I use) simply because the form of my life, in which my use of that language has its home, is not, or is not entirely, yours.

Deviations in projections

A second source of a failure to understand another may be that his or her linguistic group projects the language in ways that I do not understand, even though I can learn to speak as that group does. Let us suppose that I learn the term "love", among other things, in the context of the love that my father has for me. Then one day I hear someone say that God loves us like a father. I can certainly learn that *if* I am to talk of God's love as believers do then the right comparison is with the love of a father. So I can learn to use words as they do, in the sense that I can learn that that sequence of words is acceptable to them. But although I still think I understand what they are saying, I may find it simply unbelievable, because I am tempted to ask why, if God loves us as a father, he allows his children to suffer. *My* father wouldn't allow that, if he could help it, *because* he loves me. Yet I find communities do persist, in the face of suffering, in using the language of love in speaking of God. If I do not understand this projection of the term "love", I do not understand *them*, even though there is a sense in which, in learning to speak as they do, I understand what they are saying. I shall discuss, when I come to Winch's views on religion, the question of whether religious people are speaking sense at all. For the moment I wish only to note that one ought to be wary in saying that, because I do not see the point of a use of words, it has no point. It might be impossible for me to be brought to see why people as well as ponds are called "deep". That will not show that this use is nonsensical.

Understanding a primitive society

We are now in a position to grasp what Winch wishes to claim about the possibility of understanding another society.

In discussing social studies as science Winch claims that understanding a social phenomenon requires one to understand it from the point of view of the participants. (Winch 1958: Ch. 3). But now, it might be asked, what, having understood it, one is supposed to do next. Here there are two possibilities. One is to bring that social phenomenon – suicide, marriage, punishment, science – to the bar of some tribunal of universal rationality. The other, which is Winch's position, involves a *dialectic* with it, from which we might learn, since, as he put it "seriously to study another way of life is necessarily to seek to extend our own" (Winch 1972: p. 33). I take these in turn.

Pareto and the nature of logicality

Winch writes that "there is a powerful stream of thought which maintains that the ideas of participants must be discounted as

Understanding another society

more likely than not to be misguided and confusing" (Winch 1958: p. 95). Durkheim approaches this view when he writes, in a passage quoted by Winch,

> I find extremely fruitful this idea that social life should be explained, not by the notions of those who participate in it, but by more profound causes which are unperceived by consciousness. (quoted in Winch 1958: p. 23)

Winch attributes to Pareto the view that the notions of the participants in an activity being studied by the social scientist are, as Durkheim puts it, "unhelpful" because *illogical*. In *Mind and society*, Pareto argued that the reasons that people give for behaving as they do have less influence on their actions than they think. Consequently a sociologist investigating those actions should pay as little attention as possible to those reasons. It is in this context that Pareto makes a distinction between logical and non-logical actions, the discussion of which takes Winch immediately to his conclusions about what is involved in understanding another society. For Pareto's account reveals a general difficulty in attempts to draw a clear distinction between logical and non-logical conduct. Here is the remarkable passage that is central to Winch's thought:

> Criteria of logic are not a direct gift of God, but arise out of, and are only intelligible in the context of, ways of living or modes of social life. It follows that one cannot apply criteria of logic to modes of social life as such. For instance, science is one such mode and religion is another; and each has criteria of intelligibility peculiar to itself. So within science or religion actions can be logical or illogical: in science, for example, it would be illogical to refuse to be bound by the results of a properly carried out experiment; in religion it would be illogical to suppose that one could pit one's strength against God's and so on. But we cannot sensibly say of the practice of science itself or that of religion that it is either logical or illogical; both are non-logical.... What Pareto tries to say is that science is itself a form of logical behaviour (in fact *the* form *par excellence*) whereas religion is non-logical (in a logically pejorative sense). And this, as I have tried to show is not permissible.... His way of discussing the distinction between logical and non-logical conduct involves setting up scientific intelligibility ... as the norm for intelligibility in general; he is claiming that science possesses the key to reality. (Winch 1958: p. 100–2)

It is important to understand this passage correctly, not least because some, missing the application by Winch and Pareto of logic to *conduct,* take him to be talking about the application of logic to argument forms.

The meaning of "logic"

Winch says that criteria of logic are peculiar to such forms of life as science and religion. There is a sense of the term "logic" that is going to make this seem absurd. "Logic" often refers to the subject that interests itself in the validity and invalidity of patterns of argument. What are referred to by "criteria of logic" are the rules that determine whether the conclusion follows from the premises. So it might seem that Winch is asserting that whether an argument is valid or not depends on the activity in which it occurs, so that in science, say, an argument is valid if the conclusion follows from the premises, and in religion it is valid by some other criterion.

This is not what is meant. That is why Winch says that what can be said in *any* form of life, be it religion, art or science, is "limited by certain formal requirements centring around the demand for consistency" (Winch 1972: p. 34).

What then is meant by "criteria of logic"? Consider here what philosophers meant when they talked of investigating the "logic" of our language. They wished to find out the conditions under which it would be correct to say something, for example, that one knows. Let us, contrary to fact, suppose one popular account *were* correct. We are entitled to say that we know something if: (i) we believe it; (ii) the belief is true; and (iii) we have good grounds for the belief. This gives us the *logic* of the term "know". For there is a good sense in which, given this account, it would be illogical to say "I know it, but it is not true". If I use the word "know" properly, then when I claim to know something I am also implicitly saying that it is true. If I then add that it is not true, that yields a contradiction. I flout the logic of language.

It is in that sense that Winch claims that criteria of logic are internal to practices. If someone says that God can rightly be disobeyed, we do not know whether that is or is not a violation of the logic of the term "God" unless we know the rules for the use of that term. Where am I to find these other than in the practices of those who use this term? If, as the term is used in the language of

Understanding another society

believers, it does not make sense to talk of justifiably disobeying God (a matter to which Kierkegaard's *Fear and trembling* is germane), then anyone who says that it does violates the logic of that language. Winch writes that what can be said is:

> limited by certain formal requirements centring around the demand for consistency. But these formal requirements tell us nothing about what in particular is to count as consistency, just as the rules of the predicate calculus limit but do not determine what are to be the proper values of p, q, etc. We can only determine this by investigating the wider context of the life in which the activities in question are carried on.
> (Winch 1972: p. 34)

The conjunction of p and not-p is a formal contradiction. However, whether or not any actual instance of this formula in the living language is actually a contradiction depends on what is being said. Asked whether it was raining, my grandmother would sometimes reply "It is and it isn't". Whether she was contradicting herself depended on what she was saying. Since she was saying "It is drizzling" in her own peculiar way, she was not uttering a contradiction. As Winch remarks, if logic is

> abstracted from the ways in which men live, it loses its significance as logic, even as applied to relations between statements; for a statement is something which men make in the course of their lives. (Winch 1972: p. 56)

What it does and doesn't make sense to say in a particular region of discourse is determined by the rules followed by those who operate discourse. Though it might be logically improper for a *scientist* to say "I believe this as a scientist, though I have not the slightest shred of observational evidence for it", it *may* not be improper for a *religious* person to say this.

Getting the point

This, though, does not take us to the root of the matter. For we have not yet shown what the problem is in understanding terms. Don't we simply need to look at the way they are used in a particular discourse? Here a new problem arises about *seeing the point of a form of life*.

Winch asserts that in order to understand whether p and q are or are not consistent we need to know the meaning of the terms substituted for p and q. That requires us to investigate the use of these terms in the discourses that are their homes. But Winch's continuation of this passage is also of great importance:

> This investigation will take us beyond merely specifying the rules governing the carrying out of those activities. For ... to note that certain rules are followed is to say nothing about the point of the rules, it is not even to decide whether they have a point at all. (Winch 1972: p. 34)

Suppose I hear someone say, "God loves us". I listen to those who use the term "God", and observe that they do use the term "God" in this way and reject expressions like "God is not a loving being". Then, whenever I hear someone refer to God, I can conclude that they will also say that they are referring to a being who loves us. But I may still be totally in the dark about what they mean by "God", even though I can map the relationships between the terms used in some religious form of life. How can I ascertain that these utterances have a meaning, and, having settled that they do, how can I determine what meaning they have?

One possibility, which Winch ascribes to MacIntyre (Winch 1972: p. 31), is that we take the standards for meaningfulness of *our* language and see if the use of the terms in question measures up to those standards. That doesn't help. Suppose that someone claims to be a scientist. The test of this will be whether his or her practices meet the requirements that *we* have for being a scientist. Presumably, if someone claims to be religious, we apply our standards for the intelligibility of religious sentences. But, as Winch asks, who is the "we" here? For, if we do not understand that language, we have nothing to apply. Similarly, if a culture speaks of the witchcraft that permeates its life, are we to apply the standards according to which that kind of talk is intelligible? But not all of us have such standards.

Here two strategies are tempting. One is to say that *one* of our sets of practices, the practices of natural science, is definitive as the test of meaningfulness. The other is to appeal to some general considerations about the conditions under which we can know of anything at all whether it is intelligible.

Science as setting the standard of intelligibility

Suppose we say that a statement about a thing is meaningful if it is supportable by observational evidence. By some such criterion for "factual meaning" A. J. Ayer thought himself to have eliminated theism. For theism refers to what transcends the observational world and, by the meaning of "transcendent", no observational evidence could be available to support the pronouncements of theists.

That, though, runs into problems. First, even if this were the intelligibility standard for scientific statements, it is not clear that it is the intelligibility standard for all statements. It is not clear what observation of the facts supports the value judgement that murder is wrong. Yet that utterance is meaningful, although not, by Ayer's criterion, a meaningful *statement*. Further, we need to do more than simply assert that religious claims and witchcraft claims *are* like the empirical claims tested by science, so that the standards of science are the right ones to bring to them. An examination of the forms of life in which such claims arise would have to show this.

Perhaps it will be shown. Robin Horton (Horton 1979 and Horton in Wilson 1970), has, for example, argued that the facts, when examined, show certain tribal religious practices are on a par with "western" science as ways of making sense of the world. (Although I suspect that he does not always distinguish the claim that science is a way of making sense of the world from the claim that whatever tries to make sense of the world is a form of science.) Cioffi (1970) argues that any propensity to give up certain kinds of witchcraft rituals when penicillin comes along, shows that those rituals were a form of falsifiable technology. These writers, however, are making precisely the point that Winch is making, namely, that we have to understand a practice in terms of those who participate in it *before* we know what criteria of assessment to apply to it.

Our criteria

But the fun really begins with MacIntyre's, and, as we shall see, Gellner's (1973) and Apel's (1990) claim that there are independent standards in terms of which to evaluate the intelligibility of practices, both in our own and in other cultures. MacIntyre writes that

> beliefs and concepts are not merely to be evaluated by the criteria implicit in the practice of those who hold and use them. ... There are cases where we cannot rest content with describing the user's criteria for an expression, but we can criticize what he does. (MacIntyre in Wilson 1970: p. 68)

What are these criteria? They are "our own criteria" (1970: p. 71), the "established criteria of my own society" (1970: p. 71). One test is whether what is going on in an alien culture is "internally incoherent" (1970: p. 71). This is going round in circles. We ask whether someone might live, and express in words, a form of life, which, although it might seem incoherent to us, is in fact coherent. How do we test whether it is coherent? We ask whether by *our* understanding it is incoherent. If it is, then it is incoherent *simpliciter*. However, the question was, "What gives us the right to assume that what seems incoherent to us *is* incoherent, especially when others collectively see a point in living their lives that way?" (Winch 1972: 27ff.).

What can be made clear?

Yet the inclination, which I share, persists that some way must exist of determining, at the least, whether the expressions characteristic of a set of practices have a meaning, even if we cannot understand what that meaning is. What is that to be?

One possibility would be to say that an expression has a meaning if I could be brought to see what that meaning is. That is certainly true, and understanding it properly goes to the root of Winch's account of understanding a social institution. But it is no help to us at the stage, at which our question is whether something we do not understand is or is not meaningful. For at that stage all we have been told is that *if* the expression could be made clear to us, it has a meaning. Nor would it in the least help to argue that what shows me that something is meaningful is its actually having been made clear to *me*. Certainly people do dismiss Mahler, say, because they see nothing in him, and dismiss religion and formal logic because they do not understand what is said in them. But that has no bearing on whether there *is* anything to understand.

The criterion of reality

But there is another criterion of intelligibility that takes us to deeper controversies that have surrounded Winch's work. For, it is argued, the ultimate test of the intelligibility of an assertion, regardless of its home, is whether it does or does not *correspond to reality*.

Reality

Evans-Prichard, having first noted that *we* impute rainfall to physical causes whereas certain other human beings impute it to the influence of God, ghosts or magic, wrote:

> The social content of our thought about rainfall is scientific, is in accord with objective facts, whereas the social content of savage thought about rainfall is unscientific since it is not in accord with reality and may also be mystical where it assumes the existence of supra-sensible forces.
> (quoted in Winch 1972: p. 80)

Winch does not deny that any attribution of existence is subject to a check against an independent reality:

> We should not lose sight of the fact that the idea that men's ideas and beliefs must be checkable against something independent – some reality – is an important one. To abandon it is to plunge straight into a protagorean relativism, with all the paradoxes that this involves. (1972: p. 11)

Checking against reality, moreover, is not only embedded in the practices of science:

> God's reality is certainly independent of what any man may care to think, but what that reality amounts to can only be seen from the religious tradition in which the concept of God is used and that use is very unlike the use of scientific concepts, say, of theoretical entities. . . . It is within the religious use of language that the concept of God's reality has its place – though . . . this does not mean that it is at the mercy of what anyone cares to say. If this were so, God would have no reality.
> (Winch 1972: p. 12)

Winch, however, gives a more radical reply in a passage in which all these matters come to a head. He points out that, in an account like those of Evans-Prichard and Pareto, reality is what gives language sense, so that we can use our understanding of what it is for something to be real in order to determine whether an expression or set of expressions does or does not have sense. Then he continues, in one of the most famous passages in modern philosophy:

> reality is not what gives language sense. What is real and unreal shows itself in the sense that language has. Further, both the distinction between the real and the unreal and the concept of agreement with reality themselves belong to our language. . . . We could not distinguish the real from the unreal without understanding the way this distinction operates in the language. If then we wish to understand the significance of these concepts we must examine the use they actually do have, in the language. (Winch 1972: p. 12)

This, as I argued in Chapter 1, is certainly entailed by the considerations Winch has adopted from Wittgenstein. For "real" and "exists" are terms in use. They must, therefore, get their meaning from the practices of those who use them. This does not mean that there are no real things. There are, and, for some of them, we establish whether they really exist by observation. But whether that is the only criterion of reality will depend on whether or not there are other contexts in which the term "real" is used.

Evans-Prichard wished to say that the concept of reality stands outside the uses of language and is used to determine whether they are meaningful. How, if it is a concept, *can* it stand outside the use of language? Winch observes that for Evans-Prichard:

> The criteria applied in scientific experimentation constitute a true link between our ideas and an independent reality, whereas those characteristic of other systems of thought – in particular magical systems of thought – do not. It is evident that "true link" and "independent reality" in the previous sentence cannot themselves be explained by reference to the scientific universe of discourse, as this would beg the question. We have then to ask how, by reference to what established universe of discourse, the use of those expressions *is* to be explained; and it is clear that Evans-Prichard has not answered this question. (Winch 1972: p. 13)

We can, however, appreciate why it might be *thought* that reference to a practice-independent reality might seem necessary, if we follow a progressive sequence of questions we might ask about a practice we do not understand.

Questions about practices

There are four questions we might ask of a set of practices, say the witchcraft practices of the Azande, and the expressions embedded in those practices.

First we may ask, even though we do not understand those practices, whether they *are* a coherent form of life and whether the expressions embedded in them are meaningful. The answer Winch gives is that since the Azande function perfectly well with that set of practices, that constitutes *prima facie* evidence that this is a meaningful set of activities.

Second, we might ask how that practice should be characterized. Is it perhaps an early form of science, where science is conceived as the attempt to make sense of the world and to extend control over it? Winch argues that this is not our only alternative. We *could* try to represent a belief in the efficacy of oracular pronouncements as empirical hypotheses. Then, when an oracular statement ("sow the crops now and they will flourish") persistently lets us down, the failure to give up the practice of oracular consultation will be evidence of irrationality. But, alternatively we *could* try to show that the practice had a quite different point, or one that only partially overlapped with our science. Winch's point is that it does not *have* to be science in order to be rational activity. (Is going to art galleries an irrational activity because it is not science (see Winch (1961–2)?)

Some have argued that Winch mischaracterized witchcraft, wrongly denying it the status of proto-science. Even if that were true it does not undermine Winch's core contention, which is that we must not *assume* that it *has* to be science. If it is argued, as many of those cited in the further reading have argued, that a proper examination of the role witchcraft has in Zande life shows it to be a form of science, or even a form of superstition, then that is not at odds with Winch's claim that to understand the meaning of social practices is to understand their role in the lives of those who are engaged in them. Nor by showing these practices to be a form of science do they show that science to be the only way of making the world intelligible. Nor does Winch deny that changes in societies (such as the use of medicines to treat diseases) might undermine traditional practices and beliefs (Winch 1970: p. 258). Practices, he believes, whatever views to the contrary have been imputed to him, overlap in a person's life and culture (1970: p. 258). What we cannot rule out, however, is that good things may be lost, even if that loss is outweighed by the gains (1970: p. 258).

It is, perhaps, worth saying that any full discussion of these matters will pretty soon get into some very deep waters. Thus it has been argued that Zande witchcraft, with its division of the world into those who are witches and those who are not, is, pressed to its conclusion, *illogical*. For if the rituals deem a person to be a witch, then his or her kindred are witches. But then, given the interbreeding which occurs in enclosed communities, the logical conclusion will be that everyone is a witch or no one is. To that Winch makes the rejoinder that the Azande don't press things to conclusion in this way, so that the contradiction does not emerge. At first sight that looks very weak. For the temptation is to reply that even if *they* don't press the matter to its illogical conclusion, *we* can. The illogical conclusion is *implicit* in the practices. At that point the matter then moves into much deeper and murkier waters. For here I am sure that Winch would invoke some comments to be found in Wittgenstein's remarks on mathematics, comments related to what, in the *Investigations*, Wittgenstein refers to as "the civil status of a contradiction". For Wittgenstein argues that it is a mistake to think of contradictions *already* there in the rules like, to adopt Hild Leslie's felicitous formulation, cash waiting to be drawn out of a cash point. Given the analysis of the notion of rule following that I have earlier outlined, nothing is "already" there. A contradiction can only appear in the course of applications of rules in the course of human life. That allows Winch the rejoinder that although *our* operations, given our interests, might engender a contradiction, the operations of others, given their interests, might not. And whether that gambit does or does not work, it reveals the way in which the discussion of these matters soon ramifies into more general philosophical issues of the greatest complexity.

There is a third question. Granted that we have come to the belief that the utterances of another culture are meaningful, can we always determine what meaning they have? And that leads immediately to a fourth question. Can we ever be in a position to speak critically of those practices?

Here I return to what I called "the enlightenment project", and its conception of a rationality that is not, as in Winch's account, relativized to such practices as religion, science and art, but that transcends particular cultures and practices within cultures in order to provide criteria that, in being independent of practices, can be applied to them without circularity. Only if there is such a rationality, it is thought, can we avoid some kind of cultural relativism. And I wish to show that the denial of the existence of such a practice-independent rationality does *not* commit Winch to any damaging kind of relativism.

Gellner I: Culture independent rationality

For an example of the enlightenment project in full cry we may take Ernest Gellner. He speaks of a "place" from which we can subject *any* sub-system of the world to rational scrutiny. In that place there exist:

> no privileged places, times, individuals or groups which would be allowed to exempt cognitive claims from testing or scrutiny .... Among civilised members of the republic of the mind it is recognised that no idea is so silly as not to deserve any hearing at all, and none so elevated as to be exempt from discussion .... It is assumed that like causes will have like effects, thereby making generalisation and theory building possible .... Ideally the system might even one day turn out to have an apex, an all embracing theory. (Gellner 1982: p. 188)

Gellner asks,

> What reasons have we to believe in such a world – and its unique validity – over and above the contingent and in itself plainly inconclusive and indeed suspect fact that it happens to be the vision within which, at least in office hours, most of us think and work? (Gellner 1982: p. 188)

Two considerations are offered in support of the claim that there is such a place. One is epistemological:

> Initially anything may be true. We ask: how can we pick out the correct option of belief, seeing that we have no prior

87

indication of what it may be? The answer is contained in the epistemological tradition which has accompanied the rise of modern science, at first to help it along, and later so as to explain its miraculous success. (Gellner 1982: p. 189)

The other reason is sociological. Diverse cultures, though not sharing their beliefs, nevertheless have little difficulty communicating. "The world contains many communities but they visibly inhabit the same world and compete within it" (Gellner 1982: p. 190).

> Some are cognitively stagnant, and a few are even regressive; some, on the other hand, possess enormous and indeed growing cognitive wealth, which, is, so to speak validated by works as well as faith: its implementation leads to a very powerful technology. There is a near universal consensus about this, in deeds rather than in words: those who do not possess this knowledge and technology endeavour to acquire it.
> (Gellner 1982: p. 190)

This commitment to the universal place began as "one tradition among many". But

> It prevailed . . . . Within it, and on its terms, we investigate and interpret all other visions. It provides the single context, within which we investigate and interpret all other visions . . . . The fact that it generates a kind of technology which helps its adherents to prevail also indisputably constitutes a consideration. (Gellner 1982: p. 191)

The eventual conclusion is that:

> The conceptual unification of the world is, precisely, the work of one particular style of thought, which is not universal among men but culture specific . . . but . . . although the conceptual unification of the world does have specific sociohistorical roots, it is evidently accessible to all men [sic], and is in fact now being diffused generally. (Gellner 1982: p. 200)

These views deserve a lengthier analysis than I can give. I would, in a longer discussion, want to ask about the truth of the picture it gives of academic life as one where "no idea is so silly as not to merit some hearing at all". For just that picture is called into question when academic friends who I respect argue that certain views, those expressed for example in *The bell curve,* do not

Understanding another society

deserve discussion in the academic community. It is unclear what argument Gellner will, non-circularly, appeal to when that claim is made. One might note, too, that the hearty endorsement of sciento-technology occurs at the very moment when questions are asked about the ethical basis of further extensions of control, in human cloning, for example, and about the deleterious effects of over-use of technology. Gellner, to be sure, writes that his view

> asserts that a given vision is valid and practically effective, but it does not identify validity and effectiveness. There is in fact no reason to suppose that effective science does increase the survival-prospect of the species that carries it. (1982: p. 191).

But it is not clear to me from his account what, other than effectiveness, *is* the test of validity.

That touches on the central point, raised by Winch, which is that it not clear how the quasi-scientific world view espoused by Gellner, and which is the touchstone of universal rationality, is going to handle questions about itself. For, as Winch argued in *The idea of a social science,* the claim that science gives us *the* mode of access to what is real and true is not one for science to arbitrate. Here we might simply note the stacking of the cards against anything recalcitrant to the proposed methodology in the remark that

> enormous cultural differences, on the other hand occur in ... areas, where societies, as one is tempted to say, are free to indulge their fantasy: mythology, cosmology, metaphysics, and in some measure, social, political, ritual organisation.
> (Gellner 1982: p. 193)

Gellner II: The homogenization of culture

Let us grant, as Gellner foretells, that there will be an homogenization of humankind, so that the notion of a different cultures, with alternative ways of making sense, becomes harder and harder to sustain. Let us even grant what seems clearly false; that this homogenization distils from the now different cultures a single culture operating with the standards of techno-scientific rationality that Gellner favours. Would that homogenization ensure that the sorts of problems that Winch is raising about understanding another society would vanish away?

Not at all. Even if the forms of life from which our languages take their sense were to condense to a uniformity of Levi-Strauss jeans, McDonald's, televised soccer, net surfing and Florida holidays, the resultant language, expressive of that homogenized form of life, will, in order still to be a language, still have to be projected by its individual users into new contexts. And there is simply no guarantee that the projections will be shared. Life is simply too complex to guarantee that. What Winch said about understanding another society was not meant to conceal the fact that we have similar problems in understanding our own society and the lives of individuals in it. That is the force of his later paper "Can we understand ourselves?" (Winch: 1997a). For the line between what is alien and what is not is "quite indeterminate" (Winch 1997a: p. 202), so that:

> it is important to notice that, whatever the problem, it is not only one that arises when we are dealing with a historically or geographically remote culture. Mistakes and uncertainties are as liable to arise as concerning our own culture as concerning another ... for example assembling once a year at Stonehenge to celebrate the summer solstice.
>
> (1997a: p. 197–8)

Apel and the Principle of Universal Consensus

Winch's work had a striking impact on sociological investigation in continental Europe, particularly on what is called the "hermeneutics" (literally, the search for meaning). (Apel tells me in a letter of the substantial impact that Winch's own interpretations of Wittgenstein's later philosophy had on his approach, as well as that of Habermas.) None the less there is a disagreement between Winch and Apel over Apel's claims that there is a kind of method that leads to "ultimate consensus about human validity-claims" (Apel 1990: p. 72).

Winch might have agreed that one's ethical position ought, in some sense of "valid", to be a valid one. What Winch strikingly denied was that the assertion that someone validly held an ethical position entailed the conclusion that anyone who did not share that position would be in the wrong. This is where the dispute with Apel seems to lie.

For Apel wishes to claim that

the notion of serious argumentative discourse implies the regulative idea of a universal consensus to be reached about all controversial validity claims, as for example those involving meaning, truth and even the rightness of norms.
(Apel 1990: p. 81)

What is valid is "valid without limits; valid, that is to say, for everyone" (Apel 1990: p. 81). Apel rightly remarks that this is at odds with Winch's views, since,

> Winch's intention ... is to show that there are cases – presumably the paradigm cases of moral discourse – where it makes no sense to expect, or to postulate, a possible consensus by arguments about the right position. (1990: p. 73)

Here then we have a case in which someone believes, in opposition to Winch, that a derelativizing postulate of consensus is part of rationality.

One reason, invoked by Winch, for querying the regulative idea of universal consensus, to which we will return in Chapter 4 in discussing Winch's moral philosophy, is that there seem to be moral situations in which one has to make choices between conflicting ideals; say, in Winch's example, Gandhi's other worldly idea of asceticism and Orwell's humanistic ethics, where there may be no question of right or wrong upon which to agree. In this chapter, however, I want to raise a more general problem about Apel's postulate of the possibility of universal consensus and his claim that this alone makes sense of the notion of "serious argumentative discourse".

I have no doubt that if two people dispute what is the square root of 927, they work under the presumption of possible agreement. It may also be the case that philosophical arguments are carried out under this presumption. But in other cases it seems to me that we work not *under the belief* that consensus might be, and, if we are genuinely to engage in discussion, *must be* attainable but *in the hope that*, or even *to explore if* it might be. (Sometimes not even that: sometimes I may wish to understand what you see in a person to whom you are attracted without particularly wanting, and certainly not hoping, to end up by fancying him or her as well.)

That *hope* is the appropriate posture in some cases is suggested by the very fact of the possibility of non-shared projections of language. If I can project my understanding of musical excellence, gained from the same experiences of Bach, Mozart and Beethoven as you have had, into the music of Mahler and you can't, it does not seem in the least entailed that our discussions have to be conducted under the auspices of a belief (or even a hope) that we might come to a consensus.

Between universal and relative

To say that is to say that the genuine engagement does not, as Apel supposes, require any belief that differences will vanish. But that then brings us to the issue that lies behind everything we have so far said. For if we cannot always, and perhaps do not even want to, resolve disagreements, whether between individuals or between cultures, are we committed to relativism?

What relativism is, is a complex question (Hollis & Lukes 1982). For my present purposes something suggested by the discussion of Apel is of interest.

There is a propensity to believe that if a matter is an objective one, then, when there is a dispute as to which of two things ought to be believed, procedures exist that will, when applied, determine the matter in favour of one or the other alternative. For this reason mathematics and science have been thought to be objective, having procedures like deduction, induction and experiment by which disputes can be settled. Disputes in ethics, aesthetics and religion seem not to have methods for their resolution. So there we find relativism.

Winch denies that, whatever the dispute, we are guaranteed a resolution of it, which is to deny also that procedures exist that, if followed, can be guaranteed to resolve it. That, on the present construction of the matter, would seem to entail that he is a relativist. But this is *not*, as he explicitly says, what is entailed (Winch 1987b: p. 188). The whole thrust of his work is anti-relativist. He distances himself, for example, from "Protagorean relativism". Speaking of his "Understanding a primitive society", he writes that the argument of that essay was

> not, absurdly, that ways men live together can never be criticised, nor even that a way of living can never be characterised as irrational. Still less do I argue that men who belong to one culture can 'never understand' lives led in another culture.
>
> (Winch 1972: p. 3).

How is this possible?

The answer is that to establish that there are disagreements on aesthetic or ethical matters, say, for which no guaranteed resolution procedures exist, is not to establish the relativism of beliefs about these matters. To show that, we have to show not that no resolution of these disputes can be *guaranteed* (which is true) but that no resolution of them is *possible* (which is false). Once we have shown that *the possibility* always exists for a resolution, that defeats relativism. For that view is that certain disputes will for ever resist resolution. That is precisely the point that Winch makes:

> We may feel convinced that disagreement is more widespread and intractable in ethics than elsewhere, but this . . . hardly seems to point to any relativistic conclusion. It could be that such issues, are so difficult and tangled that it is often merely difficult or even practically impossible, to arrive at a solution of them. . . . We need something stronger than this . . . to justify the conclusion that talk about "agreed solutions" is conceptually out of place here.
> (Winch 1987b: p. 186; see also Marshall 1990, p. 14)

We have to grasp, first, that the ways in which we resolve disputes in aesthetics, and, I shall argue, in subsequent chapters, in religion and ethics, are not like the way in which two people might go about finding out what is really the square root of 987, or the way in which one might determine experimentally whether a certain theory of relativity is true by seeing whether light rays bend on passing the sun. This is a corollary of Winch's (and Aristotle's) claim that the methods used have to be appropriate to the nature of the subject. What are these methods?

Insight

I indicated earlier two ways in which understanding another might fail. One reason was deviation in life history. Because my life history included a certain kind of relation to soccer and yours did not, you don't understand my valuations. The other is in the case in which we project our words differently. A striking case given by Winch is that in which Gandhi projected the notion of a right life in ways differently from George Orwell.

Given this we can see that one essential preliminary, if we wish to resolve a disagreement in valuations, is simply to understand the kinds of lives that generated the differences. We can do that, if it can be done at all, by getting people to see connections between their lives and ours. And this task will differ to the extent that our lives do and do not overlap. Here I wish to return first to my example of my relationship with soccer.

Suppose, because of my life history; I am *deeply* attached to that sport. Many sorts of divergences from me are possible. Someone, equally passionately addicted, but brought up in a later age, might wonder why I support Ipswich and not some more fashionable club. Here the lack of understanding might be remedied by appealing to something in the other's life that illuminates this. I might have to talk of homesickness for particular places associated with his or her upbringing, from which come the notions of allegiance to place. When we deal with someone who is equally passionate, but about a different sport, the task is easier. We can talk about the phenomenon of tribal allegiance, of terraces, wind, rain, friends at a match, characters and so forth, and we simply understand that these, by accident of history, deflect into different sports. (We may have no interest in converting the other so as to ensure conformity.) All these sorts of things may or may not work. But the charge of relativism sticks only if it can be shown that they *could not* work, and all the evidence is to the contrary.

The same applies if someone makes a projection of language that we do not follow. We both, let us say, use "wonderful" in the same way of Bach and Beethoven. But then, when we come to Mahler or Wagner, I project it one way, you another. Again we talk. We try to get people to see what we see. We do this by gestures of the hand, analogies, descriptions, metaphors (as when Bob Sharpe illuminated Mahler for me by remarking that he is the musician of a certain kind of modern urban culture). These procedures work. That they don't always, and are not guaranteed to do so, leads to charges of relativism. But those charges stick only if it is proved that, no matter how long we tried, nothing *could* work. Not only could that not be proved, but all the evidence is the other way. Even in the most recalcitrant cases something may lead us to say "Now I see the point of it", as when someone now sees why people enthuse about Proust, solely because of passing the age of 40.

Suppose (a matter to which I return, when, in Chapter 7, I discuss realism and anti-realism) it is said that, when our lives do run together and we say things like "That music *is* wonderful", we are not referring to some real feature of the world. On Winch's account this is not going to be as easy a charge to make as is sometimes thought. For the charge invites the question "What criteria for something's being real are operative here?" It will not do simply to say "Those employed in the physical sciences". For the terms "real" and "true" have their uses in aesthetics, for example, as well. People are prepared to say that Mozart really is wonderful and that Oasis really aren't that good.

Limiting conditions of life

We may now see why, in "Understanding a primitive society", Winch so clearly indicates that the essence of securing understanding is getting someone to see, or, at the very least glimpse, a sense in the utterances and practices of people from different cultures by relating those practices to our own lives.

He remarks that we are not "powerless to find ways of thinking in our own society that will help us to see the Zande institution in a clearer light" (Winch 1972: p. 38). The task is to come to see "the point of the rules and conventions followed in an alien form of life" (1972: p. 40). And he promptly does precisely the kind of thing that I have done in explaining my passion about soccer to another. For the Azande, crops are important: coming from an agrarian county I *empathise* with it, as will any fruit farmer whose blossoms (and whose very livelihood) depends upon the whims of a late frost. One has to take a stance towards that possibility. Winch invites us to think of the stance taken by the Azande in their oracular dealings as analogous to utterances in Judeo-Christian cultures of "If it be thy will". No one has to accept this assertion just because Winch makes it. It is open to anyone, in the activity of dialectic, to draw attention to features of the situation that suggest other analogies.

Sometimes Winch's analogies are more particular. MacIntyre raises a puzzle about why certain aborigines carry with them a stick or stone, which is treated as if it embodies the soul of the carrier and where, if the stick or stone is lost, the loser anoints himself as if dead. MacIntyre calls this "thoroughly incoherent". Here Winch tartly remarks that

> he is presumably influenced by the fact that it would be hard to make sense of an action like this if it were performed by a twentieth century Englishman or American; and by the fact that the soul is not a material object like a piece of paper and

cannot, therefore, be carried about in a stick as a piece of paper might be. (Winch 1972: p. 45)

Yet what would an aborigine make of the fact that we wear a piece of gold round the finger, which we call a marriage ring, and grieve if we lose it? And just as we express our sense of our love of another by the wearing of rings, so might an aborigine express something about the sense of his whole life by carrying that stick and behaving that way on its loss.

This reference to the sense of a life as a whole leads to something else that Winch suggests may advance understanding. For when we meet others, in whatever culture, we meet those who live a *human* life. That human life, Winch claims, is bound by what he calls "limiting conditions"; birth, death and sexual relationships.

For although "the specific forms which these concepts take, the particular institutions in which they are expressed, vary very considerably from one society to another", none the less they are "inescapably involved in the life of all known human societies, in a way that gives us a clue where to look, if we are puzzled by the point of an alien system of institutions" (1972: p. 43).

In these shared limiting conditions our lives overlap in ways that make understanding others possible, if not guaranteed. Winch appropriately finishes "Understanding a primitive society" with a striking passage to this effect from the sixteenth-century Neapolitan philosopher Giambattista Vico:

> We observe that all nations, barbarous as well as civilised, though separately founded because remote from each other in time and space, keep these three human customs: all have some religion, all contract solemn marriages, all bury their dead. And in no nation, however savage and crude, are any human actions performed with more elaborate ceremonies and more sacred solemnity that the rites of religion, marriage and burial. For by the axiom that "uniform ideas, born among peoples unknown to each other, must have a common ground of truth", it must have been dictated to all nations that from these institutions humanity began among them all, and therefore they must be most devoutly guarded by them all, so that the world should not again become a bestial wilderness. For this reason we have taken these three eternal and universal customs as the first principles of this Science.
> (quoted in Winch 1972: p. 47)

Onward to ethics

We *can* come to understand the practices of another society. But to understand is not always to forgive. We might understand why cruel pains are inflicted, in this or that culture, on young boys on initiation into manhood, perhaps by having parallels drawn to university examination systems. That is not to condone the practice. What then of *those* value judgments. Are *they* not the imposition of our views on another culture?

Towards the end of "Understanding a primitive society" Winch remarks, "Here the difficulty concerns the relation between our own conceptions of good and evil and those of other societies. A full investigation would thus require a discussion of ethical relativism" (Winch 1972: p. 42). And, taking that cue, it is to Winch's ethics that we now turn.

Further reading

Winch's "Understanding a primitive society" spawned an industry, in which various issues concerning relativism, rationality and what other societies are up to in practices, say, like witchcraft, are too often run together.

Dividing them up, we can ask first for a clearer understanding of what is being meant by accusations of relativism. I have tried to give some indication of one interpretation in the foregoing. Those who wish to read around this matter will find food for thought in two collections, Wilson (1970) and Hollis & Lukes (1982). See also "Rationality and cultural relativism" in the *Routledge encyclopedia*.

As to the remaining issues it seems to me essential to separate two sets of questions that are rarely distinguished. One is the set of questions about Winch's general account of what it is to understand someone and whether understanding another culture is possible. (To that Winch gives a firm "Yes"). For that general account could be right even if the particular interpretations are wrong. Some of the essays in the two collections I have mentioned have a bearing on this question. One or two other contributions worth noting are R. Trigg, *Reason and commitment* (Cambridge: Cambridge University Press, 1973), discussed in Winch (1987b), pp. 195ff. John Kekes, in two papers, has argued the shortcomings of Winch's position. They are "Rationality and coherence", *Philosophical Studies* **26**, pp. 51–61, 1974 and "Towards a theory of rationality", *Philosophy and Social Science* **3**, pp. 275–88, 1973. Much of what is said in these apparently critical papers, seems to me compatible with what Winch has wished to argue. Those interested in Quine will be interested in P. Roth, "Pseudo-problems in social science", *Philosophy and Social Science* **16**, pp. 59–82, 1986, for its introduction of the notions of indeterminacy of translation. It does not seem to me to give a happy account of rules. Also to be noted are A. Derksen, "On an unnoticed key to reality", *Philosophy of the Social Sciences* **8**, pp. 209–25, 1978 and P. Almond, "Winch and Wittgenstein", *Religious Studies* **12**, pp. 473–82, 1976, which roundly argues that Winch's view is "incoherent". Even more robust, to give something of the tone of the discussions, is A. Saran, "A Wittgensteinian sociology", *Ethics* **75**, pp. 195–200, 1965, which describes Winch's work as "inept advocacy". See also D. Henderson, "Winch and the constraints of interpretation: Versions of the principle of charity", *Southern Journal of Philosophy* **25**, pp. 153–73, 1987, which raises the interesting question of what, on Winch's view, it would be to attribute an error to another culture.

The second set of questions, where the fun really starts, concern whether, even given that he has provided a coherent account of what it is to understand another, Winch has correctly characterized various societies, including the Azande. The consensus among many of those who have made studies of such societies seems to be that he is not right. Notable contributions include: C. Williamson, who has provided an explosive article on witchcraft entitled "Witchcraft and Winchcraft", *Philosophy of the Social Sciences* **19**, pp. 445–60, 1989; J. Skorupski, *Symbol and theory* (Cambridge: Cambridge University Press, 1976); H. Mounce, "Understanding a primitive society", *Philosophy* **47**, pp. 347–62, 1973 (and note Winch's reply in Winch 1987b: pp. 202ff. and Rhees 1997: pp. 103ff.); B. Dov Lerner, "Winch and instrumental pluralism", *Philosophy of the Social Sciences* **25**, pp. 180–91, 1995, on which see P. Phillips, "Winch's pluralist tree and the roots of relativism", *Philosophy of the Social Sciences* **27**, pp. 83–95, 1997. These last two papers debate the issue whether the concession that there are many standards of rationality entails that witchcraft is not a form of instrumental rationality. In contrast I found Kai Neilsen's attempt to show that there is no conflict between such apparently diverse figures as Winch, Lukes and Hollis a refreshing change.

See his "Rationality and relativism", *Philosophy of the Social Sciences* **4**, pp. 313–31, 1974. Finally there is a pivotal exchange between Jarvie and Winch in R. Borg & F. Cioffi, *Understanding and explanation in the behavioural sciences* (Cambridge: Cambridge University Press, 1970).

The first interchange between Apel and Winch was in the symposium reprinted in Brown (1997: pp. 3–88). One nice point here is that Apel had supposed that surely Winch was at least seeking agreement about his philosophical claims. To which Winch replied, "I find myself, in my professional life, surrounded by many people of high intelligence, intellectual seriousness and honesty and philosophical commitment, with whom I shall never have a genuinely profitable philosophical discussion" (Brown 1979: p. 69).

Small note: Since Pareto is so rarely defended against Winch, I mention A. Baker, "The philosophical 'refutation' of Pareto", *Mind* **69**, pp. 234–43, 1960.

The mention of Quine above is a reminder that, in the light of Winch's philosophy, it is pertinent to consider Davidson's influential account of what it is to understand others. For a way into this see S. Evnine, *Donald Davidson* (Cambridge: Polity Press, 1991). Winch's approach would, I think, strike at the notion of interpretation that lies at the heart of Davidson's account.

Chapter 4
"Good examples are indispensable": The ethical life

The disconsolations of ethics

Three things about ethics, as it is often studied, are responsible for the fact that the subject often does not endear itself to those who are required to study it. On every one of these points Winch's ethical thinking offers a more inviting perspective.

First, ethics is too often narrowly focused on questions about particular right and wrong actions, for example, whether to keep a promise or whether to lie, where these are detached from the whole life of a person and from questions about what makes that life a life worth living. Bernard Williams has it right: "It is not a trivial question, Socrates said: what we are talking about is how one should live" (Williams 1985: p. 1). Winch's contributions to ethics, focused on here, are to do with "what is involved in a man's attempt to arrive at a moral understanding of his own life and of the relations between this and his understanding of his relations with his fellow men" (Winch 1972: pp. 3–4).

Second, the examples used in ethics are often irritatingly trivial (whether to return a library book, for example) and such that no one of any sense would waste a moment's sleep over them. (Winch castigates the reliance on trivial examples (1972: p. 154).) Hence the stress in Winch's work on the need for "good examples". Few were the equal of Winch in finding interesting examples, often from the world's great literature. One of these, indeed, the discussion of the harrowing case of Melville's Billy Budd, has attained the status of a classic. We shall, of course, have to ask what the legitimacy is of taking fictional examples (O'Neill 1986, Phillips

1987). But Winch is right. We need good examples if we are to come to understand morality. Part of the appeal of Sartre's ethics resides in the interest of Sartre's examples, often described with the novelist's eye. That, too, is something that does much to explain the appeal of Iris Murdoch's philosophical and fictional work. Third, after taking an ethics course, a student once quoted to me a passage from Fitzgerald's *Rubáiyát of Omar Khayyám*:

> Myself when young did eagerly frequent
> Doctor and Saint, and heard great argument
> About it and about; but evermore
> Came out by that same Door as in I went.

The student was not complaining, as some do, that ethics does not supply ready made answers to pressing moral questions. Rather the complaint was that she could not see how the theories studied bore on practice *at all*. Even if I do not expect ethics to tell me how to act morally, nor to decide hard questions for me, I might expect it to help me understand what acting in that way amounts to, and how ethical decision making should be conceived. That is not notably forthcoming. A. J. Ayer (1936: Ch. 6) tells us that moral statements (like "murder is wrong") are emotive expressions (like "murder (hiss! boo!)"). But whether that fits moral life as we live it is not discussed; nor are we told what it would be to live by that understanding of morality, nor, even, what the possibilities would be of community were such an understanding to correctly characterize the ethical life.

These questions, however *are* central to Winch's work. This is why his collection was entitled *Ethics and action* (1972). He attends to the nuances of moral life as it is lived and offers a compelling picture of what it is to differ morally and what the possibilities are when differences occur.

The ethical life does not wait on philosophy. It is an unavoidable exigency that we live in communities where we cannot avoid each other. It is equally unavoidable that our actions affect others, whether it be through the thump of a 100 watt bass speaker in an adjoining room or by questions of priority in going through doors. And it is simply not to be avoided that we find ways of dealing with those conflicts of interest. We will do so whether or not philosophers think about them. As Winch clearly demonstrates, ethical concepts have a life and force prior to any philosophical theories about them (see, for example, "He's to blame" in Winch 1989a).

The ethical life

From those transactions arises the ethical language and its gets its life from them, and not from philosophy.
Philosophy has two things left to it. One is negative. For it cannot be denied that philosophical theories impinge upon practice. If the theory is bad, then the practice is damaged. The quantifying calculative mechanisms of a certain sort of obtuse utilitarianism produced the likes of Gradgrind in the educational system, and still does. So one task is to expose bad theorizing.
The other thing is positive. We do philosophy because we wish to understand ourselves. True, what we seek to understand philosophically is, I have argued, already there. But we can know without knowing what we know. What we are seeking is an understanding of what we are doing when we act ethically and what the possibilities are when our ethical paths diverge. When we have that we understand ourselves as ethical beings. We will understand "what is involved in a man's attempting to arrive at a moral understanding of his own life and of the relations between this and his understanding of his relations with his fellow men" (Winch 1972: pp. 3–4). And since we are, in the account to be found in Wittgenstein and Winch, only what we are because we are social beings, and because ethical action is one central form that sociality takes, to understand ourselves as ethical beings is to understand ourselves.
It is convenient for the purposes of exposition to divide what follows into three overlapping parts. First, there are the negative comments that Winch makes about the major theories of ethics. Second there is his own distinctive contribution. Third, a discussion of how Winch's work relates to ethics as it is now being done.

Part I: Negative comments on ethical theories

There are comments in Winch's ethical writings on most of the major theories of ethics. The comments largely focus upon two such accounts of ethics: virtue ethics and theories of ethics that stress the universalizability of ethical judgments.

Virtue ethics

Here the central figure in ancient philosophy is Aristotle, although he continues a line of thought begun in Plato. The central figures in recent philosophy were Philippa Foot and Alasdair MacIntyre, both of whom have moved on from their original positions, and with the latter of whom Winch was in a life-long symbiotic relationship of discussion. The central idea of one kind of virtue ethics is best understood by looking at it as an answer to a question that Glaucon asks Socrates in Book One of Plato's *Republic*, a question that shapes all subsequent moral philosophy.

Grant that if, as individuals, as opposed to leaders of nation states, we lied, murdered, stole and cheated, life would soon become intolerable. So we prevent that by catching and punishing people. That would give us the self-interested motive for staying in line. But suppose we could get away with it? Suppose, as in the story told in the *Republic*, we have a ring that rendered us invisible. Why not, as we really want to do, indulge our true inclinations?

The kind of answer given by virtue ethics, can be glimpsed if I ask any of my readers whether she or he would happily be without one of her or his hands. Certain avant-garde artists aside, most would say not. But if I ask *why* not, one answer might be that, evolved humans being what they are, I need all my parts if I am to function properly. A virtue ethics argues, by parity of reason, that such virtues as truth-telling, honesty and generosity are needed for our proper functioning, no less than are our hands and eyes. There are basic needs, common to all human beings, which are served by the virtuous life. Consequently, to lie, cheat and steal impede our proper functioning no less than would cutting off a hand. Behaving virtuously is, therefore, the reasonable way to behave.

The account in some of Alasdair MacIntyre's work is based on this line of thought (MacIntyre 1966). MacIntyre shares one important thing with Winch, namely, the view that moral considerations are somehow linked with the ways in which we make sense of our lives. It is within shared traditions in societies that our concepts of good and evil arise. Those societies give us conceptions of what it is to live a good life; tell us the virtue necessary in order to live that life. In one kind of ancient Greek city state a good life would consist of this and that kind of action. In Lutheran Germany the conception of a good life would be somewhat different and the virtues upon which stress would be laid, acting from the stern voice of duty, for example, would be somewhat different.

On to this MacIntyre grafts a somewhat dyspeptic analysis of

The ethical life

our modern predicament (MacIntyre 1982). Whereas in earlier cultures there was a shared moral vocabulary, a shared concept of the story (what MacIntyre calls a "narrative") that we could tell about what the journey from cradle to grave in a good person's life would be like, our modern world is fragmented into a plurality of cultures. Our moral disputes are irresolvable because different sub-groups appeal to the values of a different sub-cultures, there being no way to weigh these different values against each other. There is one strong similarity between MacIntyre's position and that of Winch. Both embed the meaning-giving rules for the use of an ethical vocabulary in socially shared practices. No less than MacIntyre, Winch implies a gloomy view of the possibility of moral certainty in a rapidly changing world. Thus Winch writes that:

> What is ruinous to a settled mode of behaviour, of whatever kind, is an unstable environment. The only kind of life that can undergo a meaningful development in response to environmental changes is one which contains within itself the means of assessing the behaviour it prescribes. (Winch 1958: p. 64)

Fixed humanity

Whatever the similarities, Winch is none the less opposed to the kind of virtue ethics that has been introduced above. Virtue ethics must be committed to the possibility of something called "human nature"; for it is in terms of the needs and interests that *define* what it is to be human, that one decides what it is rational to do to further those needs and interests, it being the hope of a virtue ethics that what it is rational to do will turn out to be acting virtuously.

That commitment to some fixed essence of humanity, in which we all share, posits a kind of Archimedean point from which we can judge whether the particular virtues possessed by this or that society represent the best life for us, given our essential human nature. Thus it is that, although MacIntyre believes that an ethical life has sense only within the meaning-giving practices of particular societies, which would seem to relativize ethical values to those societies, he also makes judgements between those societies. He favours the virtues of the kind of society in which Aristotle lived and disfavours the virtues, characteristic of Lutheran Christianity, exemplified in Kant's society. And Winch asks what the grounds are for this preference. For if we start with the assumption that morality gets its sense from the particular forms of social life in which it is embedded, by what criterion are we to judge that the moral life embedded in the meaning-giving institutions of ancient Greek city life is superior to the moral life embedded in the meaning giving institutions of Kant's eighteenth century Königsberg? Why not more consistently say that, just as Aristotelian ethics was right for Aristotle's society, Kantian ethics was right for Kant's society? The answer is that, having a notion of a fixed human nature, MacIntyre believes himself to be in a position to judge whether this or that system of virtues best serves that nature, whereas human nature is constituted by these shifts.

Winch queries the belief in an essential human nature. Indeed he thinks that denial is entailed by the story that MacIntyre tells of the way in which, as societies change, so their concepts of what is virtuous change also. But if the notion of the virtues is used in order to tell us, for this or that society, what it is to live as a human being, then the emergence of a different set of virtues will entail that the notion of a human nature has changed. Winch writes:

> If you take the view that it belongs to the nature of human beings to have more or less fixed needs and wants, you may be able to "explain" particular moral codes as different ways in which these needs may be ministered to in different social contexts. But once you allow the concept of human needs to float freely, like a currency with no fixed parity, alongside the changing moral codes, then those needs will as much (or as little) require explanation as the codes themselves.
>
> (Winch 1972: pp. 28–9)

MacIntyre, then, claims that human nature changes as new historical and social conditions arise. Moral concepts must, therefore, have an historical setting and change as society changes. They are "embedded in behaviour ... partially constitutive of forms of human life" (Winch 1972: p. 76). This is to say that the notion of morality and the notion of human nature vary together, so one's view of human nature will be a function of one's morality. In that case, far from the possession of a notion of human nature being a key to the understanding of the notion of morality, the possession of a notion of morality is a key to understanding of the notion of human nature. Thus Winch writes,

> What we can ascribe to human nature does not determine what we can and what we cannot make sense of; rather what

The ethical life

we can and cannot make sense of determines what we can ascribe to human nature. (1972: p. 84)

Limiting conditions
It might seem that Winch's denial that there is an essence of human nature is undermined by his view that human life is, as we have seen, bounded by what he calls "limiting conditions", which "determine ethical space" and which are "inescapably involved in all life"; which are a "constant" (Winch 1972: p. 43). In *Ethics and action* he writes:

> These notions . . . give shape to what we understand by human life; a concern with questions posed in terms of them is constitutive of what we understand by the morality of a society. . . . It does not seem to me merely a conventional matter that T. S. Eliot's trinity of "birth, copulation and death" happen to be such deep objects of human concern. (1972: p. 44)

But although these notions tell us in which directions to look, if we wish to understand another culture, they do not allow us to talk of some fixed essence of human nature. For, first, we are told, although these notions are a "constant" they take "different forms". We are told nothing about human nature if we are told that the dramas of our lives are played out against a necessary backdrop of birth, sexual relationships and death. For different ways of embodying birth, death and sexual relationships in a human life will constitute different kinds of human life constitutive of different human natures, although the kinds will overlap in very complex ways.

Second, the particular forms that human life will take depend upon very general but not fixed facts of nature, facts that may cease to obtain. Thus we might consider how our moral notions, and the conceptions of the possibilities of human life, would be changed if motherhood aged sixty and beyond became common, or if the age of death were raised towards 150 years, or birth by labour were made optional, or even that man were not born of woman but woman of man.

Convention
This bears on the way in which Winch argues, in the important paper "Nature and convention" (Winch 1972), that our moral ideas cannot be "merely" conventional. Those ideas are founded on the

limiting conceptions of human life that do not seem to be optional. It is not, he says, merely a conventional matter that T. S. Eliot's trinity of "birth, copulation and death" are deep objects of human concern. Nor does it seem entirely conceivable that "the sorts of attitudes taken up in our society to questions of the relations between the sexes might be reserved for questions about the length people wear their hair" (Winch 1972: p. 43). And if it be replied that the proliferation of hair emporia shows that the latter questions *have* become central, the reply is that this is because questions of fashion are bound up with questions of sexual relationships. Samson did not pull down the temple in a fit of pique over an uninvited adjustment to his coiffure.

Two other things arise here.

Decision

First, the claim that, say, justice is merely a human convention, is likely to suggest that a system of justice is a sort of optional extra, which, if we could get away with it, we might decide not to have or abide by at all. Conventionalists make the possibility of such decisions central to ethics.

To that, Winch replies that decision is not the fundamental conception in morality. When Sartre declared the fundamental principle to be "choose anything, but choose", where my choice was in some absolute sense free from my history, my culture, my biology, and the other aspects of what is called my "facticity", he seemed simply to ignore the fact that decision is only possible in the context of a meaningful way of life:

> A moral decision can only be made in the context of a moral way of life. A morality cannot be based upon decisions. What decisions are and what decisions are not possible will depend on the morality within which the issues arise and not any issue can arise a given morality. (Winch 1972: pp. 54–5)

Primitive bases

The notion of morality as conventional overlooks, for Winch, the roots of morality in primitive, unchosen, behaviour. I shall return to this when I discuss the importance for Simone Weil and for Winch of her notion that the concept of a person carries with it the non-chosen phenomena of what she calls "hesitation" when confronting another; a matter as we shall see, related to the stress Winch, following Wittgenstein, lays on the notion that we do not

The ethical life

choose to act to other people *as if* they were human (Winch 1987b: pp. 140–53).

For the present I note that Winch argues that our developed notions of morality and justice are related to primitive reactions; to what he calls "the primacy of certain kinds of response within the learning process" (Winch 1989b: p. 162). A child "spontaneously reacts to certain kinds of behaviour in various ways, some of them hostile" (1989b: p. 162). One such reaction expresses itself in, and gives meaning to, utterances like "He's to blame"; what might be called the "playground sense of fairness". Such a reaction, Winch thinks, is continuous with "very fundamental moral responses" (1989b: p. 163). That looks right. It does not undermine the possibility of reflecting on such responses and so coming to changed conceptions of, say, punishment. For "our concept of punishment offers us considerable resources towards criticism of our actual ways of thinking and acting in relations to offenders" (1989b: p. 164). Winch remarks, however, that one should not underestimate "how much we might have to change once we start this criticism, how much we are taking on" (1989b: p. 163). For if the notion of punishment is closely interwoven with many other moral concepts, the change is hardly likely to be localized.

We have, then, in Winch's writings, important questions raised about the notion of virtue ethics. The second major theme in his writing is his treatment of the notion of universalization in ethics, a treatment that reveals even more clearly the distinctive quality of his ethical thinking.

Universalization

In taking on the notion of universalization, Winch takes on various philosophers. The first is Kant.

Kant

To gain a glimpse of what is at issue here, consider whether you feel a difference between a person who gives a coin to a beggar because he or she knows that someone he or she wishes to impress is watching, and someone who gives the coin to the beggar because that seems the right thing to do. For Kant, the latter acts morally, the former does not. Hence Kant's central claim that a moral action is not one that merely accords with what duty would require, but one that is done because that is the right thing to do.

That tells us that an action is morally right if done from duty. The imperative to act well is not hypothetical – do this *if* you wish to impress the boss – but categorical – do this whatever. How, then, do we decide which actions acting from duty requires of us? Kant's answer is to ask whether it would be coherent to will everyone to act in the way I am thinking of acting. Thus lying is out because the notion of wanting everyone to lie all the time makes no sense. Kant asserts that a moral rule must be universal in its application in at least this sense: if I say it is morally right for me to do something then I am committed also to saying that it is morally right for anyone in my position to act in that way.

Hare

Universalization as a criterion of the moral also characterizes the philosophy of R. M. Hare. For Hare, moral language is a matter of action-guiding prescriptions or imperatives. If I ask "What shall I do here?" the answer will be the imperative "Do this!" But moral judgements are *universal* prescriptions. Saying someone should do this, if it is a moral judgement, commits me to saying that anyone in the same position should do that. This is a point from which Winch's distinctive moral philosophy takes its departure.

Utilitarianism

Let utilitarianism be the theory that, since we are motivated by the desire for happiness, then, as Mill famously put it in Chapter 1 of his *Utilitarianism*, "actions are right in proportion as they tend to promote happiness, wrong as they tend to promote the reverse of happiness". A rational moral theory will seek to discover which actions will most effectively advance the promotion of happiness. The task of the legislator or moralist is so to arrange things as to maximize the happiness of all – the greatest happiness of the greatest number. It is essential to that idea that if I think as a legislator and a moralist, I must be impartial. I act partially if I treat my own case differently. With that view (athough this is not Winch's (see Winch 1996: p. 17)) if I believe, for the greatest good to be done, that people should not be able to buy a better education, but I send my children to fee paying schools, "Harmanizing" my conscience in whatever way I can, I do not act morally. If I think as a utilitarian moralist, having in view the greatest happiness of the greatest number, then I must not be partial. Hence utilitarianism has universalizability built into it – which is why Hare has claimed

The ethical life

that Mill and Kant may be closer than is usually allowed (Norman 1998: p. 180).

Sartre
As a final example, we may note that Sartre at one time seemed simply to offer the advice, "choose anything, but choose". Later, he added to this the claim, with what consistency I do not know, that when we choose we choose for everyone. That looks akin to what I have just said is the position of the universalizing moralist.

Winch on universalization

Winch on Kant

In *Nature and convention* Winch argues that truth as a virtue cannot be deduced from the necessity of truth telling to language. To be sure, if none of us told the truth, then language, including moral language, could not survive. Here there is an apparent endorsement of what Kant says about the incoherence of willing lying as a general policy. Later, as the result of some penetrating observations by Roy Holland, acknowledged in the preface to *Ethics and action,* Winch came to think differently. In that preface, he observed that merely noting the impossibility of everyone always lying does not capture the full force of the way a policy of not lying might function as *virtuous* conduct. For it would not explain why *an individual* might feel truth-telling as an obligation. That point, as we shall see, introduces a distinctive Winch concern with the *individual* moral being, "the kind of moral significance that can attach to my own acts, distinct from the significance of the act of others" (Winch 1972: p. 6). So, "To say that the virtue of truthfulness must play some part in the life of any society is not to describe the peculiar part it plays in the life of any particular society" (1972: p. 69).

When I introduced Kant, I invited the reader to consider the difference between an act, dropping a coin into a beggar's hat, done to impress someone, and the same act done simply out of duty, and I asked which we would say is the moral act. The inclination is to say the latter, in which case we end with the notion of duty for duty's sake and Kant's ethics. Winch's answer is that we do not have just these two alternatives. To illustrate this he gives an example, it being one of the characteristics of his philosophy that it is conducted by examples, which *remind* us of our tendency to forget things, our "too narrow views of what can and cannot be said, thought and done" (Winch 1972: p. 83). Indeed "all we can do ... is to look at particular examples and see what we do want to say about them" (1972: p. 182).

The example comes, as so often in Winch, from great fiction, in this case Ibsen's Mrs. Solness who *does* act from duty, but who is none the less a moral cretin. Her response when dealing with others is "I will put myself out for you, it is my duty". Winch remarks that we would think better of her if she just did the right thing from simple goodness of heart. So we are reminded that there aren't just two possibilities: giving to impress and giving out of duty. There is also giving because, as the ancient mariner put it, when he found his salvation at the moment that he spontaneously blessed the sea creatures, "a spring of love sprang from my heart, and I blessed them unaware". And wouldn't we, he asks, using an example from Simone Weil, wish that our parents spent time with us out of love rather than out of duty?

It does not follow from this that we are to replace the general rule "act from duty" with the general rule "act spontaneously". For, in Winch's view, "there is no general kind of behaviour of which we have to say that it is good without qualification" (Winch 1972: p. 181).

Winch on universalizability

Winch does not in the least deny that the universalization principle often applies. We need to guard against a certain sort of partiality. Often we do want to say that what goes for us goes for others too. But he points out (Winch 1972: p. 159) that in a wide variety of situations, in which we act morally, what goes for me may not go for others.

Here again a very powerful example is given, the example of Vere, the captain in Herman Melville's *Billy Budd,* who must decide between what a military code and what his feelings of compassion demand of him. Winch says that he could not have decided as Vere did, yet does not, as the universalization principle seems to demand, want to say that Vere was wrong. Both he and Vere can be right. I might come to find out what it is possible for me to do in certain moral situations. But I need not thereby find out what others ought to do. It should be carefully noted, however, that only in the specific context of a moral dilemma of the kind involved

The ethical life

in *Billy Budd* does Winch say that what is right for me might not be right for you. Nothing in Winch's discussion licences the conclusion that this is the case in *any* moral context.

Objections

To this there are two kinds of objections.

Apel (1990)
One sort of objection takes the line that the kind of judgement upon which Winch focuses *is* universalizable. Apel argues in this way. As we have seen, Apel wishes to show that the possibility of genuine argument has, as a precondition, the object of attaining a universal consensus. Winch's case presents a problem. Here we have not two judgements converging on *one* rightness but, explicitly, two opposed judgements and the claim that *both* are right.

Apel's main consideration is that in philosophy, unlike life on board a man-of-war, we can continue such moral arguments indefinitely and "eventually come to a consensus" (1990: p. 91). But this confuses two claims. One is that there is always the possibility, if we continue an argument, of arriving at a consensus, although we won't know whether there is one unless we find it. There is no guarantee of that. This seems to me to be Winch's position. The other possibility is that, when we argue, we must believe there actually to be some one consensus position, the rightness of which an indefinitely continued argument must reach. The latter is Apel's position. I am not sure what would verify it. No amount of cases in which we *did* reach a consensus would establish that this is always possible.

Opposed judgements
The second line of objection takes up Winch's claim that two opposed positions, his and Vere's, can both be right. That looks as odd as the claim that someone asserting p ("It's raining here now") and someone asserting not-p ("Its not raining here, now"), here and now being the same place and time, could both be right. Doesn't Winch's position go against the thought that if one person is right, another who says something opposed to that must be wrong?

To deal with this objection we need to look at Winch's positive account of a moral life and of the kind of thinking, argument and judgement characteristic of it. In that positive account I detect two things. One is a general account of what the moral life entails. The other is some more particular accounts of particular questions within the moral life, about punishment, about whether, as Socrates denied, a good man can be harmed, about whether, as Christ seemed to say, one who thinks of adultery is as bad as one who commits it. I begin with the more general account.

Part II: The positive account of morality

Moral argument

In "Understanding a primitive society" we encountered a view of the way in which we might begin to understand another, perhaps puzzling, social institution. That account carries over directly into the discussion of morality, with the addition of a greater emphasis on the use of examples. If we are confronted with moral dilemmas, and discrepant moral judgements, moral thinking consists of a dialectic in which we try to extend our understanding of morality to cover new cases, and in which our understanding of morality itself might be challenged by those new cases. In this, Winch's work foreshadows the work of David McNaughton, who speaks of "moral vision", where this incorporates the view that "the only method of arriving at correct moral conclusions in new cases will be to develop a sensitivity in moral matters which allows one to see each particular case aright. Moral principles appear to drop out as, at best, redundant and, at worst as a hindrance to moral vision" (McNaughton 1988: p. 62).

That account, like Winch's, is particularist. One does not come to learn general principles that one applies by rote to particular cases; one comes to see the character of the actions that one has done. As in the case of King David, who had behaved abominably to Uriah the Hittite, it is a matter of being brought to see, in his case by a story told by Nathan the prophet, the character of his actions.

However, we do not understand this fully unless we grasp what it is to see some general principle exemplified in a particular action. The account Winch gives, in which that kind of seeing is related to the way in which rules are applied by projection into new contexts, has a deep explanatory power. It makes moral practices

The ethical life

intelligible by relating them to the more general and cognate notions of language and meaning.

Here the example of the parable of the good Samaritan is instructive. "Who", Christ is asked, "is my neighbour?" Here the question is to what cases the word "neighbour" should be applied. Christ does not give a rule. That would not help since, as we saw earlier, *any* application of any such rule in new particular cases requires insight.

The man who passed by on the other side might have said, "As I have learned the customs of my tribe I am not required to help people of a certain race". The parable of the good Samaritan produces a more creative application of the rule. An example is produced and we are brought to that creative application of a rule. Here the word "we" suggests that a moral life involves a *dialectic* with others.

Tolerance

How tolerant are we required to be in this dialectic? Gellner, as we saw, wrote that "among civilised members of the republic of the mind, it is recognised that no idea is too silly as not to deserve any hearing at all, and none so elevated as to be exempt from discussion" (Gellner 1982: p. 187).

That solves the question in one way. And yet, as one of my students remarked, we don't find the notion that Hitler might have been right all along the line *seriously* discussed in universities. And I find it difficult seriously to entertain, let alone discuss, the notion that paedophilia is a legitimate way of life.

Here let us take this remark by Winch on the practice of child sacrifice in pre-Aristotelian society: "The main problem is . . . one of understanding what was involved; not just one of taking up an attitude, for without understanding we would not know what we are taking up an attitude to" (Winch 1972: p. 54).

Suppose someone were to say to me that certain societies engage in the morally improper activity of leaving old people to die in the snow. I might, however, find that this is done as a form of love, which is consented to by the old, who have no wish to undermine the chances of the newly born in situations of survival existence. I find out that when I understand what is happening they and I do not differ in our attitudes to human beings. In that sense,

115

whatever the activity, it is right to say that if we do not understand it, we don't know what we are doing in taking up an attitude to it. Certainly that society and mine express our care for the old in different ways (although given the practice of shipping one's relatives off to some under-funded state institutions for the old, I am not entirely sure their society and mine share an *enlightened* attitude).

It is easy enough to take up an attitude of disapprobation to something and it is often entirely justified. Certainly, the one who strikes such an attitude has the pleasurable feelings of rectitude. What, however, of the target of the attitude?

Sometimes the mere fact of disapproval is salutary. Although someone may not see what it is that people dislike about his or her inclination to turn every innocent remark into a *double entendre*, that dislike may be enough to modify the action. But often the mere fact of disapproval is as water off a duck's back. Disapproval is not moral argument. For that to occur one has to engage in the kind of dialectic that seeks and attempts to convey understanding. Winch clearly has that in mind when he contrasts three reactions to being punished (Winch 1972: pp. 217ff.). One who says, "I'll carry on offending but I'll be damned careful not to be caught again" has learned (or been taught) nothing morally. One who says "I stop offending because I'll not risk getting caught again" is in the same position. One who says "I did wrong, I must change" admits to having learned something morally.

I suspect that no one can, on principle, be excluded from a dialectic. It is hard to engage with those who have done what seems to us unbearably evil, especially if done to those we love. But that is to say that in certain situations we fence ourselves off from moral engagement.

What is hard to face is that in the dialectic we put ourselves at risk. To enter into a genuine dialectic with a non-pacifist or a meat-eater is to run the risk of being brought to see things differently. If that is not a danger when talking to those of viler dispositions, that is partly because we so rarely meet those of such dispositions who are happy. More typically the cases we encounter divide between those (schizophrenia possibly) where physiological imbalances preclude any moral dialectic at all, or cases in which there is already an unhappiness with what is being done that craves insight, understanding and a wish for redemption.

Winch said of "Understanding a primitive society" that his

The ethical life

argument was not "absurdly, that ways men live together can never be criticised, nor even that a way of living can never be characterised in any sense as 'irrational'" (Winch 1972: p. 3) (although he has been taken to task for the absence of examples, which leaves the reader to work out how such criticism would operate in practice). "Criticism" here, however, does not merely mean saying that something is wrong or irrational. It requires understanding and the risks of the dialectic that are sometimes required if we are to attain that understanding. It is aimed at producing insight. The parable of the good Samaritan is a model of such criticism. That, however, raises the question of the status of such parables.

Examples

Examples in moral philosophy are often fictional. Christ did not begin, "Last week, you may recall, a man was mugged on the way to Beersheba". He begins, "A certain man fell among thieves", where the question "Which man?" shows an ignorance of the conventions of fiction equalled only by those who apply for a vacancy for a bar person in *Cheers*. Then, however, there is this problem: reading a fiction about someone's reaction to a crisis in life, I might say, "Yes, that's right", meaning, "That is how I and others *would* and should act". I feel illuminated. But how do I know that the reaction in question would seem right to me in the actual event.

In Chapter 1 I distinguished between the truths we find out by experience and the implicit truths that we already possess, and of which we might be reminded. I do not think, with some uninteresting exceptions, that the former kind of truth can be taught to us by a fiction. True I might learn from a novel, praised for its factual accuracy, something about the streets of San Francisco. But what I usually learn is something about *possibilities implicit in what I know*.

Thus, I doubt, first, I could find out much about what I might in fact do if this or that were to befall me. Reading of Dorothea's marriage to Causabon in *Middlemarch* I might think, "I won't make that mistake", a declaration, to amend Dr Johnson somewhat, that might represent a triumph of hope over rational expectation. But what I *can* come to is an understanding of how I *now* am, an understanding that may cast my past actions, through which my character expressed itself, in a wholly new, and, I might think, truer light to me.

I have been much impressed by something T. S. Eliot said in "Little Gidding" (*Four quartets*) about "the gifts reserved for age" of which the last was a kind of insight which involves (lines 138–43):

> ... the rending pain of re-enactment
> Of all that you have done, and been; the shame
> Of motives late revealed, and the awareness
> Of things ill done and done to others' harm
> Which once you took for exercise of virtue.
> Then fools' approval stings, and honour stains ...

Fiction has a special role to play here (as, possibly, does historical writing). For a work of fiction invites us imaginatively to inhabit its point of view. I am invited to apply it to myself, and it may fit. Of course I can go wrong in thinking that I have come to a self-understanding. I may be too hard on myself or too hasty. But only a dialectic with others can correct that.

Part III: Moral philosophy now; realism

Yet I *do* say that I get it right and wrong. What is the justification for that claim?

Winch says that he and Captain Vere come to opposite conclusions about whether Billy Budd should hang and yet are both right. That, it might be thought, undermines the possibility of rightness and wrongness here. For if a judgement is right it must tell us how something *really* is, and there are not two incompatible ways for things really to be. The judgement that a thing is really square excludes the judgement that it is round. But Winch seems to allow that an action (giving a court martial judgement) can be really right, from Vere's point of view, *and* really right from Winch's *different* view. To be sure, the discussion focuses upon a case of a moral dilemma, in which both Vere and Winch confess to be pulled in two ways, and licences no general conclusion about what should be said in cases where there is not such a dilemma. None the less something in that discussion, with the notion that two opposite views can both be right, seems to flout the proper use of the term "real".

A major topic of current discussion in ethics and, as we shall see

The ethical life

in Chapter 7, more generally, in philosophy, is realism. On the one hand there are those, like John Mackie (1977), who deny that there is a moral reality to which our moral beliefs might or might not correspond. There are, for him, no real, objective, moral properties. It will follow that the "this action is wrong" does not tell us about a property of the world. At best these are projections of our emotions, sentiments and attitudes on to the world. On the other hand, there are those who for various reasons espouse moral realism. What bearing do Winch's views have on this much debated issue?

I begin with a statement by an able philosopher of ethics about what a realism about ethics would have to show:

> What the realist must maintain is that a moral utterance is made true by something independent of the particular mental state which consists in the speaker being committed to the utterance. To put it simply, for the realist, moral beliefs cannot be true just because we think they are; there must be something that makes them true. (Norman 1998: p. 205)

This repeats something said long before by Winch. Having said what Norman says, namely that, as Winch put it, "something is not made right just by thinking it" (Winch 1972: p. 164), he continues:

> We should not lose sight of the fact that the idea that men's ideas and beliefs must be checkable by reference to something independent – some reality – is an important one. To abandon it is to plunge straight into an extreme . . . relativism. . . . The check of the independently real is not peculiar to science. The trouble is that the fascination that science has for us makes it easy to adopt its scientific form as a paradigm against which to measure the intellectual respectability of other modes of discourse. . . . God's reality is certainly independent of what any man may think, but what that reality amounts to can only be seen from the religious tradition in which the concept of God is used. . . . This does not mean that it is at the mercy of what anyone cares to say; if this were so, God would have no reality. . . . We could not distinguish the real from the unreal without understanding the way the distinction operates in the language. (Winch 1972: pp. 81–2)

Norman says (1998: p. 222) that we should not be too occupied with ontology – questions about reality. But if Winch is right, this is where the matter *must* begin, that is, with a clear understanding of the notion of reality. For if we are not clear about that notion, one danger is that we might think that one way of using the term "real" (the kind of way that it might be used in the observational sciences) is the key to understanding that notion. Then, since the moral does not conform to that, morality is not to do with reality.

Consider, too, the force of Winch's contention that the concept of reality is to be grasped by coming to understand how we operate with the terms "real", "unreal", "reality" and "true". What we *can* be sure of is that, however those terms are used in ethics, the appropriateness of their application is not determined by the kinds of tests appropriate to the questions about whether the terms have been used as scientists, say, use them.

When Mackie says that, if they refer to reality, moral judgements would have to refer to "queer" sorts of properties, observable by something called "intuition", it seems that he is modelling the use of ethical property terms on the use of terms like "heavy", "red" and the like. The question is whether that is the appropriate model. And I stress that the answer might be "Yes". But, equally, I stress that this cannot be known in advance of looking and seeing how the moral discourse functions, before, that is, investigations of the kind that underpinned Winch's remarks about ontology.

If we assume that ethical properties, if they exist, must be like the kinds of properties to which we refer when we talk about a thing as being heavy or red, then we immediately encounter another problem. For those properties are, so to speak, *inert* evaluatively. From the fact that something is red, nothing follows about whether it is any good or not. Further, relatedly, the fact of its being red gives of itself no reason for wanting it or for doing anything by way of getting it. As Mackie says, it is difficult to think of moral properties as both factually there (like redness or squareness) *and* as action guiding (Mackie 1977: p. 38). The "thereness" only tells us what something is. From that nothing follows about whether it ought to be like that.

This is only a problem if we think that what we are doing when we say that something is the right thing to do is referring to something like (but not quite like) a natural property. That way we get what Michael Smith calls "the moral problem" – namely how to get the facts of the matter, which as facts are inert, hooked up to values (Smith 1994).

This is not a place to discuss complex attempts, of the kind Smith offers, to solve that problem. I note only that Smith's

The ethical life

account leaves intact Hume's distinction between beliefs, which are about "objective matters of fact" and motivations. But what I cannot find is any full account of what the force is of the expression "objective matter of fact", although there is more than the hint of a suggestion that this is a notion that does not vary according to the region of language in which it is used. But if, as Winch argues, there is a question about whether reality *is* a context independent notion, there is equally a question about whether "objective fact" is such a notion. The belief that it is may be what generates the problem.

If a group of terms within a region of the language, ethics, has a settled use in that region, it will do so because those who speak ethically have a use for those terms and wish to mark something by their use. That is compatible with their coming to think that they do not now wish to use terms like "right" or "guilty", perhaps because they think those terms are ideological or embody a false consciousness or are for some other reason questionable. But those terms would not have emerged without their use having had some point. If those terms include "right", "true", "real" and the like, they, too, will get their sense in their region of the language because of the purpose they serve *there*.

Now let us look and see what happens in morality. As Mackie himself concedes, we say things like "You are right. I acted badly", or, "It is true that my remark was insensitive but . . . ", or "That's no real excuse", or "He really is an odious man". Mackie says that this language implies that we are speaking of properties although there are no such properties. We are simply mistaken (Mackie 1977).

We do use, in our ethical discourse, terms like "real", "right" and the like. But I doubt whether, in the course of using that moral vocabulary, as opposed to speculating philosophically about it, most people think that they are *referring to properties*. Quite apart from the fact that the term "property" is not as perspicuous as many suppose, that sounds too grand.

My guess is, rather, that when we use such terms we are signalling the fact that we find some point in saying that we have come to *see* that we behaved badly, or that someone is odious.

In what circumstances do we say such things? Well, someone tells me a story after which I say, "Yes, I see what you mean. I did behave disgracefully". It is from these propensities that talk of morality, and aesthetics, too, as being involved with truth and falsity, right and wrong, gets its point.

Is this enough to allow one to speak of objectivity and realism in morality? For many it is not. It won't do for some, to begin with, because we have no *methods* by which to prove to someone who claims not to see that this is how an action should be seen. Certainly we have nothing like induction or deduction. Christ did not say, "Since the last one hundred people you helped were your neighbours, this one probably is". Nor would it have been much help to argue that since all men are neighbours and this is a man, therefore it is a neighbour. But we do have a process that I have called dialectic and it does produce insight. It does not always get someone to see, but then, nor does a mathematical proof.

More significantly there is the question whether, when I have been brought to see my actions in a certain light, I can *know* that this is the right way to see them. One might, indeed, be mistaken. I can think my actions done for the good of another, be brought to believe that I in fact intended them for their harm, and be wrongly so brought to believe. But that is not a problem to which ethics is especially subject. I can think that I have got a complex proof right, be brought to say that I believe I have made a mistake, and be wrong in thinking this.

However, it does look as if any claim to see my actions in a certain light, perhaps as the result of being told a parable, might be mistaken. That, far from showing that right and wrong have no place in ethics, seems to suggest the contrary. Moreover, various possibilities exist here. One would be to invoke the notion, canvassed in Wittgenstein's *On certainty*, that certain beliefs, like the belief that there are objects, are not to be doubted, but rather constitute a context in which doubt becomes possible. Similarly, one might say that a parable might bring an ethical outlook home to us with such force that doubt about it is not something we could seriously entertain. After reading Tolstoy's short story about the matter, I might be so struck with the horror of prostitution that I could not seriously ever again engage with any work that was in any way sympathetic to that institution. I do not wish to exploit that possibility, if only because *On certainty* seems to concede that our seemingly revelatory foundational experiences *can* come to be doubted. That shakes, and I think rightly shakes, the foundations of any hope of having self-authenticating epiphanic moral revelations.

A better possibility is to claim that one can have a perfect title to say, on hearing a parable, "Now I understand", even if one later comes to feel that the story got it wrong. This seems to me to be of a

The ethical life

piece with the claim that one can have a perfect title to say that one is seeing a pig, even if that claim later turns out to be false. The error here is to believe that claims to have received moral insight, and claims to see the world, require incorrigibility for their legitimacy. The claim that revelation sorts with incorrigibility seems to me not to do justice to the fact that our moral views, and more generally our views of life, are constantly brought to the bar of experience and can alter in consequence. We can never be sure when this is going to happen. One example of this is the case in which my belief as to how one should morally comport oneself in certain imagined circumstances, when unjustly imprisoned for example, may simply not turn out to be true when that actually happens.

We engage with each other in moral interchanges, interchanges that can effect a change in our views. These interchanges are complex, and the agreements and disagreements that are reached are often patchily overlapping and sometimes fugitive. They must be so, since we all bring to the interchanges our individual and constantly updated psychological histories. I bring to the rich dialectic of the moral life my present moral and metaphysical posture and that dialectic can affect it, and the continuing dialectic may affect it yet again. At each stage I may feel a revelation. Although I must always be conscious that this revelation is at risk of what time and other insights may bring, I can still accept it, if I can live it.

Thinking doesn't make it so

Next, it might be asked, if we think of our ethical judgements as open to assessment as right and wrong, whether there are, as there are in other contexts in which the terms "right" and "wrong", "true" and "false" are used, tests of rightness, other than the say so of the judger, for those assessments. For as we use the term "true" we distinguish the question whether something is true from the question whether someone thinks it is. Norman correctly observes, as, we have repeatedly seen, did Winch, that if moral realism is to make sense, moral beliefs cannot be true just because we think they are (Norman 1998: p. 205).

In this connection, Winch stresses the importance of the question of whether the way in which a person makes a judgement

Peter Winch

reveals whether he or she is a person who cared about making a *moral* judgement. I am not obliged to take seriously any half-baked, off the cuff comment. Moral concerns require seriousness. Second, we might ask whether someone's ideas about right and wrong differ too much from ours, for that might raise questions about their sense as *moral* judgements. Third, we need to consider sincerity and insincerity, the latter seeming to us to disqualify a remark as relevant to our deliberations. I suspect that these all amount to the test of whether the person making a moral judgement has been or is willing seriously to engage in the dialectic of morality. If one isn't thus engaged, then no amount of thinking one is right counts as being right.

Captain Vere again

Let us return to Winch's discussion of Captain Vere's decision to recommend death for Billy Budd. Here two opposing judgements are expressed, both of which are said to be right. How is that compatible with moral objectivity?

One thing is for sure. If the way in which terms like "true" and "false", "right" and "wrong", "real" and "unreal" are used as they are said to be used by scientists to talk of the world (although whether that *is* the model has been questioned (e.g. Bloor 1983), then we cannot make the judgement that this is a genuine disagreement about a matter of fact. But in fact we have operative models of situations in which we use terms like "true" that are not unlike the case in which Winch disagrees with Vere. First, two people might agree that Bach, Mozart and Beethoven are great musicians, see what the other sees in them, and yet disagree about Mahler. That does not stop them thinking that what they believe about Bach, Beethoven and Mozart is right, nor that it is true that these are great musicians. More interestingly, two people might agree that tomatoes are red, bananas are yellow, Paul Newman's eyes are blue and peas are green and yet have disputes about whether the curtains are green or blue. That disagreement may be irresolvable by all the usual methods (taking them into better light), and inexplicable by reference to defects of eyesight. That simply does not undermine the objectivity of the colour language, an objectivity that allows a policeman to testify that the light was red when I went through it. I can say that *both* people are right about the curtains, and even that eventually one might come to agree with the other. Certainly their disagreement is compatible with there being an objective colour language. Equally I could say that Winch and Vere are both right, without that undermining my ability to say, in other cases, that someone gets it wrong.

Particular insights

Thus far I have tried to explain Winch's general views about ethics. I conclude this chapter by observing that in a number of essays, to many of which I shall return in later chapters, Winch addresses himself to more particular problems. Three examples are the essays "Can a good man be harmed" (Winch 1972), "Trying", which discusses the question whether it is as sinful to think of committing adultery as actually to commit it (Winch 1972), and the essays that discuss punishment, namely "Ethical reward and punishment" (Winch 1972), and "He's to blame" (Winch 1989a). In each of these three things are exemplified. First, there is again the use of serious examples. Second, almost invariably something is brought to the discussion from other regions of philosophy, whereby it is proved that ethics needs the illumination that, say, epistemology and the philosophy of mind can bring. Thus, the question whether doing evil is as bad as thinking evil is illuminated by a discussion of the view that the will lies outside the physical world of action and sometimes causally intervenes upon it, a view to which I shall return in the chapter on Simone Weil. There I shall discuss also the bearing on ethics of an understanding of Wittgenstein's remark that "my attitude towards him is as towards a soul", a remark to which a notable Winch paper is devoted (Winch 1987b). Third, those essays do not merely outline what a moral dialectic must be. They contribute to it, so that I come to understand why there is a difference between thinking and doing evil (whatever actually doing evil might be) and what the force of punishment might be. I shall touch again on this treatment of particular ethical issues. For the moment I conclude this chapter by commending the essays on particular issues as an example of a serious and talented thinker doing what philosophy always seemed to promise to do, namely, illuminating the deep issues of human life.

Further reading

Winch's treatment of universalization in ethics is notably challenged by Apel (1990). The original exchange between Apel and Winch occurred in Brown (1979). There are also comments in J. Atwell, "A note on decisions, judgments and universalisability", *Ethics* 77, pp. 130–34, 1967; R. Montague, "Winch on agent's judgments", *Analysis* **34**, pp. 161–6, 1974 (this interestingly enquires about reasons for not universalizing judgements); K. Kolenda, "Moral conflicts and universalisability", *Philosophy* **50**, pp. 460–65, 1975 (this argues that the obligations that Winch feels in contrast with Vere are non-moral inclinations because non-universalizable); M. Levin, "The universalisability of moral judgments revisited", *Mind* **88**, pp. 115–19, 1979 (this argues, I think compatibly with what Winch says, that a universalizable ought fills out the objective side of the subject–object distinction). Also note D. Norton, "On an internal disparity in universalisability formulations", *Review of Metaphysics* **33**, pp. 519–26, 1980.

Winch had argued that ethical decisions had to be made from within traditions. That led to a further engagement with Popper in the article "Popper and the scientific method in the social sciences" in *The philosophy of Karl Popper*, P. Schlipp (ed.) (La Salle: Open Court, 1974), vol. 2, pp. 889–904, which engendered a reply from Popper in that same volume that was stormy even by his standards.

Winch's use of stories is challenged in O. O'Neill, "The power of example", *Philosophy* **61**, pp. 5–29, 1986. There is a riposte in D. Z. Phillips, "The presumption of theory", in Gaita (1990). See also Bob Sharpe's "Moral tales" (Sharpe 1992).

On Winch's remarks on particular ethical issues see M. Paton, "Can an action be its own punishment", *Philosophy* **54**, pp. 534–40, 1979, which, with its author's typical acuity, queries Winch's claim that ethical reward and punishment cannot be regarded as consequences of wrong actions but lie in the action itself. Also striking is T. Champlin, "Punishment without offence", *American Philosophical Quarterly* **13**, pp. 85–7, 1976, which, to Winch's question whether the innocent be punished, gives a resounding "Yes!", although not one that, I think, necessarily disturbs Winch's position.

Much insight can be gained from the way in which Winch, in a tradition deriving from Wittgenstein, did ethics by reading some of

The ethical life

the essays in Gaita (1990), including Gaita's own essays and the remarkable essay by Cora Diamond, with its use of Dickens's *Our mutual friend* to make its point. Note, too, footnote 23 to Phillips's paper (Gaita 1990) for more on ethics after Wittgenstein. On that matter see also Sabina Lovibond's "Wittgensteinian ethics" in *The Routledge encyclopedia*. See also H. Glock, *A Wittgenstein dictionary* (Oxford: Blackwell, 1996), pp. 107–11. The realism debate in ethics is usefully approached through a collection, G. Sayre-McCord (ed.), *Moral realism* (Ithaca, NY: Cornell University Press, 1988). Finally, I commend N. Dent, "Duty and inclination", *Mind* **81**, pp. 552–70, 1974, for a most sensitive discussion of the role of acting from inclination in morality, and one very much in the spirit of Winch (who is named in the article).

Since completing this text I have read the striking discussion of ethics in Jackson (1998). He writes, *inter alia*, "if two people agree on the descriptively given facts and are not confused, and one uses 'right' to describe a given situation and the other does not, they mean something different by the term" (Jackson 1998: p. 161). It is instructive to consider that passage in the light of the account that I have given on Winch's work both in ethics and in the analysis of such notions as fact and meaning.

Chapter 5
"The concept of God is used": The religious forms of life

> I trust that if we next enquire where religion is chiefly to be sought among its fruits, only one answer will be found self-consistent and correct. The answer is, seek it where the vital contacts of man with the world are formed as feeling.
> (Schliermacher 1969: p. 110)

The condition of religion

Peter Winch's discussion of religion takes place against a background in which, most notably in secularized philosophy, religious belief is not taken seriously. In those quarters, it is widely believed, religion is a superstitious leftover. Like the Matthew Arnold of "Dover Beach", all one hears now of the sea of faith, which was once "at the full", is its "melancholy, long, withdrawing roar ... down the vast edges drear/And naked shingles of the world". It was in this context that Norman Malcolm expressed the sentiment, expressed, too, by Winch, that:

> In our western academic philosophy, religious belief is commonly regarded as unreasonable and is viewed with condescension or even contempt. It is said that religion is a refuge for those who, because of weakness of intellect or character, are unable to confront the stern realities of the world. The objective, mature, *strong* attitude is to hold beliefs solely on the basis of the *evidence*. (Malcolm 1993: p. 177)

If the belief be that the sea of faith has receded, a refuge for the few who still hold out against a predominantly secular tide, that belief is simply false. Even *were* it true that, in large parts of England, religion had been reduced to scattered remnants of the old summoned by mellifluous bells to consolations of their evensong, that is not true in other parts of the world. Indeed in that world something like six billion people assert themselves to be religious, of whom some three billion attest to theism in some form or other.

There is another aspect to this that makes the discussion of religion a pressing matter. Hans Kung has remarked that there will be no peace in the world until there is peace between the world's religions. The great religions are like the tectonic plates on which the solid masses of the earth float and move. Where those physical plates move against one another the effects of their frictions are great. No less is this true of those places where the tectonic plates of the earth's religions meet and grind against each other.

One way to solve those problems would be to eliminate religion. This would seem to require persuasion rather than force, the survival of the Russian Orthodox church, and indeed of Christianity itself, being evidence that attempts at physical extirpation merely increase obduracy. Persuasion, if one wants to attempt it, can, however, best work if it starts from an understanding of those who it seeks to persuade. This simply repeats, in the area of religion, what Winch has said in ethics, namely, that we can only take up an attitude to something if we understand it.

The other way to solve the problem would be for those who are religious to find a commonality in their religions. Whether that is possible or not, the task will again presuppose the possibility of understanding as between religions. We can best approach Winch's work on religion as a contribution to the question of what it would be to understand something like a religion. It is thus simply continuous with what he has said about understanding in other areas of culture.

Meaning questions in religion

When one hears someone say God exists and someone else deny the reality of God, one encounters the use of terms, like "real" and "exists". Our question is whether such terms have a meaning and what it would be to understand them.

The religious forms of life

There are various questions here. Often what religious people say seems puzzling to the non-believer who claims not to understand it. Of course, my not understanding an utterance is not of itself a criterion for it being meaningless, else the meaningfulness of the utterances of the musically gifted would be undermined by the reactions of the tone deaf. But it leads us to ask such questions about conditions that must be met for an utterance to have meaning, and ask questions, too, about the conditions under which we are prepared to allow that an utterance has a meaning even if we do not understand it, and questions about whether religious utterances meet these conditions. I can also ask, granted a suspicion that religious utterances might have a meaning that I do not understand, whether I might at least begin to be able to penetrate that meaning. In this there is a resemblance to questions that Winch was asking when he talked of the problems of understanding another society.

I wish to stress Winch's assertion that, in discussing such questions, he is "not advocating the attitude of the believer but trying to understand what it is" (Winch 1987: p. 130). Certainly, discussion of the fundamental questions about the conditions under which an utterance has sense, and about whether the utterances of the religious meet those conditions, do not require a religious sensibility.

With other questions this is not so clear. One who wishes to get some sense of the meaning and point that religious utterances actually have, must, as Wittgenstein said of himself, have the possibility of religion in her or him. In the same way, to penetrate the sense of the practices of another culture I need to have some sense of what Winch calls the "limiting conditions of human life", namely, birth, sexual relationships and death. If I did not have the possibility of religion in me, I *could* not begin to understand its sense in the lives of those who are religious.

The *strong* attitude

I will approach Peter Winch's treatment of religion by characterizing more fully the attitude to which it is opposed.

Malcolm speaks of the strong attitude as being one that asks for evidence. I would rather say that it looks for *proof.* For evidence is evidence only in the service of proof. Winch himself (Winch 1987b:

p. 114) sums up the strong attitude as one which, when confronted with claims about the existence of God, asks for proofs. Since, it is argued, these can't be verified or falsified, proved or disproved, they have no clear meaning and are thus not rational.

The inference to the irrationality of religion

We are presented with something like the following picture. The use of religious language is seen, by virtue of the meaning of the terms used, as committing the believer to certain "existential" claims; these claims are articulated in theologies. Unless those theologies are verifiable or at least falsifiable, there is in principle no way of telling whether those existential presuppositions are warranted. Thus the religious believer's language has no clear meaning and his belief fails of rationality. My aim is to undermine this position. (Winch 1987: p. 114)

Winch's thinking about religion is, therefore, addressed to the temptation to argue thus:
1 An assertion in a field of human interest, and that field itself, are rational, intelligible, objective etc., if proof procedures exist by which it can be shown whether such assertions are true or false.
2 The natural sciences and mathematics have such proof procedures, namely induction and deduction.
3 So they are rational forms of life.
4 These proof procedures are non-effective in determining the truth or falsity of religious assertions.
5 So these assertions, and indeed religion itself, is irrational.

To understand Winch's claims about religion is to understand why he is unhappy with this inference.

Let us, although there are problems even here, allow 1 and 2 and the inference from them to 3. Should we also allow 4?

Winch allows 4, I think for two reasons. First, there is the fact that deductive and inductive arguments *for* the existence of God have not, as arguments, fared well in recent discussions. Discussions as to why this is so form a popular staple of undergraduate courses. Good discussion of the traditional arguments can be found in Gaskin (1972), Mackie (1982) and, from a more sympathetic point of view, Swinburne (1979).

If proof has fared badly in religion, disproof has fared no better.

The religious forms of life

The most common method is to attempt to deduce a contradiction between the following three propositions: God is morally good; God is omniscient and omnipotent; and evil and suffering exist. This triad does not, in fact, constitute a formal contradiction (Pike 1963). It does so only if we add that a morally good, omniscient and omnipotent being would have no reason to allow evil and suffering. The standard defences of theism in the face of evil (theodicies) attempt to construct reasons that would excuse the almighty from blame for the suffering. I am not sure what kind of view of the almighty one has if one envisages the possibility of bringing that being to the bar of justice and demanding it excuse itself. (Hence Camus' remark that he who brings God to judgment kills him in his own heart.) More to the point is that the argument implies that God is a member of the moral community of human beings and can enter into moral activities, including blaming and being excused. Against that view the story of Abraham and Isaac (at least in Keirkegaard's version) and the book of Job seem to give explicit warning.

Winch argues that the sense of a practice has to be understood by the way in which it is woven into the lives of those who see a point in it. Talk about God is no exception. He remarks, as a general methodological principle for the investigation of religion, that "how a term refers has to be understood in the light of its actual application with its surrounding context in the life of its users" (Winch 1972: p. 113).

Now consider this. Some years ago I had occasion to spend time visiting a hospice for the dying, where one learns that even if death cannot be lived through, it can be lived right up to. If anyone had occasion to call God to judgment, it was some of the dying and their relatives. What was singularly absent from many of the religious among them, however, was any hint of a suggestion that the existence of suffering counted against the existence of God in such a way as to demand an excuse from God. Reference to God entered in a quite different way. That being so, it is not only difficult to construct a disproof in formal terms by deducing a contradiction between God's goodness and the existence of evil. The task *may* also rest on an entirely mistaken conception of the place played by the notion of the goodness of God in the lives of those who speak of that goodness.

The second reason why I think Winch does not spend any great amount of time on the traditional arguments for or against the existence of God is that he clearly believes that such formal processes of argument are not that upon which belief is by and large founded. In this, as in much else that he writes about religion, he is clearly influenced by Rhees.

> Those who hold to rational theology seem to argue that a man might be brought to a belief in God ... by formal argument alone, even though he had never known anything like the attitude of "trust in God". Here I cannot follow them, and I wonder if I understand at all what they are saying.
> (Rhees 1997: p. 36)

The inference again

This all means that 4, as well as 1–3 of the inference I sketched above might be accepted. But Winch's point is the inference from 1–4 to 5 is simply invalid. For it to be valid the argument must assume the premise that induction and deduction, as they are used in mathematics and the natural sciences, are the only ways we have of showing something to be true or false, so that science and mathematics become the measure of all things. But that is precisely what Winch has argued against, from *The idea of a social science* onwards.

Philosophy and religion

Everything Winch says about religion, then, is a corollary of what he says about the task of philosophy in *The idea of a social science*. It has been suggested that Winch's views on religion do not represent a worked out position. This is not so. Having said what he said about philosophy, what he says about religion naturally and coherently follows.

According to *The idea of a social science*, we try to make sense of the world. Science helps us do this, as does religion, and as does art. Two things immediately follow. First, we have no reason, in advance of investigation, to assume that one way of making sense of the world, science, say, has a priority. Second, if we want to see how an activity helps us to make sense of the world we have to look at that activity in its own right. When we do this we find that these activities make existence claims; claims about reality. It is tempt-

The religious forms of life

ing to think that there is only one way of making such claims and only one set of standards in terms of which any existence claim should be judged. But "real" is a term in the language and has a meaning. The claim to be investigated is that "real" is used according to the same criteria in all areas of language. To investigate this we need to see what makes meaning possible. What underlies meaning is agreed projections in the use of words. If we wish to discover what the term "real" means in a practice, we have to look at that practice; at the ways language is used. If we do we may well find that the rules that govern the terms "real" or "exists", when people talk about the reality of God, are not those that govern those terms when talking of the existence of planets. Finally, if we wish to understand a practice or an institution, we have to come to understand the point that those who practice it see in their practices. This can be done by finding analogies; finding some point of contact between our lives and theirs. Nothing will guarantee that this understanding will be forthcoming. If it is not, however, we have no reason yet to say that the institution in question has no meaning.

By this account, it is always possible that someone might project a term into new contexts and that some others will, and some will not, see the point of that projection. In that event the practices of the group that see the point in a projection will seem enigmatic to those who do not. Those who do see that point will feel that those who cannot must suffer from a blindness of insight. In those circumstances all they have, by way of methods, is ways, like those we have seen in ethics, in which we try to get someone to see what we have seen (with the attendant risk that they will get us to see it their way). This will be a matter of drawing analogies, stressing similarities and dissimilarities, describing cognate phenomena and so forth. It will not be a matter of induction or deduction. Hence the inference to the irrationality of religious discourse fails. For it was predicated on the assumption that deduction and induction were the only ways of making the sense of an utterance clear. But religion, no less than ethics and aesthetics, might have a dialectical method designed to produce, but not such as to be guaranteed to produce, insight.

Those who are unable to see the point of a projection cannot, simply on that ground, conclude that those who claim to do so are hallucinating. If they find that others live a life with those projections, talk to each other, share practices, weave their words into

135

the actions of their lives, agree in further projections, that establishes the presumption that they are *speaking sense*.

An analogy may help. There are people who claim to be able to tell certain things about wines just by tasting them. They take a wine that is to my palate dry and project the word "sweet" on to it. They make ever subtler discriminations and develop an extraordinary complex and flexible language that fits that activity. The language is often metaphorical. In fact, none of that way of talking makes much sense to me.

But although the language makes no sense to me, and although I suspect there are charlatans who use it, I am not in the least inclined to deny that there are those to whom it *does* have a meaning. How else can I know this other than by seeing that they use words in a certain way, that they agree in the often highly distinctive metaphorical projections that they make, that it is woven into their lives in various ways? That I cannot use this language, and don't really know what they are doing in using it, is no reason for saying that it has no meaning.

A silly example may reinforce this point. An explorer goes into a remote village, sees an unfamiliar game of cards being played and attempts to work out the rules simply by watching. He sees one man deal one card to each player. Each man puts a sum of money on to the table. After a time, which varies greatly, one person takes all the money and the procedure is then repeated. At midnight they all go to bed. Some days later the game is played again.

Would you, even though you knew many other games, be able to work out the rules? For I promise you this is all you will be likely to observe. And if you had no idea what was going on, would you be entitled to say nothing was going on? And if you thought something was going on, what would tell you this other than evidence of the existence of a collective practice that you did not understand? For a game *is* going on. Each player receives a card. Each player bets. They all wait. The first card on which a fly lands, wins the pot.

The principle of charity

Why is the charity extended to wine tasters not always extended to those who are religious and speak accordingly? One answer might be that there is too much divergence in what religious people say

The religious forms of life

for us to talk of agreements in projections. One reply to that is suggested by Winch. He envisages the possibility of asking not what constitutes this or that religion, but what might lead us to talk of a use of language as "religious" in the first place

> I am concerned with meaning and religious language, not the language characteristically used in this or that particular religion. I want to ask primarily: how do we identify a use of language as religious in the first place. If we start by asking about words like "God" . . . we are open to the objections that such expressions do not have analogues in all religions insofar as our aim is to arrive at a characterisation of religious language as such. (Winch 1987: p. 107)

We should not start with terms like "God". Since there are nontheistic religions, an examination of theism would not give us an account of religion as such. If, however, we did concentrate on what might lead us to say some response is religious, it might emerge that there is more similarity between religions in the projections of language than a superficial look at their differences might suggest.

A second reason for thinking that the incomprehension of a nonparticipant confronted with the words of the connoisseur of wine appreciation differs from the incomprehension of the non-believer confronted with the words of a religious language is that, in the case of wine tasting, we know, simply by virtue of the fact that we are acquainted with the language of preference, something about what is going on. If I can make fine discriminations between different rock groups, I can be told that what the wine taster does is something like that. But I have no idea what is going on in religion.

One might, as Winch does, try to meet that objection head on by claiming that there are features of our lives that give us some insight into religion. As we shall see, the projections that are made into religion are of words like "love", "dependence", "acceptance", "awe", "forgiveness" and "prayer". Since I understand them out of their religious contexts, I understand something of their projected meanings, no less than, because I understand "prefer" with respect to clothes, I can understand something of its use with respect to wine tasting. Winch quotes Wittgenstein as saying in his notebooks that "we are in a certain sense dependent, and what we are dependent on we call God" (Wittgenstein 1979: p. 74). Whether or not I understand why the term "God" was brought in here, I do have some sense of being at the mercy of things, and indeed of sometimes feeling exempt from those contingencies. Again, if I am told that God gives "not as the world gives", then I may well meditate on how the world might give and get some sense what is being said.

Once we grasp all this, Winch's remarks about religion fall into two broad categories. First there are reminders of what he has established generally about the meaning of words and practices. Second there are remarks, akin to those in the second part of "Understanding a primitive society", that try to get us to see the point of religious practices and expressions.

The foundation of religion in practices

We are told repeatedly that if we wish to understand religion we have to do so in terms of the point seen in their practices by those who are religious. Even if theologians import a special set of theoretical technical terms to talk about religion, eventually, as I argued earlier, these will have to get their sense from the way in which they are related to the practices we are exploring, as liquidity preference was said by Winch to be related to the activities of entrepreneurs. For, "theological doctrines are not developed independently of their possibilities of application in the worship and religious lives of believers" (Winch 1987b: p. 115).

Examples of the injunction to understand religion in terms of the sense given to words by those who use them are legion in Winch's writings on religion. Thus we are told that "what makes a belief a religious belief is understood by investigating its roots in religious practice of concepts at work in religious beliefs" (Winch 1972: p. 110). For "how a term refers has to be understood in the light of its actual application" (1972: p. 113).

But all these are derivative from something said right from the beginning, in *The idea of a social science,* and in "Understanding a primitive society". In the former we read:

> criteria of logic are not a direct gift of God, but arise out of and are only intelligible in the context of ways of living or modes of social life. It follows that one cannot apply criteria of logic to modes of social life as such. For example, science is one such mode and religion another; and each has an intelligibility peculiar to itself. So within science or religion actions can be logical or illogical; in science, for example, it would be illogical not to be bound by the results of a properly carried out experi-

The religious forms of life

ment; in religion it would be illogical to suppose that one could pit one's own strength against God's.... But we cannot sensibly say that either the practice of science itself or that of religion is either logical or illogical.   (Winch 1958: p. 100)

In the latter we read:

> God's reality is certainly independent of what any man may care to think, but what that reality amounts to can only be seen from the religious tradition in which the concept of God is used, and this use is very unlike the use of scientific concepts, say of theoretical entities. ... It is within the religious use of language that the concept of God's reality has a place.
> (Winch 1972: p. 12)

Having put this so emphatically Winch, when later writing explicitly about religion, is content merely to issue reminders from time to time that science does not give us the only model of understanding. We have to look at and try to understand practices as they are, not as the scientifically minded would like them to be.

Understanding religion

What can we understand about religion? Four things at least are worth extracting from Winch's remarks.

I Not another thing

Winch remarks that talking about God is not like talking about something like the planets. Nor is praying to God like an ambassador asking for an audience (Winch 1987b: p. 119). God is not another thing; not a person as we are, but on a greater scale. There are two reasons for this claim.

The first makes reference to the way religious people speak of God. A particularly vivid example comes from Anselm's *Monologium* where he says of God's existence:

> it has no place or time, and has not taken to itself distinctions of place or time, neither here nor there nor anywhere, not then, not now, not at any time. Nor does it exist in terms of this fleeting present in which we live, nor has it existed, nor will it

139

exist in terms of past or future, since these are restricted to things finite and mutable which it is not.

(Anselm 1962: Ch. 5)

Second, more often the claim is something like this: that we could not make sense of theistic religion if we supposed that God were some spatio-temporal entity. Religion, on Winch's account, is to do with things like the meaning of one's life or the sense of the world. It would make no sense to treat God *as one more thing*, however powerful that thing would be.

In a memorable episode of *Star Trek,* the Enterprise takes its crew to a planet on which the Greek god Apollo languishes. His problem is that he is bored with eternity, much as was Mrs Makropoulos in Capek's novella, *The Makropoulos case.* By that we learn that a spatio-temporal entity of whatever power cannot fill the role of an object of religious devotion. What the religious person wants is a way of coming to terms with what there is, and merely to add another thing to what there is would be to give that person one more thing to come to terms with. And if what is added is another person, that person too, in so far as it is part of the spatio-temporal order, will have the same problems about the meaning of life that religion was meant to cure.

Von Danniken has talked of "the chariots of the gods", the hypothesis that there is a race of super-farmers of the universe. Hence the question of whether God is an astronaut. Whether there is such a race of beings is simply a scientific hypothesis. Whatever they are, although we might call them gods, they are not fitted to occupy the role of God as that occurs in religion. Even were they to live for ever, that would not help. As Wittgenstein remarked, nothing is solved about the meaning of life by living for ever. If I have a problem about the meaning of life, everlasting life will give me an everlasting problem.

The diagnosis that Winch offers is this. We hear someone say that God exists, that God is like a father, that God sees everything, and we take them as suggesting that there is one more super-entity to be listed in the inventory of the furniture of the universe. To that Winch replies (for example, Winch 1987b: p. 119) that if we pay attention to the way in which religious people speak we will see that the ways of speech do not imply, and could not if the needs of religion are to be served, that the object of religion is just one more thing. Later I shall deal with the accusation that Winch is trying to have it both ways. The religious person tries to refer to

God both as an extra entity and to deny that this is what God is.

II The religious use of pictures

Pictures have an important function in religion. Here we may take Winch's example of God reaching out a finger to Adam in Michelangelo's Sistine Chapel frescoes, where his discussion takes its departure from Wittgenstein's remark in *Culture and value*: "these pictures can only serve to describe what we are to do, not justify it" (quoted in Winch 1987b: p. 65; see also Winch 1987a).

A picture need not always be helpful. Someone might think that God sat for a picture as a model sits for a portrait and so come to an extraordinary view of the almighty. (Rather as if, as Wittgenstein put it in another context, someone hearing that God sees everything were to ask about God's eyebrows). Winch says, therefore, that the representation of God "does not enter as a picture" (1987b: p. 78). It is not "related to some event" (1987b: p. 79). Yet the picture can "describe what we are to do". How is this to be understood?

Let us think of a situation where a person has strong feelings, of love perhaps, but cannot express them. Then one day he or she reads e. e. cummings's "Somewhere I never travelled":

> (i do not know what it is about you that closes
> and opens; only something in me understands
> that the voice of your eyes is deeper than all roses)
> Nobody, not even the rain, has such small hands.

She or he might think, "That is how I feel". Who can deny the power of music, pictures and poems to evoke that response? But here it is not a question of a *correspondence* between the work and some reality already existing in me independently of it. If I am a poet struggling to express a thought, it is not until I find the thought that I know what I wanted to express. The work of art clarifies it for me.

Now consider the picture to which Winch refers. What I had not noticed about this picture, until Winch pointed it out to me, is how different the representation is of God from what has gone before in much theistic art. Hitherto God might have been depicted high above me, on a throne, distant and remote. Here God reaches out in love and is greeted with love, as if embodying the new commandment that we love one another. And I could imagine someone finding that this pictorially speaks to him or her; brings to consciousness and expresses a feeling about God and creation. That thought about God, though, is represented but not justified. For if one did not see that representation as right, find some fit between it and one's life, what could justify that way of seeing? Winch remarks therefore that Michelangelo's picture shows that

> God's power is his love. Here we understand in terms of the connection between love and the worship of the believer. Here the picture confronts reality, but not like an accident diagram.
> (Winch 1987b: p. 121)

III Religion and ethics

It is an important feature of Winch's account of religion that religion and ethics come into a special sort of relationship. He does not say that someone who wishes to act ethically needs to ask what God's wishes are in this or that matter. Rather ethics is rooted in certain primitive reactions and the notion of punishment, and indeed ethics itself, might be rooted in such spontaneous reactions as are expressed by "He's to blame". But once we have that notion of punishment it can relocate itself to a religious site. There "guilt and punishment lead a second life" (Winch 1972: p. 196). A person might come to think of afflictions as punishments that are not to be avoided but that might be beneficial, as any punishment might be to someone who accepts its justice. Similarly the ethical value of patience might take on a religious tone when it involves not a kind of quietist settling for an easy life (Winch 1993: p. 125) nor the "quiescent acceptance of avoidable evils, but an attitude to the unavoidable, a voluntary acceptance of unavoidable suffering" (Winch 1972: p. 206). Ultimately, I think, Winch may suspect that the ethical life is at least kindred to religion. For he writes that "to will the good is to see the limit beyond which one cannot go" (Winch 1972: p. 203), where that involves a relationship to one's life as a whole (Winch 1972: p. 206). These notions are also involved in religion.

IV The analogy with expression

But how then are religious utterances to be taken if they are not like the straightforward statements about spatio-temporal entities

The religious forms of life

that on their face they appear to be? A first point that Winch makes is that religion is rooted in primitive reactions, perhaps the feelings of awe one feels in great landscapes or seascapes, the feelings of absolute safety that can come upon us, our sense of contingency and so forth. Theology is not (better, *should* not) be developed independently of these responses. Theology is not independent of what Winch calls the "autonomous" practices of worship and the religious lives of believers, although, as it develops, it affects tradition and tradition affects it (Winch 1972: p. 115). In this connection I am reminded that the authority of the controversial encyclical "Humanae vitae", which proscribes artificial methods of contraception, has been queried by some as genuinely authoritative because it has not been taken into the lives of the faithful.

What Wittgenstein meant when he talked of foundational "primitive" experiences is a matter of some debate. (For an excellent survey, see Säätela 1998: Ch. 3). Sometimes he appears to be speaking of something pre-linguistic, like snatching a hand away from a hot stove. Sometimes he spoke as if the reactions were those that might be made by socialized beings; like Winch he speaks of justice being related to the behaviour of children in playgrounds. Winch's discussion of the role of these experiences in religion seems to me to tiptoe between the two sorts of cases, although I do not think this affects the point he wishes to make.

Thus, he likens these experiences and the responses that are their modes of their expression, and from which religion somehow arises, to pains and their expression. If one were to ask about the meaning of "I am in pain", that would have to be explained by saying that people have primitive reactions, which they articulate by crying and holding the injured part, and that they come to replace this behaviour by utterances such as "I am in pain", if only because to replace the primitive expressions with a developed language is to increase one's expressive possibilities. Pain replaces crying and does not describe it. Here Winch speaks (1987: p. 111) of an "analogy" between the development of a language for articulating one's pains and other aspects of one's life of feeling, and the development of a language in which the primitive reactions upon which religion alone can be based can be articulated.

Here is a vivid example of what I think Winch is after when he talks of religious expressions getting their sense from spontaneous reactions to experience. (It is worth comparing this example with

Winch's discussion of the way in which a mother expressed her love for her dead son (Winch 1987: pp. 65ff.).)

In Virginia Woolf's *To the lighthouse*, Mrs Ramsay sits in the evening, knitting as the light fails and the light of the lighthouse sweeps across her. As she performs those repetitive actions, under a repetitive sweep of light, so she becomes meditative and feels liberated:

> Beneath it is all dark, it is all spreading, it is unfathomably deep; but now and again we rise to the surface and that is what you see us by. Her horizon seemed to her limitless. There were all the places she had not seen; the Indian plains; she felt herself pushing aside the thick leather curtain of a church in Rome. This core of darkness could go anywhere, for no one saw it. They could not stop it, she thought, exulting. There was freedom, there was peace, there was, most welcome of all, a summoning together, a resting on a platform of stability. Not as oneself did one ever find rest ever, in her experience (she accomplished here something dextrous with her needles), but as a wedge of darkness. Losing personality one lost the fret, the hurry, the stir; and there rose to her lips always some exclamation of triumph over life when things come together in this peace, this rest, this eternity; and pausing there she looked out to meet that stroke of the lighthouse, the long steady stroke, the last of the three, which was her stroke, for watching them in this mood always at this hour one could not help attaching oneself to one thing especially of the things one saw; and this thing, the long steady stroke was her stroke. Often she found herself sitting and looking, sitting and looking, with her work in her hands until she became the thing she looked at – that light for example. And it would lift up on it some little phrase or other which had been lying in her mind like that – "Children don't forget, children don't forget" – which she would repeat and begin adding to it, It will end, It will end, she said. It will come, it will come, when suddenly she added, We are in the hands of the Lord.
>
> But instantly she was annoyed with herself for saying that. Who had said it? not she; she had been trapped into saying something that she did not mean. . . . What brought her to say that: "We are in the hands of the Lord?" she wondered. The insincerity slipping in among the truths roused her, annoyed her. She returned to her knitting again. How could any Lord

have made this world? she asked. With her mind she always seized the fact that there is no reason, order, justice: but suffering, death, the poor. No happiness lasted, She knew that. (Woolf 1992: pp. 69–71)

Here I make two remarks, both integral to an understanding of what Peter Winch had to say about religion. First, for myself, I feel I have *some* grasp of why, given that twilight experience, and given her cultural heritage, Mrs Ramsay might feel she had to utter those words. (Someone from a non-Christian tradition would not have referred to "the Lord", although other words might have been available.) Those words were the *only* ones that seemed to her at that moment to say what she wanted to say. They got that meaning from *that* experience in *those* circumstances. Winch's suggestion is that religious utterances arise in this way, as a primitive response that articulates an inner life of feeling, no less than the pain language articulates the inner life of sensation (Winch 1992a: pp. 69–71).

Second, Mrs Ramsay immediately rejects her mode of thought. But the novelist is careful to add "with her mind she seized the fact that there is no reason, order, justice". Here we learn that someone might try to intellectualize something that was not delivered by the route of the intellect, and Mrs Ramsay, an analytical philosopher's wife, will have been well versed in those possibilities. But it would equally be possible to say that, in thinking that way about the experience, one falsified it.

Winch remarks that "a historian or sociologist of religion must himself have some religious feeling if he is to make sense of the religious movement he is studying and understand the considerations which govern the lives of its participants" (Winch 1958: p. 88). But he also remarks, as if discussing the example I have given:

> The ways in which expressions are used with religious significance may serve to articulate a standard from the point of view of which the disorder and wretchedness which so largely characterise human life in its fundamental aspects may have to be assessed and come to terms with. (Winch 1987: p. 131)

He then adds, "though what sort of 'coming to terms with' this is I have neither the space nor the competence to say more about" (1958: p. 131). I share that feeling. But I have been at pains to say that the inability to inhabit a religion, rather than visit it as a tourist, does not mean that I have to deny that its utterances have a sense and a truth, nor that I cannot begin to sense what that might be.

It should be noted that throughout all this, Winch speaks of an analogy. All he wishes to say is that if we wish to understand how a religious language might have developed and what its character is we might think of the way in which a language can be founded from and arise out of primitive responses. From that propensity to respond, whatever sense a religious use of words might have is derived. That will not tell us what has developed. For that we shall have to look and see. There are those who point out, either with relief or regret, that this replaces the notion of religious language as a fact stating language with the notion of such as language as "merely" expressive. To that Winch, in ways that I shall shortly describe, would reply with the question of what here is the force of terms like "fact", "merely" and "expressive". That, however, leads to a consideration of possible objections to Winch's account.

Objections

I have no doubt that Winch has given a coherent account of religion. Religion arises, no less than do aesthetics and ethics, from responses made to the world that inform the language arising from them and to which they give sense. Where else could it come from? Moreover, to understand that language is to understand what responses those who use it are trying to articulate by it. Then it emerges that they are not necessarily to be understood as referring to some extra entity, and, if they are lured into thinking that they are, it is not clear how such reference is related to the concerns from which a religious life arises.

This view is deeply controversial. On the one hand there are those who welcome it as putting the final nail in the coffin of religion. For them, religion poses some kind of challenge because it seems to refer to an entity not accessible to observation and not deductively or inductively provable. That was precisely the way Ayer, for example, put it in *Language, truth and logic* (Ayer 1936: Ch. 6). But now, the claim is, no such reference is being made. All a religious person is doing is expressing his or her feelings, and not making truth claims (Mackie 1982: Ch. 12). That undermines religion. On the other hand there are those who react with hostility to this account just because it seems to put a nail in the coffin of

The religious forms of life

religion. They want to talk about a being "out there", and, as successive bishops have discovered, any abrogation of that claim seems to many to give up what is central at least to theism and to invite contempt. That is what Simone Weil was referring to when she said that attempts to purify the notion of God could seem like atheism. It is time then to look at some criticisms.

Having it both ways

Mill wrote:

> Here then I take my stand on an acknowledged principle of logic and morality that when we mean different things we have no right to call them by the same name and to apply to them the same predicates. ... Language has no meaning for the words "justice", "mercy" and "benevolence" save that in which we predicate them of our fellow creatures; and unless that is what we intend to express by them, we have no business to employ the words. If in applying them of God we do not mean to affirm these very qualities differing only as greater, we are neither philosophically nor morally entitled to affirm them at all. ... I will call no being good who is not what I mean when I apply that epithet to my fellow creatures.
>
> (Mill 1957: pp. 91–2)

More recently Flew wrote

> "Someone tells us that God loves us as father loves his children. We are reassured. But then we see a child dying of inoperable cancer of the throat. His earthly father is driven frantic in his efforts to help, but his heavenly Father reveals no obvious signs of concern.
>
> (Flew & MacIntyre 1955: pp. 98–9)

The charge here is that Winch wants it both ways. On the one hand he claims that there is a use in a religious context for a term like "father" or "love", which also has a perfectly good meaning in non-religious contexts. It is natural to assume some kind of connection of meaning, else, as Mill asks, why use *that* term. But, Flew complains, when we come to look at the use in religious contexts, we find that all meaning connections with the term in its ordinary context seem to have been severed. So we have no idea what is being said. (Here, incidentally, we have an echo of the problem that led to the theological doctrine of analogy. Since God shares none of the properties of his creatures, being wholly other, how could we talk about him at all using the terms, like good, that apply to earthly creatures?)

One answer here, deriving from Winch's work, is to take the case, to repeat an example, in which we all use the term "deep" to talk about things like mine shafts and ponds. We agree in the projections we make and use this term with no sense of strain. Then one day Wordsworth speaks of "thoughts that do often lie too deep for tears". Here "deep" is relocated. I might feel that Wordsworth seems systematically to have severed the use of the word from the criteria I have learned for its use. Suppose I said, "I don't see what you are saying". Of these deep thoughts I ask, "Are there rulers for them?" "No", I am told. "Plumb lines?" "No." "Will I get vertigo contemplating them?" "Not in that sense." "Can I end it all by throwing myself into them?" "Not in that sense either."

Although I might not, in not following this projection, understand what is being said, yet I have no right to deny that something is being said if others follow the projection Wordsworth makes and use it themselves.

Where then is the basis of Mill's and Flew's criticism? Is it that the religious person cannot make his or her meaning clear to the non-religious? But, then, is Wordsworth's poem meaningless because some literal minded Gradgrind cannot understand it? Is it that I have no idea how I might be brought to see it? Well there are ways we might try. These are not unlike the ways we have described in talking about insight in ethics and aesthetics and how it might be conveyed by analogy or metaphor, or might even have to wait upon the grace of fate that some event in life might get someone to see the point (as age might open the closed book of Proust). And life might close the book, too. Is it that we do not understand the notion of projection? But then we do not understand the notion of language either. Is it that the meaning has changed? But when Wordsworth used "deep" did he change the meaning? Wasn't that the only word that would do?

Why then is it not simply thus: someone learns to use the word "love", and then, because of some experience speaks of the love of God, where that love never fails. I do not understand this. But others appear to do so. Why then do I not extend to that extended use the charity I extend to Wordsworth's?

The religious forms of life

The non-factual

But in the end the most profound objection to Winch's account rests on the belief that it replaces the factual with the expressive and that in so doing it amounts to a denial that God "really" exists, "out there".

A first thing to do is to query the way this is often put. It is often said that, by Winch's account, religious language is "merely" expressive. Built into that is the following sort of view: the factual is what is real and important. The factual, the real and important, is also the objective. For the objective is what is in the object, in what is out there. The expressive is subjective, is *not* out there. It is inside a person. Expression may tell us how it is with a person, but is no guide to objective reality. "I'm in pain" does not tell you about a world independent of me. It tells only about the person, the subject, issuing the utterance.

That view is entirely commonplace. It underlies the inclination to think that emotions are mere expressions, and are neither reasonable nor unreasonable. It underlies the inclination to think that science is more basic than the arts, because the arts, having to do with the inner life, are more subjective. As such they can be relegated in the curriculum, as if the matter of the harmony of our lives were much less important than our appropriation of reality.

From the fact, if it is a fact, that science is one area of human activity, the area that deals with how the world objectively is (of which more later), and the expression of emotions and the rest of the "inner" life is another area of activity, nothing whatsoever follows about which is the most important. So even if religion were only related to the life of expression, that cannot be a way of relegating it in relation to science, unless we have some reason to think that science is the only form of life that in the end matters. And that, as I have explained, is a judgement that it is not for science to make. Nor is it a true judgement. Science has its importance, and so does the expression of an inner life: and a poet who gives a way of articulating our feelings of loss, love, grief, joy or whatever, contributes to the task of giving intelligibility to life, as much as does any scientist. To think otherwise, to think that merely because religion is expressive it *must* be inferior to science, is to assume a priority in science that needs proving, and that cannot in general be proved.

That takes us to the heart of the matter. For integral to the

149

complaint with which we are dealing is the belief that science deals with what is factual, what is out there, what is real, so that in divorcing religion from science Winch denies it any factual status. Isn't that to make religion out to be different from what believers took it to be, namely a matter of it *being a fact* that something called "God" "actually" exists?

But now we are back where we started. For from the very outset Winch wished to claim that we cannot take the notions of "fact", "real", "actual" and "exists" for granted. Nor should we take for granted the claim that science has a unique right to the use of these terms. Nor can we take for granted that fact that, even if other areas of existence turn out to have a use for these terms, the scientific one is prior.

First there is the question of whether religious people do use the term "real", "exist", "fact" and the like. And they do. "God exists" is certainly said. Second there is the question of whether the criteria that govern the application of these terms to, say, God, are the criteria that govern the application of these terms to things like planets. The answer is "No". God is not observable as are the entities with which observation concerns itself.

Does it then follow that religious people aren't using the word "exists" meaningfully? Possibly, if they think that this commits them to an extra spatio-temporal and potentially observable entity. But, as an earlier quotation from Anselm revealed, we are specifically debarred from taking it thus. But whether or not religious people are using the term "exists" meaningfully does not *necessarily* depend on whether they are using it as a natural scientist does, that is, in such a way as to make empirical observation germane to questions of the truth of the claim that something exists, else "There exists a prime number between 11 and 17" would also be a meaningless use of the word "exists".

Here we might go two ways. One way is to say that since certain living practices use the word "exists" that establishes a presumption as to its meaningfulness, although we have no idea what it means nor how it got its meaning. The alternative is to say that we do have some idea of how it might have got its meaning.

In line with what I have earlier argued, we might try this. We learn the word "exists" in ordinary mundane practices. Let us say that as we learn that term we learn that what exists is somehow there, whether we are or not. Let it even be that we learn the word as tied to certain observational and calculative methods of establishing existence. But then out of some experience of life, perhaps the experience that Wittgenstein and Winch make much of, namely, of feeling absolutely safe, someone says (as Mrs Ramsay found herself spontaneously led to say) that there is a God who loves us. That is expressed by using the word "exists" in those circumstances. We might do so because the safety seems to come to us and not from us; our mere wishing for it cannot guarantee to make it come to us or continue with us. That might give the word "exists" a use and point here, even if those who have different experiences cannot see its point.

It would be foolish to think that things are different with terms used in science, so that religion is worse off here. Of course, a religion might change in its nature or appeal, but science changes, too. What remains is that if someone sees a point in a projection and others see that too, then there is, prima facie, a point.

Reality

And, finally, someone might object to the whole philosophy upon which all this is founded, a matter to which I shall return in Chapter 7. For, it might be said, reality now becomes relativized to language. What exists, in science, religion, whatever, becomes a function of what we see a point in saying.

Winch writes "I am not saying that the 'existence' of what is spoken of simply consists in the fact that people talk in a certain way: I am saying that what 'existence' amounts to is expressed, shows itself, in the language they speak" (Winch 1972: pp. 113–14).

But isn't this view that something exists because people talk a certain way? How can Winch simply deny that?

In the *Philosophical investigations* Wittgenstein has his interlocutor ask "so you are saying that human agreement decides what is true and what is false" (Wittgenstein 1953: ss. 241). He replies with the far-reaching remark that "it is what human beings say that is true and false and they agree in the language that they use. This is not agreement in judgments but in forms of life".

That says no more and no less than this: *reality* is not true and false, objective and subjective. It is what we *say* that is true and false. And, as we use our words, it is simply untrue that "real" means "constituted by our say so", and, as Winch remarks, if it did mean this, it would be unclear that we could have a language. For

(Winch 1972: p. 13) "we cannot imagine a language which had no way of distinguishing between the real and the unreal".

Our observational use of language imports a distinction between the real and the unreal that separates reality from what anyone might happen to think or say. Does religion have a use of the word real that allows us to distinguish what is real from what any particular person might think is real? Winch says "Yes":

> God's reality is certainly independent of what any man may care to think. ... It is within the use of language that the concept of God's reality has a place – though ... this does not mean that it is at the mercy of what anyone cares to say. If this were so, God would have no reality. (Winch 1972: p. 12)

There are really things out there, but we can *say* this only because we have a use for the term "real". What goes for the reality of shrubs *might*, on Winch's account, go for the reality of God also.

Further reading

Another version of the claim that religion is now not taken seriously in a certain sort of intellectual culture is to be found in D. Z. Phillips, "Wittgenstein, religion and anglo-american culture", in *Wittgenstein and the philosophy of culture*, K. Johannessen & T. Nordenstam (eds) (Vienna: Verlag-Hölder-Pilcher-Tempsky, 1996), pp. 201–17. Phillips, like Winch, was closely associated with Rush Rhees, and his work bears illuminating affinities with Winch's analyses. For more on Phillips, see Tessin and von de Ruhr (1995). Thanks to Phillips we now have the remarkable collection of mostly unpublished writings on religion by Rhees. Winch, in what must be almost the last thing he wrote, remarks, in his dust jacket commendation of this body of writing: "I know of nothing else remotely like it in the field, whether for philosophical acumen, intellectual honesty or religious insight". Everything Winch has to say on religion is illuminated by a reading of these papers by Rhees.

Some have imputed to Winch the view that religion is a "language game", a term coined by Wittgenstein's translator. They have further said that this makes religion a form of life cut off from other games, like science. Winch certainly does not believe the latter, which he characterizes as "sealing the door between the

The religious forms of life

chapel and the laboratory to make sure that there is no intermingling of the incense and the hydrogen sulphide" (Winch 1972: p. 121). He also expressed some scepticism about the helpfulness of certain introductions of the notion of language games (Winch 1993: p. 112). See also G. Anscombe, "Cambridge philosophers: Wittgenstein", *Philosophy* **70**, pp. 395–407, 1995, and her comment (p. 406) that to say that a language game is played is not to justify it. I have tried to avoid the use of the term "language game". For those who wish to pursue it I commend P. Sherry, *Religion, truth and language games* (London: Macmillan, 1977), especially Chapters 1 and 2. His view is far less sympathetic to Winch than mine is. On the same subject there is a rousing attack on the notion of religion as a language game in J. Cook, "Wittgenstein and religious belief", *Philosophy* **63**, pp. 427–52, 1988. Cook argues that it can't be a language game, not because there are language games and religion isn't one of them, but because the notion of language games is not well founded.

Winch argued that one can't ask whether a practice is rational and answer it from within a practice. This is denied by M. Durrant, "Is the justification of religious belief a possible enterprise?", *Religious Studies* **9**, pp. 449–55, 1973. Another such denial occurs in J. Watt, "Winch and rationality in religion", *Sophia* **13**, pp. 19–29, 1974. The same conclusion is reached by J. Shepherd, "Religion and the contextualisation of criteria", *Sophia* **15**, pp. 1–10, 1976.

My term "projection" is clearly related to what Wittgenstein (1953: part II, p. 216) calls "secondary sense". This is very usefully discussed in B. Tilghman, *Wittgenstein, ethics and aesthetics* (London: Macmillan, 1991), Chapter 7. See also S. Cavell, *The claim of reason* (Oxford: Oxford University Press, 1979); P. Lewis, "On experiencing the meaning of a word", *Open Mind*, 1980, pp. 3–9; O. Hanfling, "I heard a plaintive melody", in *Wittgenstein centenary essays,* A. Phillips Griffiths (ed.) (Cambridge: Cambridge University Press, 1991), pp. 117–34; and L-O. Åhlberg, "The analogy between ornament and music", *Nordisk Estetisk Tidskrift* **12**, pp. 95–110, 1994.

Winch speaks of language as related to reactions. It is important not to assume that when Wittgenstein spoke of "primitive reactions" he wished to speak only of the pre-linguistic reactions of language learners. On this not uncommon misunderstanding see the most admirable discussion in Säätela's *Aesthetics as grammar* (1998: pp. 138–213).

Of four last matters, first, much is made of Wittgenstein's talk of "being safe whatever happens" and its relation to religion. There is an excellent discussion of this matter in L. Ashdown, "Absolute safety", *Philosophical Investigations* **18**, pp. 162–72, 1995. Second, for a different perspective on many of these matters see C. Barrett, *Wittgenstein on ethics and religious belief* (Oxford: Blackwell, 1991). Third, Winch wrote further about pictures and representation in Winch (1987a). Fourth, for a rousing denunciation of post-Wittgenstein philosophy of religion see Mackie (1982: Ch. 12). This sustained attack by a brilliant philosopher ought to be read in conjunction with, and as a set of negative comments on, my attempt to do justice to what I think to be Winch's attempt, influenced, via Rhees, by Wittgenstein, to understand religion.

Chapter 6
"The interval of hesitation": Peter Winch's Simone Weil

Simone Weil

For those who do not know of the life and work of this remarkable woman I begin with an imagined description of her thoughts during her last moments in the sanatorium in which she died, in 1943, in Ashford, Kent:

> Tuesday 24 August was a warm summer's day. As Simone Weil lay in her bed, her mind moved beyond the distant hills. She saw again the Paris in which she grew up, the cafes of the Boulevard St. Michel, her paper strewn room in the spacious flat of the rue Auguste Comte, with its view over Paris as far as Sacre Coeur, at the Lycée Henri IV where she listened to the thoughts of Alain, and the École Normale with its passionate political commitments. She saw again her school in quiet Le Puy, her little class in the summer house at Roanne, and the workers of St. Etienne with their red flag. She saw again the grinding factories of Alsthom and Renault, the miserable little room in the rue Lecourbe, and the joyful days of the Popular Front. She saw the Abbey of Solesmes besides its quiet river and heard the Gregorian chant. She saw the flat in Marseilles with the sound of the sea and the cries from the beach coming in through the open windows. . . . She saw New York and the Hudson River and her anxious waiting parents. She saw London with its parks, its pubs, its telegrams and its anger. And she saw Ashford with its green trees and green fields on

155

which the sun was declining. At half past ten her heart stopped beating and she died. (McLellan 1989: p. 266)

That, of course, does not do justice to an extraordinary life, which began with a rigorous training in philosophy and moved into school teaching; which was combined with an extreme political radicalism; which learned first hand the awfulness of factory life; which took her to the civil war in Spain and into the French resistance; and which, through profound religious experiences, brought her to religion.

Winch and Weil

Winch frequently remarks that one ought to distinguish substantive questions about morality and religion, questions about what one should, in the particular circumstances of one's life do and believe, from philosophical questions about what it is to act and believe. Likewise one is to distinguish questions about what there is, and how it is, from philosophical questions about what it is for something to exist, so that philosophy, although it might tell us that what it is to be real differs from science and religion in not expressing views about what is real.

That thought is there from the beginning.

> Philosophy is uncommitted enquiry.... To take an uncommitted view of... competing conceptions is peculiarly the task of philosophy; it is not its task to award prizes to science, religion or anything else. It is not its business to advocate any *Weltanschauung* [worldview]. (Winch 1958: p. 103)

Writing more particularly of ethics he writes:

> I think it is an important task for philosophy to make clear the distinction between corrupt and non-corrupt forms of the thought that someone is worthy of admiration. But neither it nor any other form of enquiry can show what is worthy of admiration. The idea that it can is itself a form of corruption. (Winch 1972: p. 191)

And in the case of religion he writes:

> The ways in which expressions used with religious emphasis may serve to articulate a standard from the point of view of

Peter Winch's Simone Weil

which the disorder and wretchedness which so largely characterise human life in its fundamental aspects may be assessed and come to terms with. Although what sort of "coming to terms with" this is I have neither the space nor the competence to say more about. (Winch 1987: p. 131)

Although Winch made that distinction I am not sure that he was at ease with it, nor, as we shall see did he always observe it. Some anxiety is expressed about it at the beginning of his book on Simone Weil, *The just balance* (1989b), and also towards the end of that work, when he remarks on a methodological difficulty he has with where to draw the line between philosophy and religious meditation (Winch 1989b: p. 5). That may explain something many have wondered about, which is why that book breaks off where a second volume, which would have dealt with Simone Weil's writings on religion, might have begun.

Leaving aside the question of where such a line is to be drawn, and even whether it should be drawn at all, the remark reveals a tension to which anyone approaching Simone Weil's work (and I suspect anyone approaching much of what is called "continental philosophy") from Winch's particular philosophical position and with Winch's sense of the relevance of philosophical speculation in great issues of ethics and religion, is likely to be subjected.

For on the one hand, as we shall see, Simone Weil is a toughminded philosopher, interested, in ways that any philosopher in any tradition would recognize, in epistemological and ontological issues, the understanding of which Winch believes to be an essential prerequisite to any understanding of such things as ethics, religion, science and the arts. But on the other hand there is an aspect of her work that touches upon something that Winch believes to be peculiarly characteristic of the search for *understanding* in ethics, religion and the study of societies.

In my exposition I pointed out that the method of coming to that understanding was related to what is traditionally called dialectic, in which one seeks to find, or to give, a certain insight, which, when attained, is reflected in such phrases as "Now I see it". In that dialectic both sides will use such things as analogies, metaphors, stories and examples that stress similarities between something we do understand and the phenomenon we are seeking to understand, as when Winch tries to illuminate an aboriginal practice by comparing the carrying of a stick called the soul in one culture with carrying a wedding ring or a lock of hair in another (Winch 1972: p. 45).

But there is another component of that strategy. In an account of the various strategies of getting someone to see something in a work of art, Frank Sibley, after mentioning the use of comparisons ("It brings to mind those languorous afternoons in Provence"), analogies ("It's as if the paint had been thrown at the canvas"), remarks that sometimes we simply *point* to the feature that we claim to see and are trying to help another to see, (as when someone asks me to help them see what moves me to admiration of Rothko). And as a result of the pointing, the other can indeed come to see. *Of course* we simply point to what we want someone to see. Aesthetics is a perceptual matter. We have to see the grace of a line, hear the harshness of the music, if we are to have the experience. So I can say to someone, "Look at the delicacy of this line as compared with this in another work". And, in saying that, I can produce insight.

Precisely that can happen where what is in question is the understanding of a morality, a religion, or a society which we cannot find ourselves as yet inhabiting. (This is why, presumably, McNaughton calls his book on ethics *Moral vision* (1988)). One simply points out, as Simone Weil does in speaking of the factory system, that a certain sort of organization embodies a certain sort of oppressiveness. And having had it pointed out to us, we see it, much as Tolstoy might get us to see the vileness of a form of prostitution (as opposed to getting us to believe that it is vile) by showing it to us in a short story.

Wittgenstein writes that:

> Philosophy simply puts everything before us and neither explains nor deduces anything. The aspects of things that are most important to us are hidden because of their simplicity and familiarity. (One is unable to notice something because it is always before one's eyes). And this means that we fail to be struck by what, once seen, is most striking and most powerful.
> (Wittgenstein 1953: ss. 129)

Simone Weil's work, then, is not merely an investigation of questions instantly recognizable as questions about the foundations of knowledge and about our relationship to the world that is known by us. It contains also striking remarks that often elicit that feeling of having been reminded of something, or recognizing

Peter Winch's Simone Weil

something, that was there to be seen but that we had not seen. Those reminders are likely to elicit the words "That's right".

I have discussed already the question of how, if one says "That's right", one might or might not be entitled to one's claim. For the moment I wish only to point out that, across a wide range of topics, ranging from the nature of the state, the nature of factory oppression, morality, religion and justice many, including many philosophers, have clearly been moved to assent by her remarks. She is, as we shall shortly see, illustratively quoted by Winch as often having brought something into clearer focus for him.

Having now said this, I sense contrary tugs in Winch's philosophy, which become clearly apparent in his engagement with the work of Simone Weil. On the one hand there is his view that philosophy has to do with the conditions of intelligible and meaningful behaviour and of the understanding of behaviour in various regions of our lives, where that will be a matter of understanding what it is, in those various regions, for something to be real, of saying what it is to know that something is real, and of understanding assertions to that effect. These questions are conducted without reference to questions about what *is* real, what *is* the case, what *is* known. They are questions about the possibilities. On the other hand there is a pull not merely towards saying that answers will be delivered by a certain sort of dialectic, but also of intimating what those answers might be, as when he says, for example, that technology frees us from one sort of oppression (as when central heating delivers us from oppression by the natural impact of the weather) only to deliver us into another kind of oppression (the regular stoking of a stove) (Winch 1972: p. 42). I cannot see how that could have been avoided by someone who not only stressed the need for dialectic, but must also have thought deeply about substantive issues.

Two uses of Simone Weil's work

There are two employments of Simone Weil's work in Winch's philosophy. One is his citation of particular remarks by Simone Weil, which have, for him, that illuminating reminder effect that I have attributed to her writing. These, however, contrary to things Winch sometimes says about philosophy, illuminate substantive issues. For in those remarks we are reminded, and so brought to

159

knowledge, of how things are for good or ill in our world. The other employment, evidenced in his last book, *The just balance* (1989b), is the sustained philosophic analysis of her thinking, where philosophy is conceived, as Winch conceived it, right at the start of his various philosophical enterprises, as an ontological and epistemological enquiry into what there is and what it is to know it. I take these in turn.

The first use: reminders and illuminations

There are eight cases in his essays in which Winch mentions some thought of Simone Weil's in a way that seems to me to verge on a violation of his avowal of the neutrality of philosophy. The reference to her in "Text and context" (Winch 1987b), although illustrating an important point, seems to me rather peripheral. The other seven are not.

I Oppression

In "Understanding a primitive society" Winch writes that when we investigate another society, we often find that it has other ways of doing things (sowing, tending and reaping crops), perhaps less technical than ours. Having said "my aim is not to engage in moralising" he continues by saying that, when we encounter such societies:

> We are confronted not just with different techniques, but with new possibilities of good and evil, in relation to which men may come to terms with life. An investigation into this dimension of society may indeed require a quite detailed inquiry into alternative techniques (e.g. of production), but it is an inquiry conducted for the light it throws on those possibilities of good and evil. A very good example of the kind of thing I mean is Simone Weil's analysis of the techniques of modern factory production in *Oppression and liberty* [*Oppression et liberté*], which is not a contribution to business management, but part of an inquiry into the peculiar form which the evil of oppression takes in our culture. (Winch 1972: p. 42)

For, he continues, (and he remarks that the point is "beautifully

Peter Winch's Simone Weil

developed by Simone Weil in *Oppression and liberty*"),

> technical independence is yet another form of dependence. Technology destroys some dependencies but always creates new ones, which may be fiercer – because harder to understand – than the old. This should be particularly apparent to *us*. (Winch 1972: p. 104).

But two things are worth remarking, given that this work is part of a quest to understand Peter Winch's philosophy. First, the remarks Weil makes and which Winch cites are *not* neutral. They involve the claim that there is a certain kind of evil in our society. Second, Winch does not say it *is* apparent to us that our society involves questionable relationships of dependence but that it *should* be apparent (although it might not be). That is to say that one may need someone to make the obvious clear. Why should that someone not be a philosopher?

II Legality and justice

Winch wrote numerous things that fall squarely into the area of political philosophy. The article "Hobbes and Rousseau" (Winch 1972) is one clear example. (See also Winch 1958–9, 1990 and the very important 1991). In that penetrating account of these two philosophers, Winch is led to remark that Hobbes was not able to recognize the difference between legality and justice. Of course not. For Hobbes there was no justice until a legally constituted state made justice possible. There is no *natural* justice. In what Hobbes calls the "state of nature", a state reminiscent of the trading floor described in Tom Wolfe's *The bonfire of the vanities*, or the world of Gordon Gecko in Oliver Stone's *Wall Street*, there is no justice, only the war of each against each. Rousseau, he thinks, has a different view. So, too, does Winch, if only, as we saw, because he thinks that notions like blame and fairness rest on primitive pre-social reactions, so that if one child is less well rewarded for the same act it will simply protest that this is not fair.

Now Hobbes's account leads to the difficulty of seeing how a properly elected, constitutional government can act unjustly provided it acts legally. And it is here that Winch invokes Simone Weil's remarks about the government of France in the period leading up to its capitulation in the Second World War, remarks that

161

he himself later translated into English (Winch 1987b). She writes of the government of France that

> After 1937, the government did not merely *de facto* abandon the forms of legality – that would not matter much, for the British government did the same, and yet there never was a British Prime Minister who was more legitimate than Winston Churchill – but the feeling for legitimacy was gradually extinguished. Practically no Frenchman approved of Daladier's usurpations. Practically no Frenchman became indignant about them. It is the feeling for legitimacy that makes one indignant about usurpations.
>
> (quoted in Winch 1972: p. 107)

Her point is that at that time a perfectly legal government lost *authority*. A gap emerged between legality and propriety which should not, on Hobbes's account, be possible. So Hobbes's account is false. It claims, as a necessary truth, that legality and justice go together. We find cases that go against that claim, so it is not true. And again we find in Winch's account the two features that I have mentioned before. First there is the admission to have found illumination from some penetrating remarks by Simone Weil. But second, we seem to have arrived at a substantial claim, in breach of philosophical neutrality, namely that since justice and legality did not go together in pre-Vichy France, that government was defective, as will be any government that although legal, has lost authority.

III The stern voice of duty

In the discussion of ethics we saw that there is a certain kind of ethical philosophy, of which Kant is the exemplar, which makes the rightness of an action consist in the fact that it is done from duty. Winch, in objecting to this philosophy, produces as a counter example Ibsen's Mrs Solness, who does what she does for others, not from any spring of love or good will, but from the harsh imperative of duty. But he invokes most tellingly a remark by Simone Weil about the difference between a father who plays with a child out of love and one who does so out of duty. Again the reminder has salutary force, but again it seems to entail a substantive conclusion, that a certain sort of way of engaging with others is wrong.

IV Punishment

Winch's essay "Ethical reward and punishment" (Winch 1972) began with a problem: what did Wittgenstein mean when he said that "ethics has nothing to do with punishment and reward in the usual sense"? Punishment in the usual sense, he thinks, often means deterrence, a means–end notion. Punishment is justified because it is the means to the end of preventing certain actions being performed. Already there is a strain between this and the notion of the ethical. For the ethical involves the notion of doing the right thing, but not just as a means to an end.

A convict who thinks "I won't get caught again" does not have an ethical attitude towards punishment and neither does one who thinks "I won't do it again, in case I get caught". But then there is a paradox. For now it looks as if the only person who can have an ethical attitude towards punishment is one who thinks "I did wrong and I will live better". But since that person is now repentant, isn't punishing him or her somehow otiose? And it is at this point that Winch quotes a passage from Simone Weil that has the thought-provoking air of paradox of many instructive passages from art and philosophy. (Think here of that master of the genre, Wittgenstein, and the force of remarks like "If a lion could talk we would not understand it".) She writes,

> In the life of the individual, the innocent must always suffer for the guilty; because punishment is expiation only if it is preceded by repentance. The penitent, having become innocent, suffers for the guilty, whom the repentance has abolished. (quoted in Winch 1972: p. 219)

Winch finds this illuminating as a reminder that there is a kind of repentance that *demands* punishment, where owning up to what one did creates in one a wound that can only be healed by suffering something. The most striking case of this, discussed with sensitivity in Winch's "Trying", is Oedipus. Although not even guilty in any strict sense of what he undoubtedly did, he felt some need to suffer if he were to be able to live with himself. As Winch remarks, we can understand this, even though it may seem alien to us. Again I note both the illumination he claims to receive from Simone Weil and its substantive implications; namely that those who do not have the ethical attitude to their punishment are in a less happy state as human beings than those who do.

163

Peter Winch

V The hesitation before others

In one of his essays, Winch makes a point, to which I shall return since it is central to his reading of Simone Weil as a philosopher, that there is a difference between our reactions to people and our reactions to things (Winch 1987b: Essay 10). It is not unknown for automobilphiliacs to pat the car after a long journey safely accomplished. Only regressed anthropomorphs, however, would blush when undressing in front of the family saloon. But other *people* impinge on us. The point will be familiar to readers of Sartre. If I look through a keyhole at someone undressing (to use *his* example) I may do so with no sense of wrongdoing. Let me become aware that another is watching me doing it and I am likely to become uncomfortable, to the extent of feeling shame. Other people impinge in such ways, as objects do not, on our freedom to act as we please; a fact that underlies Sartre's comment that hell is other people.

Winch remarks that this difference in our attitudes to things and our attitudes to people is not based on reasons, a remark related to his analysis and endorsement of Wittgenstein's assertion that we are not of the *opinion* that our mothers, say, are human persons. (Although in the world of the film *Men in black*, permeated as it is by aliens in the most unlikely guises, I *might* be of the opinion that some particular thing is a human person). Others have an effect on us, different from the effect of lamp-posts and cocktail glasses, merely by their presence. They induce in us, in an important phrase of Simone Weil's, a "hesitation", which is primitive. On that is founded, among other things, the whole of ethical life. Again, she is quoted by Winch as having put this in an illuminating way, and again the point has substantive implications.

> The human beings around us exert just by their presence a power which belongs uniquely to themselves to stop, to diminish, or modify, each movement which our bodies design. A person who crosses our path does not turn aside our steps in the same manner as a street sign, no one stands up, or moves, or sits down again in quite the same fashion when he is alone in the room as when he has a visitor.
> (quoted in Winch 1987b: p. 146)

Not to hesitate before another in such a way as to acknowledge his or her personhood is to be morally defective, at least in the sense of being excluded from the possibilities of participation in a moral life (although not from the consequences of moral censure). When Rosencrantz and Guildenstern acted as they did to Hamlet the most *damning* judgement he could make of them was that they made a *thing* of him and *used* him as a thing.

But perhaps the most profound of Winch's citations from Simone Weil come when he is talking of religion, partly because he was there obviously profoundly impressed by the importance of the questions about the meaning of life and death that religion addressed, and partly because the remarks on religion belong to a profound later phase of Simone Weil's work, where philosophy, in ways that puzzled Winch, merges into religious meditation. There are two major examples in Winch's essays.

VI Grace

In explaining what I took to be some of Winch's thoughts about religion I remarked that he believed the words used by religious people to express their religious life rested on a foundation of primitive responses that were simply there. One such, clearly central to Wittgenstein's emotional life, and clearly evidenced in the passage I quoted from Virginia Woolf, is the feeling of being absolutely safe, a feeling that is, I think, expressed by saying that the world cannot touch one. Winch, indeed remarks that "religion sets us apart from practical concerns, though it is connected to them" (Winch 1987b: p. 131). For the expression "the world" here includes such things as wealth, fame, health and human love, all of which can be lost. Someone, then, who has a sense of safety that comes from having money in the bank, a reputation, good health and a job, is not safe whatever happens. But to be safe whatever happens is not to be safe in that way. For the religious person, presumably, what is important is the thought (which Wittgenstein thought to be in one sense "strictly nonsensical") expressed by "not as the world gives give I unto you". It is in that sense, Winch argues, that one might understand the sense of the claim that the good man cannot be harmed.

It is, however, possible to misconstrue the phrase "safe whatever happens" as "safe whatever". But Winch remarks that this is to "try to take the eternal by storm" (Winch 1972: p. 207). For one thing *can* always happen, namely that one could lose the sense of safety (but see the reference to Ashdown in the reader's guide to Chapter 5). And it is in this connection that Winch quotes Simone Weil's remark about Peter.

> To say to Christ as Saint Peter did: "I will always be faithful to thee", is to deny him already, for it is to suppose that the source of fidelity is in ourselves and not in grace. As he was chosen, this denial was made known to all men and to himself. How many others boast in the same way – and never understand. (quoted in Winch 1972: p. 207)

And again I have to say that the illumination entails substantive conclusions. Peter, and anyone acting as he does, is arguably irreligious.

VII Religion

A remark that profoundly touched Winch appears in a passage from Simone Weil, and is quoted in "Meaning and religious language":

> Earthly things are the criterion of spiritual things. Only spiritual things are of value but only physical things have a verifiable existence. Therefore the value of the former can be verified only as an illumination projected on the latter.
> (Winch 1987b: p. 122).

That somewhat cryptic passage lies, I think, at the roots of Winch's philosophy and I have no doubt that he quotes it because it expresses precisely what lay within the progressing and painfully wrought passage of his thinking about the nature of religion. For what it says is this: the spiritual is not reducible to the non-spiritual. "For to say 'Earthly things are the criterion of spiritual things' is not to say they are identical" (Winch 1987b: p. 210). It is to say that the spiritual can only be grasped through the non-spiritual.

One thing that may be meant by this can be brought out by considering the case of the possession of value by a painting. For a painting is a physical thing, pigments, perhaps, which can be specified in terms of chemical properties, distributed in this or that order, an order that can be described in terms of spatio-temporal coordinates, on a surface that is itself physically describable. But from the fact that someone can see the pigments and their distributions it does not follow that he or she will see the value features that inhere in those pigments thus distributed. Every one of my readers will doubtless be able to recall cases in which he or she saw everything there was to see about a painting, in the sense of agreeing entirely on its physical description with someone, and yet was not able to see the value imputed by that other to the painting, even though they trusted the testimony of the person who claimed to see that value. Those value features are all that is of value when we talk about the artistic value of the painting. Yet only the physical aspects of the painting can be seen with the sense organs, and in that sense have a verifiable existence. It is *through* our perception of those pigments in that and that order that we come to grasp the value features of the painting. We *have* to see those physical properties if we are to grasp the value of the work. As Wollheim might put it, we have to see something *in* those pigments (Wollheim 1980: Essay V). To see that is to see those pigments, in that ordering, as illuminated by the values that inhere in them. That is analogous to saying that, as the world goes, only spiritual things are of value. The world, the physical world, is what is the case, is what is just there. But we have to apprehend the physical world in order to grasp its spiritual values, just as we have to apprehend the pigments of the painting in order to see its values. The religious person apprehends the spiritual values as inhering in and illuminating that physical world.

That analogy illuminates two other things I have stressed. One is that the language in which we talk of the spiritual is rooted ultimately in responses we spontaneously make. Just as no one could come to an understanding of aesthetic value who was not inclined to dance when music plays, be uplifted by great landscapes, or moved by the textures and fragrances of the world, so no one could come to a religious language who was not moved in certain other ways by the world. Second, when someone is moved and someone else is not, there is little point in trying to induce understanding *merely* by telling someone that one has seen something. One has to try to produce insight by those kinds of dialectical procedures to which I have continually referred. For a powerful example of what that means I commend the reader to John Wisdom's article "Gods", whose tone seems far from the verificationist leanings that many have attributed to it (Wisdom 1953).

Peter Winch

The second use: The systematic study of Simone Weil's philosophical development

Although those appropriations of thoughts from Simone Weil have illuminating force they do not constitute a systematic study of her as a philosopher. Clearly Winch read and studied her and found great illumination from reading her. But, we are told in the preface to the systematic study he eventually came to write, *The just balance*, that he had some difficulty in writing that more systematic work. Fortunately circumstances conspired to enable him to do so and it is to that study that I now turn.

Prefatory comment: Different emphases

I have called this chapter "Peter Winch's Simone Weil". He himself stresses that his book concentrates on "one theme", which is related to the background that he himself brought to her work. I can well imagine others thinking that to concentrate on that theme is to lay stress on what is not the most important thing about her work. Thus someone else might want to stress the critique of factory production and the lessons embedded in the work for industrial and post-industrial society. They will stress the work, of which Camus was the first editor, entitled *Oppression and liberty*. Camus, indeed, remarked of it, in his introduction, that "western thought has not produced anything more penetrating and more prophetic since Marx" (Weil 1955: p. 8). Others, including at least two popes, might have wished to stress the religious value of Simone Weil's work, in which case the thoughts of such works as *Gravity and grace* will seem more central.

It is nothing to the disadvantage of a philosopher that many different people emphasise different aspects of his or her work. And the thread that Winch follows through the works of Simone Weil is most assuredly there. What he traces is dictated by the kind of conception he has of philosophy. That began in *The idea of a social science* with a notion of philosophy as the examination of how we make sense of our relationships to other human beings and of our relationships with the material world in which we co-exist. And that conception owes its allegiance ultimately to the philosophy of Wittgenstein.

Winch assumes that it illuminates Simone Weil as a philosopher to approach her in that way and to stress the similarities of her concerns to the concerns of a line of philosophers that runs from Plato, through Descartes, Spinoza, Kant, Marx and Wittgenstein. Those concerns had to do with the nature of human beings, where these are clearly in part material beings in a material world, who none the less have the power to think. So we are led to investigate the relationship between thinking and the materiality of the human world; what thinking is; how it arises out of a peculiarly active relationship of human beings to the world and each other; and the consequences of the findings of this investigation for the proper understanding of the nature of human society and the lives we live together. In that he found coincidental affinities between the ways in which Wittgenstein and Simone Weil approached philosophical questions. In both there is the emphasis on the way the use of expressions is related to the roles they play in human aspirations, attitudes, activities, lives and relationships.

For myself, I have no doubt that because Winch had thought through and understood some of the thoughts Wittgenstein had articulated about meaning, language, mind and knowledge, he was able to see the significance of many of the thoughts in Simone Weil's work and could see, more particularly, one continuing strand in the pattern in its development. But I am equally sure that it is only because he had himself thought deeply about philosophy and was impressed by the depth and seriousness not only of philosophy but of the forms of human intelligibility as reflected in various forms of life, that he was able to see as much as he did. The same goes for his thinking about Spinoza (Winch 1995). In one of his few excursions into aesthetics, in the essay "Text and context", he wrote that:

> We need to apply our knowledge and skill to a text in such a way that it does not come between us and the text but brings the text to life. . . . My judgment must be genuinely my judgment and judgment of the work before me while yet informed of the works surroundings. . . . [and] . . . situations . . . are what they are by virtue of the place they occupy against the background of the rest of one's life. (Winch 1987b: pp. 20, 23)

In his work on Simone Weil he lived up to these prescriptions. One could imagine no more fitting application of his particular philosophical talents.

Peter Winch

The just balance

I turn now to the story Winch tells of the developing philosophy of Simone Weil. I do not intend to do more than characterize the main outlines of an account that the reader can fill in for herself or himself. This is not a précis, but an attempt to characterize her philosophy and what may have attracted Winch to it.

I The startings

Winch locates the background from which Simone Weil set out as Cartesian, as expressed in the dissertation she wrote for Alain entitled "Science and perception in Descartes".

Descartes has reasoned thus. Knowledge must be founded upon the basis of what cannot be doubted. But I can doubt the evidence of my senses, my memories and the like. So they cannot be the foundation. What I cannot doubt is that I exist. *Cogito ergo sum*: I think, therefore I am. The problem is how to found a knowledge of a world that exists apart from me solely upon the foundation of my knowledge of myself. Thus, she starts off with the Cartesian notion of a self-conscious consciousness and with the question of how such a consciousness can become aware of, conceptualize, the world.

Weil's first step is to replace "I think, therefore I am", with "I act therefore I am". That is a step in the right direction. Eventually that will yield the story told in *Oppression and liberty*. There we are told that human beings are active. Social life develops through the attempts by human beings to further and safeguard their active natures in the face of natural and social obstacles. (The outcome was enslavement. "Man", as Rousseau wrote in the *Social contract* "is born free; and everywhere he is in chains". *Oppression and liberty* has to do with an account of the mechanism of enslavement and what might be done about it).

"I think" is replaced by "I act". At this stage the conception of the relationship between my acting and anything that happens as a result of my acting is (defectively) conceived thus: acting is a kind of inner process of thought about what I would like to happen in the world. What I can always *do* (even if I am paralysed) is will this or that. Whether anything actually happens as a result of that willing is not within my control. So, although what I am is defined in terms of what I can do, what I can do comes down to what I can will, not on whether my will is effective.

This is one of the clearest points at which Winch is able to see and articulate certain points about this account because of his prolonged wrestling with the thoughts of Wittgenstein. One of his earlier papers "Wittgenstein on the will" (Winch 1972) has investigated a view expressed in Wittgenstein's *Tractatus*, which is strikingly like that expressed by Simone Weil.

Wittgenstein had said that "the world is independent of my will" and expressed the view that whether or not anything actually happened as a result of my willing was a purely contingent matter. One thing that may suggest this, or which might be a consequence of it, is the view discussed in Winch's "Trying" (Winch 1972), which underlies things said by Kant. On that view even if my actions turn out wrong, the fact that I meant them well, willed the right thing, excuses me. And that can suggest that it is the will that is really me in action, not this or that outcome for good or ill of my willing.

Two things interfere with that picture of willing. One is the striking demonstration in "Trying" that there is a very great difference between someone who unsuccessfully attempts to carry out an act of murder and someone who successfully carries it out. One is a murderer; the other isn't, and might thank his stars for the fact that his attempt failed. That suggests that the proper characterization of an action is not to be given just in terms of what the agent hoped to bring about, but in terms of what was done.

The second thing that upsets the picture is that it makes the relationship between intention and action quite mysterious and quite different from what we know it to be. If I knock on your door there is not first an action inside me, deciding to knock on the door, and then another event in the world. (If deciding were an action that I do, wouldn't I, on this account, have to decide to decide and so on ad infinitum?) I simply knock on the door. World and me come together. Thus Wittgenstein could later write "Willing . . . must be action itself" (quoted in Winch 1972: p. 134). Human action becomes primitive. It is because we knock on doors that we have the notion of human action. Once we have that notion we can identify the possibility of wanting to and not being able to, which is where willing comes from. But willing, the internal process, is *derivative* from my acting in the world. As Winch put it, using Goethe's words, in another article expository of Wittgenstein "In the beginning was the deed" (Winch 1987a: *"Im Anfang war die Tat"*).

Peter Winch

II The transcendental self

At the first, Cartesian, stage of Weil's development she is caught up in the notion that what I do is an internal act, willing, to which external events may, if I'm lucky, correspond. Thus I wish to raise my arm. *My* part of the action is saying to my arm, "Go up!" If I am lucky it goes up.

This Cartesian framework begins to crack when we come to the "I" that is the subject term of Descartes's "I think". In Weil's view, Descartes conceives this to be an entity that does the acts of thinking; what is called in much of the literature of continental philosophy "the transcendental ego". It lies outside the world (including my internal world of sensations and thoughts) and thinks about it. That transcendental self is denied by Weil. "I" becomes the self expressed in our activities. It does not stand behind the actions, including thinking, of a life. It is spread out in them. (Michael McGhee has pointed out to me that this seems more Kant than Descartes. Descartes seemed happy to speak of a primitive notion of the union of body and soul; "the seule personne".)

That transcendental ego is an object under attack in much recent French philosophy (Lyas 1997: pp. 170–84). One piece of reasoning against it begins with the thought that meaning cannot be given to words by individual acts of will. If I tell you that by "horse" I mean "dog", you are entitled to ask me what I mean by "dog", and if I reply, "mouse", you can ask again, and so on *ad infinitum*. Meaning is something I acquire, not something I invent. It subsists in speech practices of the community into which I am born and on the activities upon which those speech practices ultimately rest. To learn it I have to act in the world. I have to bump up against it; interact with the others of a speech community. Weil, too, argues in her first dissertation on Descartes, that thought cannot be pure activity. It needs a subject matter with which to interact and that (as she was later to put it), does not seek to dominate, but upon which it waits with obedience, hoping for the gift of grace that is clarity and understanding.

III The material of thought

Thought cannot be pure activity. Thought is *of* something. It works on material that must come from somewhere. In the second chapter of his book Winch deals with the extraordinarily subtle argument by which Weil demolishes the empiricist claim that the concepts of thought are formed by the act of mind working on material that is provided by passively received sensory content. Again Winch finds a parallel with the work of Wittgenstein, who may have been tempted at one time to some such view (Winch 1989b: p. 29).

We can indeed learn from sensations, but only in a developed structure of language that allows us to talk of other things such as radiators, wine and so on. Within that structure, sensation terms like "warm", "sweet" and the like can become informative. The empiricist, however, is committed to building up that structure from raw sensations. According to that account a sensation is an event limited to the present moment and detached from any surroundings. How, then, can we build up our structured notions, say the notion of time, from such material? (Winch 1989b: p. 46–7). It is no good saying that we become aware of time when we intuit that some sensation we are having also occurred in the past. For that assumes we have the concept of the past and can apply it to sensations, whereas sensory experience alone was supposed to generate such structured concepts. Indeed, we can only think of a sensation as a *present* one if we understand a whole network of relationships. That understanding is possible only in the context of human action, which is a temporal phenomenon.

IV Reactions

As we have seen, Simone Weil's concern is to understand the facts about human life that make human understanding possible. Pure Cartesian thought won't help. (What would it understand about what?) Nor will the picture of the agent forming concepts by processing a bombardment of sensations passively received (processed by what, and how?). That leads to a dilemma. It seems, especially on a Cartesian account, that the order of the world is the product of thought. But thinking can be possible only in an already ordered world.

Here Simone Weil makes a striking move: "The concepts necessary for thought and reflection require unmediated, unreflective responses for their formation" (Winch 1989b: p. 43).

That is to say, Weil rejects the claim that order is the product of *thought*. Rather, it is the product of an activity that does not in the first instance involve thought. What we start with is the human child, with a stock of propensities, born into an existing society.

Very strikingly she includes physiological reactions in that stock of propensities. By means of such reactions the body classifies before thought ever occurs. She even says that physiological actions are not merely a matter of stimulus and response. Even salivation manifests a purpose. There is also what might be called "natural" geometry. Our notion of three dimensional space comes from active movement in time. The notion of a straight line is a notion of walking as directly as possible to a point. So that, as she memorably puts it, "There is an elementary geometry in perception, as if our bodies knew the geometrical theorems which our mind does not yet know" (quoted in Winch 1989b: p. 46).

Winch points out that in the earlier stage of her development of these ideas there is still a residue in Weil's work of a kind of solipsistic individualism reminiscent of Descartes, for whom the individual faced the world as pure individual consciousness. On her present account an individual human being brings into the world a set of propensities to active movement expressive of its wants and needs. As it grows it adapts to its environment and forms concepts of the objects and processes of that environment and of the possibilities of interactions with them. At this stage, however, the involvement is conceived as one that takes place in *individual* dealings with *nature* and not people.

> The notion that nature involves systematic interconnections between objects of determinate kinds is a product of the system of connections present in language between the discriminating responses to different situations which have evolved from the original primitive reactions. (Winch 1989b: p. 54)

How this system of connections evolves is related to the thought that our primitive reactions to nature treat nature as an obstacle. Our reactions to objects is thus teleological. We act with a view to surmounting the obstacle. Our actions can be thwarted and then there are characteristic reactions (tacking round an obstacle). That, too, underpins our sense of geometry.

Geometry, of course, seems to have a necessity. But for Weil, as for Wittgenstein, and, as we have seen, for Winch, this necessity is a matter of our going on in the same way in our operations again and again. That necessity is founded upon certain sorts of agreements in practice.

Consider now, the notion of a method of inquiry. This, for Weil, is related to the difference between the notion of a constraint and the notion of an obstacle. If we recognize something as an obstacle we are on the way to investigating reasons why it is an obstacle and the methods we might use to get round it. That puts us in the way of understanding the environment. To understand it, is to understand how it might help or impede us.

Nature as an obstacle

At this point Weil moves into a different register by suggesting that, as well as nature presenting us with obstacles, such as streams to be forded, it can itself be an obstacle, like a natural object that gets in our way, but on a grander scale. If that were so then we would think how we might get round the world itself, and that might suggest the notion of transcending the world. That will be a way into religious considerations.

Those considerations are also raised by her analysis of geometry. Geometry enters the natural world by being applied. It introduces necessity into nature. We might then think that what gives a value to geometry is its empirical success. Weil suggests that is not where its value really lies. It lies rather in the contingency that the *necessity* of geometry reveals in the human condition. That suggests the existence of something non-contingent, which points the way to religion. It helps us get outside the contingent world.

Winch is quite certainly unhappy with all this. It is one thing to think of nature as containing obstacles; another to think of nature as itself an obstacle that might be transcended. Nor, as a follower of Wittgenstein, is he going to be happy with the notion that the necessity of geometry somehow shows defects in the lived world. Necessity is a difficult concept to grasp but such "Philosophical concepts will become even more difficult . . . if wrongly given the status of religious mystery" (Winch 1989b: p. 76).

V Equilibrium

Let us now think further about the notion that we acquire our conceptual apparatus by some kind of interaction. In that interaction, there are two things standing over and against one another: human beings and what they encounter. So far this interaction has been conceived as one between humans and nature. In the primitive stages, life depends on natural rhythms. We are passive to our inner and outer needs. There is, therefore, no such thing as liberation from natural necessity. Even the division of labour is a sort of natural necessity that subjects us to others. Here others are treated as obstacles that oppose us (as in Sartre's view of others as impinging on our freedom).

Weil's important notion of equilibrium amounts to the notion of two things being in a stable relation with one another *without either sacrificing its true nature*. If you make me a zombie by drug addiction, then there is no equilibrium, in this sense, between us. For human beings to be in equilibrium it is necessary that they recognize each other as human. However, in Weil's earlier, more Cartesian, individualistic account, in which a human being is conceived only as confronting nature, any proper account of the equilibrium between human beings cannot be given. Others merely threaten my projects and the only way out is to seek domination over them.

One reason that Weil cannot as yet get this right is the influence of Descartes and the view that the mind and the body are only contingently connected. In that view, we do not appear in the world as minds. Only bodies appear there, bodies being material and not mental things. Our dealings with others, therefore, can only be dealings with material things, which at best can be encountered, and be obstacles to us, just as logs and stones can be.

Here Winch is right that deep mistakes in philosophy account for the difficulties. The deepest mistake is the view that the mind of another, its thoughts, willings and the like, can be severed from what happens in the world with which it is merely contingently connected, and can only be free if it is not subjected to the world around it. Even if that made the mind free, it would make it inaccessible to others. Just as we saw that we can only obtain a knowledge of the spiritual through its connection with the non-spiritual, so we can only relate to the mind of another if the body in the world, the body that we see, is, to use an earlier phrase, illuminated by it. All we have in Weil's present account is private, individualistic centres of consciousness.

According to that account, justice can only be conceived as what individuals negotiate in order to get the best they can from others, an account of justice that Winch attributes to Rawls (Winch 1989b: pp. 179ff.). For as he represents Rawls's account, justice is the outcome of negotiated compromises of rational self-interested agents.

But it is unclear why, according to that account, we should call the negotiated outcome *just*. One way out of this, which Sartre embraced and with which Weil may have flirted, is to say that human beings can resist ordering by other people. One attempts to impose one's own order on the world in dominance. The projects of others do not have a reality for us. We can't even understand them. But all that now changes as we move to Weil's mature thought.

VI *Others*

The first step, which links Weil's later thought to the earlier, and which links it also to what Winch has said in many places about the primacy of primitive spontaneous responses as the foundation of practices, is to note that we simply *do* react differently to other human beings than we do to non-human objects. At this stage there are still, in Weil's work, residual thoughts of others as obstacles. But we also have a clear sense that there is a difference between a person and a natural obstacle. For one thing the recognition of something as a person imports a new notion of necessity; a notion of what we can and cannot do. Others inhibit me. When we meet them, there is what Weil calls the "interval of hesitation", which is immediate and unreflective. On this is founded the notion that consent is essential.

One can, Weil thinks, only hesitate in this way before something that we recognize as having the power to refuse. The roots of all this, to repeat, lie in how human beings as a matter of fact react. We do not so act towards others because we think we ought. It is because we so act that our actions become, as Winch puts it, impregnated with value. The hesitation imports a set of attitudes and establishes a notion of a human being as one to whom respect is due.

Implications of recognizing others

Having reached this point Winch thinks that although Simone Weil's thought still retains elements of individualism, she has broken through to a position where some of the implications of the recognition of the other for religion and for moral and political philosophy can be seen. His analysis is not uncritical. But it gives the sense of a dialogue in which a philosopher uses an understanding he has extracted from intense thought about some of the profound issues in philosophy to elucidate the thoughts of a philosopher who has engaged with equal passion in those issues. Rather than deal with these matters now as a serial development I shall focus on some of the ideas that emerge after the breakthrough to the notion that the recognition of others as persons is born in the primitive reaction of the interval of hesitation.

The void

There is something in the desire for particular things that can never be satisfied. From each satisfaction to the next we are successively betrayed. Nor can we ever know in advance where our good will lie. A void lies where something that might satisfy all our needs, including our needs to know, might lie. Yet from that can arise the notion of a good that is not only good conditionally, and that could never give us lasting satisfaction, but of a good that is unconditionally good; good whatever will happen. From that a sense might be born that whatever happens is good. That, as we have seen is one of the springs from which religion might rise and one of the forms in which it may express itself. But whether that goodness, which might be thought by the believer to be an aspect of God's love, is ever revealed, is not, Winch thinks, something that philosophy can ensure and, what is shown to us, if it is revealed, is not for philosophy to determine.

Incommensurability

The notion of incommensurability introduces a possible way of understanding value. A value is something that human beings can destroy by a use of force that introduces a form of disequilibrium called incommensurability. Thus one can destroy values by turning another person into a thing, where a relationship of equilibrium between us is made impossible because a thing and a person are incommensurable. Another way to establish incommensurability is to kill the other, which creates, at the least, an incommensurability between a living thing, me, and a physical thing, the dead body of another. It may also be established by robbing the victim of a power to refuse, and it may also consist in the way in which the victor in his or her triumph can lose the power to act rationally towards the conquered. What we have here is the powerful reminding of the forms that a loss of equilibrium can take and of the ways in which relationships between human beings can fall away from the norms established in the moment of hesitation.

Beauty and truth

There is an extraordinary discussion in Weil of the notion of beauty. Let us suppose that love of one's neighbour is founded upon the interval of hesitation that is constitutive of our ability to recognize another as a person and not a thing. Weil suggests that there can also be a hesitation before the natural world, which can express itself as what she calls *love of the beauty of the world*. That will come out in the sense that the world is not there simply to be used by us. That reaction, it is argued, becomes related to our notions of truth. It encourages paying careful attention to things in their own right. Winch puts the matter in a passage in which many of his concerns surface, and to which I shall return in my final chapter for a consideration of its verdict of recent philosophy. According to this view, says Winch, truth is a matter of not wanting to change or doctor the evidence. It is a matter of:

> wanting to read it honestly, however distressing. Here we should note the "honestly" which introduces "good". And that surely must be right. The concept of truth, considered as the standard according to which an inquiry or pronouncement is to be justified and something which many have been prepared to suffer and die for, would not make sense unless it were tied to a concept like "honesty". Someone who said he or she was willing to die for the truth, understood solely in terms used to present it in western analytic philosophical theories, would strike most people as crazy . . . and rightly so. (Winch 1989b: p. 176)

The supernatural

Winch points out that he has given a certain reading of the notion of hesitation. He has shown how there is a hesitation before others that yields notions of justice and value, and a notion of hesitation before the world that yields the notions of love of the beauty of the world, and he has indicated the connection of love of the beauty of the world with truth. What, however, leads from those considerations, to Simone Weil's talk; talk which is, in the eyes of many, cherished and central to her philosophy, of the supernatural? Winch concludes therefore with some remarks on that notion.

As we might suspect, neither he nor Weil thinks of the supernatural as the paranormal. Nor is it a creationist issue. Perhaps, he suggests, rather, that there is a notion of hesitating before *all* our projects; a way of thinking about those projects. That would be a way of thinking about earthly things. But since it thinks from a point outside those projects, there will be *a* sense in which it comes from outside the world, and any sense of value we attribute *to* those projects does not come *from* them. That does not mean that it comes from something that exists in some quasi spatio-temporal region. But it is in a sense transcendent. But that is as far as he can go with the supernatural.

Further reading

On the topic of Winch's discussion of Weil's philosophical development in *The just balance*, I quite unreservedly commend Rowan Williams's review in *Philosophical Investigations* **14**, pp. 155–71, 1991. This brings out the lasting influence of the thought of Alain as its shows itself in a tendency to make each person a moral monad. Williams also, as Winch does, remarks on the way in which Weil's religious culture preserved and intensified her philosophical tangles, remarking that had she begun rather than ended with the Bhagavad-Gita, a certain view of the self could not have been a temptation.

Accounts of the life and work of Simone Weil can be found in R. Rees, *Simone Weil: a sketch for a portrait* (Oxford: Oxford University Press, 1966), S. Pétremont *Simone Weil: a life,* R. Rosenthal (trans.) (New York: Pantheon, 1976) and D. McLellan, *Simone Weil: Utopian pessimist* (London: Macmillan, 1989). The last of these works has a most comprehensive bibliography of the works of Simone Weil and of her commentators. *A Simone Weil anthology*, Sîan Miles (ed.) (London: Virago, 1986) is a useful starting point. Winch himself wrote the introduction to *Simon Weil: lectures on philosophy*, H. Price (ed.) (Cambridge: Cambridge University Press, 1978) and "Le nécessaire et le bien", in *Simone Weil: philosophe, historienne et mystique*, G. Kahn (ed.) (Paris: aubier Montaigne, 1978).

Chapter 7
"Someone willing to die for truth": Peter Winch's legacy

In this closing chapter I wish to do three things. First, I wish to say something about the bearing of Winch's work on a certain conception of philosophy, a conception that attempts to blur the line between philosophy and the natural sciences. Second, I wish to ask what light might be thrown by an understanding of Winch's views on the currently vigorous debate between realists and anti-realists. Third, I wish to ask one last time about the validity of the whole approach to philosophy that Winch inherited from Wittgenstein.

I Philosophy and science

In his history of the decline and fall of the influence of Wittgenstein, Peter Hacker (1996) charts the waning appeal of the kind of conceptions central to the work of that philosopher. The tone of philosophy has, indeed, undoubtedly changed in that, as Hacker points out, many have become far less sceptical of the claim that discoveries in science can solve philosophical problems than Wittgenstein or Winch would be. Various advances in science have seemed to offer ways out of philosophical impasses, the long-standing failure to resolve which, as Kant remarked, bring scandal on philosophy. One example is the quite extraordinary discoveries about the mechanisms of the brain, and the ways in which variations in those mechanisms affect behaviour. That, it is thought, might help resolve the problems about mind and body, personal identity, consciousness and the like that have long plagued the philosophy of mind. Perhaps, after all, the advances show that mind and brain are identical.

I have practiced one of the sciences and I am often moved to awe by the achievements of my scientific friends and colleagues. Nor have I the least doubt that their discoveries, when applied, will bear on how we think of ourselves. To use one hackneyed example, I have no doubt whatsoever that were brain transplantation to become a common phenomenon, this would have effects on the ways in which we behave. We would simply have to accommodate ourselves, probably by some messy compromise, to the fact that some people have had certain sorts of things done to them. What is unclear is that science, linguistics, computational models of the brain or even philosophy will give me any indication about how we *will* accommodate ourselves (Lyas 1996: pp. 194–9).

Winch seems to me to be entirely right to claim that it is one thing for a philosopher to *know* of the advances in science, another for philosophy to *be* one of those sciences. If someone claims that science, however conceived, and whichever branch is the preferred candidate, is the proper method for solving traditional philosophical problems about the mind and its relationship to the body, about what is the right thing to do, about whether there are gods, about whether action is free, that is no more than a *claim*. Since that claim is made on behalf of science it cannot, without circularity be arbitrated by science. How else is it to be arbitrated than by a philosophical dialectic to which a scientist is but one party?

Second, *if* a brain scientist claims to have solved philosophical problems (and most have more important scientific things to do than that), such as the problem of the relationship between mind and body, or what consciousness is, that, again, is a claim. About that claim I offer two remarks.

Models

First there is a warning about models. Models, metaphors and the like abound in present talk about the mind. The brain is treated as a computer. Nerve cells become homunculized and are said to use the same inductive logic as a detective. In those models no account is given of the way *we*, as embodied and enworlded organisms, make our inferences.

Camus writes:

> And here are trees and I know their gnarled surface, water and I feel its taste. These scents of grass and stars at night, certain evenings when the heart relaxes – how shall I negate this world whose power and strength I feel? Yet all the knowledge on earth will give me nothing to assure me that this world is mine. You describe it to me and you teach me to classify it. You enumerate its laws, and in my thirst for knowledge I admit that they are true. You take apart its mechanism and my hope increases. At the final stage you teach me that this wondrous and multi-coloured universe can be reduced to an atom and the atom itself can be reduced to an electron. All this is good and I wait for you to continue. But you tell me of an invisible planetary system in which electrons gravitate around a nucleus. You explain this world to me with an image. I realise then that you have been reduced to poetry: I shall never know. Have I the time to become indignant? You have already changed theories. So that science that was to teach me everything ends up in a hypothesis, that lucidity founders in metaphor, that uncertainty is resolved in a work of art. What need had I of so many efforts? The soft lines of these hills and the hand of evening on this troubled heart teach me much more.
> (Camus 1975: p. 25)

So, too, in the models we are often offered, lucidity founders in metaphors. It is Wittgenstein, and philosophers influenced by him, such as Winch, who have offered the most acute warnings about the power of models and metaphors to mislead us.

Philosophical and scientific answers

Suppose someone, impressed by the sheer correlation between human emotional states and what is discovered about the secretion of chemicals in the brain, asserts that mind and body simply go together. Wittgenstein, contrary to what many have supposed, did not have the least inclination to deny that mind and body go together.

> The feeling of an unbridgeable gulf between consciousness and brain process: how does it come about that this does not come into considerations of our ordinary life? The idea of a

difference in kind is accompanied by a slight giddiness, – which occurs when we are performing a logical sleight of hand. ... When does this feeling occur in the present case? It is when I, for example, turn my attention in a particular way on my own consciousness, and, astonished, say to myself: THIS is supposed to be produced by a process in the brain! – as it were clutching my forehead. – But what can it mean to speak of "turning my attention on to my own consciousness"? This is surely the queerest thing there could be! It was a particular act of gazing that I called doing this. I stared fixedly in front of me – but *not* at any particular point or object. My eyes were wide open, the brows not contracted (as they mostly are when I am interested in a particular object). No such interest preceded this gazing. My glance was vacant; or again like that of someone admiring the illumination of the sky and drinking in the light.

Now bear in mind that the proposition which I uttered as a paradox (THIS is produced by a brain process!) has nothing paradoxical about it. I could have said it in the course of an experiment whose purpose was to shew that an effect of light which I see is produced by stimulation of part of the brain. – But I did not utter the sentence in the surroundings in which it would have had an everyday and unparadoxical sense. And my attention was not such as would have accorded with making an experiment. (If it had been, my look would have been intent, not vacant). (Wittgenstein 1953: ss. 412)

The latter part of this shows that Wittgenstein did not have the least inclination to deny that "mental" events (e.g. episodes of seeing) and brain processes go together. That, however, is not, as the first part of the passage makes clear, the *philosophical* problem. This is shown by the fact that when someone shows me all the massive evidence that there is of mind–brain interaction, I do not immediately greet this with relief as solving a problem (as I might the news that a new and non-additive substance has been found, the action of which on the pain receptors is to stop pain). That evidence, as the first part of the quotation I have just given shows, might *increase* my perplexity. Relief must come from a source other than scientific discovery. Winch, following Wittgenstein, would have said that it will come from reflecting on what we already know and on the way in which certain ways of talking mislead us.

Peter Winch's legacy

II Winch and the realist–anti-realist debate

I wish, next, to discuss the way in which Winch's work relates to a topic of contemporary concern; the debate between realists and anti-realists. Clearly the work of a philosopher like Winch, who placed so centrally in his philosophy a concern with the nature of reality, ought to have some bearing on these current issues. I begin with a brief remark about ethical realism.

Ethics and realism

I have talked about ethical realism in the chapter on Winch's ethics. I preface what I have to say about the more general debate between realists and anti-realists with one comment.

In discussions about objectivity in aesthetics various philosophers have remarked that we do not get very far if we think of the possibility of there being *true, objective* remarks about a thing as the possibility of referring to *properties out there in the thing*. That remark seems to be reiterated by Norman when he complains that the debate about moral realism has undergone a reversion to the "ontological vocabulary", meaning, presumably to the assumption that realism is possible in ethics only if ethical assertions refer to properties "out there" (Norman 1997: p. 117). That merely introduces another obscure notion (property) and the obscure notion of properties being *in* things, where the spatial word "in" suggests that properties are stuck in things like currants in a pudding. It is not impossible, of course, that eventually we will get the notion of properties clear, although, as Wiggins has argued, we have to clear away a good deal of lumber inherited from Locke before that is likely (Wiggins 1995: pp. 214–46). But in lieu of that, I am inclined to argue, all we need to show in order to establish the possibility of objectivity is that there is a good sense in which assertions about a thing can be said to be true or false, right or wrong, and that there are decision procedures which we might use, perhaps without guarantee of success, in determining which is which. (Kreisel, I believe, made a similar remark about mathematical truth.)

If that is the requirement, then Winch is, I suppose, on the side of moral realists, which is odd when relativism is so usually attributed to him. He is on that side for the same reasons as Richard Norman and David MacNaughton, for example, seem to be on the side of the moral realists. For there *is* a use of the terms "true" and "false", "right" and "wrong", in moral contexts and there are decision procedures that might be followed in cases of dispute (although they might not be the procedures characteristic of science and might not guarantee an agreement). It is a mistake to think that one can only be entitled to those words if, in some sense, there is something "out there".

Realism

That brings me to the connection between Winch's work and questions about realism, an issue which concerns some of the ablest minds of this generation of philosophers. I raise these questions, not in the hope of saying anything that would count as furthering their solution, save in the way in which getting people to understand and to be excited about them might advance that end. Rather, I am simply curious about how an understanding of Winch's work, which was so centrally concerned with questions about the nature of reality, might be illuminated by and might illuminate the issues in a contemporary debate.

Preliminary things

1 Language and reality
First, anyone studying the contemporary debate about realism will quickly come to understand that those who conduct that debate need have no reason to doubt that from the very first Winch located the central problem in the same place as they. For he began from the position that the fundamental question philosophy involves is a "discussion of what an understanding of reality consists in"; a discussion that "merges into the discussion of the differences the possession of such an understanding might make to the life of man" and that comes in the end down to the question of the connection between "language and the world" (Winch 1958: pp. 22–3). That indeed is why, since any social relationships are expressive of ideas about reality, any understanding of the nature of those relations is philosophical. With that last quotation we might compare the following from a recent contribution by one of the central figures in the present debate about realism: "if anything is

2 Winch as a realist

Second, on the interpretation of the notion of realism and, what is thought to be its polar opposite, idealism, offered in recent work, Winch comes out as a realist. For on the interpretation offered in some important recent work, idealism is committed to the view that "reality is . . . a reification of our own conceptual and cognitive nature, with no more claim to autonomy than a mirror image" (Wright 1993: p. 2). If that is so then Winch is a realist. For, first, he is committed to the view that reality is not "at the mercy of what any man might care to think" (Winch 1972: p. 12).

That isn't quite enough to generate realism. For an idealist might say that there is a check on the whims of this or that individual; namely some collective agreement among human beings reflecting necessary features of the human mind, from which, for various reasons, this or that human may deviate. Here the check is whether one's view coheres with the views of others. Winch, however, adds something that makes him a realist in a stronger sense. For he thinks that, in our use of the term "real", the use of that term commits us to a belief that reality is independent of us:

> "We should not lose sight of the fact that the idea that men's ideas and beliefs must be checkable by reference to something independent – some reality – is an important one. To abandon it is to plunge straight into extreme Protagorean relativism.
> (Winch 1972: p. 11)

Here, incidentally, we must note that the use of the term "antirealism" in recent discussions might give a misleading impression. For the anti-realist view is not committed, absurdly, to the view that things do not exist independently of us, but to the view that it makes no sense to posit a reality that could not be known to us.

3 The syndrome of realism

Third, Winch, as we saw, was prepared to allow that the notion of reality, and its correlative notion of intelligibility might be context variant:

> If we look at the contexts in which the notions of understanding, of making something intelligible, are used, we find that

these differ widely among themselves. Moreover, if these contexts are examined and compared, it soon becomes apparent that the notion of intelligibility is systematically ambiguous. ... That is, its sense varies systematically according to the particular context in which it is being used.
(Winch 1958: p. 18)

Hence, too, the striking remark that

God's reality is certainly independent of what any man may think, but what that reality amounts to can only be seen from the religious tradition in which the concept of God is used, and this use is very unlike the use of scientific concepts, say of theoretical entities. (Winch 1972: p. 12)

That view is an expression of the view that realism is what Wright, in a neat word, calls "a syndrome". So that we may wonder what "mathematical platonist, the moral objectivist, and the scientific realist" have in common (Wright 1993: p. 4).

Anti-realism

Realism, in the current construction, amounts to the claim that "our depictive powers may outrun our cognitive capacities" (Wright 1993: p. 3). That is to say, the realist is committed to the view that we can conceive something to be truly the case, even if we also thought we could have no way of knowing that it is the case. And sometimes this is put (the principle of bivalence) by saying that for any statement, either that statement is true or that statement is false, even if we may have no way of deciding which it is. The realist could believe the statement that Henry VIII's brother Arthur consummated his marriage with Catharine of Aragon (which he claimed and she denied) to be either true or false, even if, rightly or wrongly, he or she thought we could have no way of ever knowing which of these two it is.

Why is that problematic? Two considerations are offered. One is the "acquisition argument". How, it is asked, can the realist, as so defined, form any understanding of what it is for a particular statement to be true, if the kind of state of affairs that would make it true is conceived as being beyond our experience and, so, hermetically sealed from any contact with our consciousness of it? That argument has a clear empiricist ring to it, since it appears to share the empiricist view that the concepts we have we can only come by from experience: what we cannot know we cannot conceive. Here one is reminded of Wittgenstein's comment that the hard thing is to give an account of realism that does not fall into empiricism (cited in Winch 1987b: p. 42).

The other consideration is the manifestation argument. That argument is rooted in what should by now be familiar as a legacy from Wittgenstein. Understanding is a matter of practical abilities. To understand a term is to know how to use it properly and the proof of that is that one's use of the term manifests such an understanding.

Now in what does the *realist* (as now construed) say that understanding a statement like "Jack is thinking of putting his cigarette gift coupons towards an iron lung" consists? It amounts to understanding that *a state of affairs*, namely, a thought in the mind of another, *that potentially transcends all the evidence we might have for its truth*, must obtain if that statement is to be true. This involves the "conception" of "a potentially undetectable state of affairs ... for which there is no independent test" (Wright 1993: p. 20). But understanding an utterance like "He is in pain" does not seem to require belief in some such potentially evidence-transcendent state of affairs, but rather the ability to act in certain ways in certain situations. That will manifest my understanding of "He is in pain". What, however, would manifest a belief that his state transcends the evidence?

The relevance of Winch's work to the anti-realism debate

The debates between those who assert and those who defend anti-realism, as it is currently articulated, are lengthy, complex and, once one has made the considerable effort required to engage with them, exhilarating. It would be enough for me, if I had interested at least one reader in them. My only purpose in introducing them is to discuss the possible bearing of them on an understanding of Peter Winch's work. Here I mention three things.

1 Interpreting Wittgenstein aright
Anti-realism attacks what it calls the "realist" notion that to understand a sentence is to necessarily posit the existence of a state of affairs, sometimes undetectable in principle, that makes it

true. (To say that states of affairs exist that are undetectable in principle is to say that reality may elude our grasp, which is, I suppose, a way of making reality independent of what humans may think. Hence the characterization of the notion as "realist".) In its place is put the notion of understanding a sentence as being related to what are called "assertability conditions". For although I cannot always know whether there is a state of affairs that makes a sentence true, it can always be decided whether I have a right to assert that statement. I cannot know whether Arthur consummated his marriage, but I can have grounds that give me the right to assert that he did not.

Here an account of meaning in terms of truth conditions is distinguished from an account in terms of assertability conditions. It is part of the history given of these matters that Wittgenstein is said to have embraced the former, the account of meaning in terms of truth conditions, in his first work, the *Tractatus* and the latter, the account of meaning in terms of assertability conditions, in later works, such as the *Philosophical investigations*.

Winch writes:

> Philosophers these days distinguish between the truth conditions of a proposition and the conditions for asserting that proposition. It is often said that, whereas in the *Tractatus* Wittgenstein stressed the first of these notions, the later development of his thought involved emphasis rather on the second. I do not think this states the important changes in Wittgenstein's thought at all clearly. (Winch 1987b: p. 31)

He continues:

> "Truth conditions" is a logician's term of art. Its use may already presuppose an approach to questions of meaning which Wittgenstein is rejecting. This does not imply that he is denying that the words "true" and "false" play an important role in our understanding of propositions. To say that he *replaced* "truth conditions" by "assertion conditions" is misleading in its suggestion that he was offering an alternative theory of meaning. Whereas his point was that the notion of meaning and its connection with truth or falsity is not to be elucidated in terms of a general theory at all.
> (Winch 1987b: p. 46)

That is to say, the realist–anti-realist debate exists because of the presupposition that *either* meaning is to be spelt out in terms of truth conditions (what you understand by a statement is what states of affairs would make it true) *or* it is to be spelt out in terms of assertability conditions (what you understand by a statement is related to what gives you the right to assert it, some evidence, perhaps). In Winch's account we are not stuck with these two alternatives.

Wittgenstein writes in *On certainty*, "Really 'the proposition is true or false' only means that it must be possible to decide for or against it. But this does not tell us what such a decision is like" (Wittgenstein 1969: s. 200).

To know what such a decision is like we have to look at the ways in which the words "true" and the like are applied in particular cases, so that the criteria for their application in making statements about the past might differ from those operative when making statements about minds or infinite numbers or the funniness of remarks.

So the "realist's" thesis that a thought can be true only if there is something in virtue of which it is true can be given a perfectly acceptable interpretation. It must be remembered that, on this interpretation, what this "something" is has to be understood in the context of what we are willing to count as a case of exhibiting it, and this will vary enormously for different kinds of case.   (Winch 1987b: p. 41)

2 Ceasing to exist

Realism is now characterized as the view that to a meaningful statement there corresponds some state of affairs (possibly undetectable) that would make it true. Take, then, Descartes's assertion that a thing that exists at one moment could cease to exist in the next moment. That *seems* intelligible, and the semblance of intelligibility is strengthened when Winch, typically, draws our attention to a delicious story by Isaac Singer, in which just that happens (Winch 1987b: pp. 81–106). A shed simply disappears. And we understand the story, don't we? So we understand the sentence because we understand that a state of affairs could exist, and, as the story suggests, could detectably exist, that would make it true.

In an analysis, striking for its originality, Winch queries the contention that we do, outside the story, understand what it is for a shed simply to disappear for no reason. "If someone tried to convince me in earnest that people vanish, I do not think that I would understand what he was trying to have me believe" (Winch 1987b: p. 84). Part of our puzzlement arises from the fact that we "don't have ways to investigate people vanish" (1987b: p. 85).

Winch canvasses the possibility that we simply specify truth conditions for "the shed vanished". The problem is that no truth conditions seem forthcoming for the assertion: "At this moment it was there and the next it had vanished". This is only plausible to us if we have a story to tell about causes of the disappearance of the shed. "'The shed has simply vanished', then, simply fails to project a thought into the past" (Winch 1987b: pp. 93–4). It is unconnected with the stream of life in which notions of sheds, causality and temporality are all bound up together. In that stream of life the notion of a shed gets a meaning that makes it impossible for us to assign any sense to the notion of a shed just vanishing.

Various things could be said about Winch's account. One, favoured by Roy Holland, is that there are conceivable circumstances in which one might intelligibly believe that a shed simply vanishes (in Gaita 1990: pp. 32–41; see also Winch 1987b; Marshall 1990: pp. 13–31). My question is a different one. What bearing does this story and its treatment have on the present debate about realism?

In might seem that Winch has come down on the side of the realist. When he writes (Winch 1972: p. 105) that he has not shown that a shed could not cease to exist, only that we cannot make sense of the statement that it has, it may seem that he posits a possible realm of events that cannot be captured by our conceptual apparatus.

We are told, too, however, that moments are located in the stream of life and locked into stories about their antecedents. When we say that the shed ceased to exist at this moment and refuse to determine any way in which it does so, then we do not locate this moment in the proper place in the stream of our lives and so can only *think mistakenly* that we accord sense to it (Winch 1982: p. 104). Here we are not helped by talk of truth conditions or assertability conditions for "the shed vanished". Whether that makes sense is decided not by reference to some general theory about how utterances do and don't make sense but to how particular terms like "shed" function in our dealings with the world.

3 Truth

Winch writes, "How a term refers has to be understood in the light of its actual application within its surrounding context in the life of its users" (Winch 1972: p. 113).

I have argued, following Winch, that "real" is a term like any other in the language and gets what meaning it has from its use in the practices of the human lives in which it has a point. Let us apply what is said about "real" to the word "true".

I believe that if we examine those uses, it seems that the notion of something's being true differs from the notion, however strong, of its assertability conditions. We have a use for the notion of truth according to which what is true *transcends us* in some way, and according to which what is the case is something to which we are answerable *absolutely*. By that I mean that, if I have a right to assert something that in fact turns out to be false, I do not have to withdraw the claim that I had a right to assert it. But if I say that something is true and it turns out not to be, I *must* withdraw that claim. (This is precisely the way that Winch put the matter in a review of Alasdair MacIntyre's *Whose justice, whose rationality?* (Winch 1992: p. 285).)

That the meaning of the word "true" is determined by its use in practices that arise from our needs and interests does not prevent there emerging, in the service of some particular need or interest of ours, a conception of truth as potentially evidence-transcendent.

Whether or not that would be at odds with anti-realism, as it is now conceived, I do not know. But it does raise the questions of what the particular need or interest of ours might be that would generate such an evidence-transcendent conception of truth and what might manifest our possession of such a concept. Here we may touch on the reasons for the hostility that Winch emphatically expresses to discussions of truth in contemporary philosophy.

> Someone who said he or she was willing to die for the truth, understood solely in terms used to present it in western analytic philosophical theories, would strike most people as crazy ... and rightly so. (Winch 1989b: p. 176)

Winch, who thought of truth telling as an aspect of moral integrity, must have thought that this required something more absolute than a right to assert. Probably the nearest he got to expressing this was in his late work, in the discussion of Simone

Weil's notion of the beauty of the world, mentioned in my previous chapter. For we saw there that he thought it possible, to "hesitate" before the world, as one might hesitate before what one recognizes as a human being. That hesitation before the world would entail a respect for truth, where that was absolute and required:

> not doctoring the evidence, wanting to read it honestly, however distressing. Here note "honestly" which introduces "good". And that surely must be right. The concept of truth, considered as the standard according to which an inquiry or pronouncement is to be judged as something for which many have been prepared to suffer and die for would not make sense unless it were tied to a concept like honesty.
> (Winch 1989b: p. 176)

Whatever the truth of some standard objections to the new formulations of anti-realism, Winch may have been suggesting that this form of anti-realism, invoking the notion of assertability conditions rather than truth conditions, may overlook the way in which some more absolute conception of truth might be, to put it in Kantian terms, a regulative idea for us.

III Winch, Wittgenstein and the nature of philosophy

Winch began one of his last papers, a presidential address to the American Philosophical Association, somewhat ruefully:

> I usually decline, if only on grounds of incompetence, requests to offer generalisations about the current condition of Anglo-American philosophy. However, I feel fairly confident in saying that the works of Ludwig Wittgenstein are not the favourite reading of most contemporary philosophical professionals. And that is one of the many reasons for surprise in finding myself here today. (1996: p. 1)

There is indeed an immense gulf, which hardly anyone can fail to see, between Wittgenstein's conception of the subject and that of what Winch thinks of as the present mainstream. Indeed, conception diverges so drastically, that "some fail to see that there is any argument there at all" (1996: p. 1).

Peter Winch's legacy

To be motivated by the conception of philosophy that Winch inherited from Wittgenstein simply *is* to take a quite different view of philosophical issues from that which is now largely current. But it might be objected that Wittgenstein's and Winch's mode of philosophizing is problematic. So I conclude this work, as I began it, with a look at that charge.

The philosophy queried

I begin with one last reminder to the reader of a central assumption that seems to me to lie behind the view of philosophy inherited from Wittgenstein by Winch.

Part, but only part, of the account I have given asserts that Wittgenstein's way of doing philosophy is founded on the claim that it is a fact that our language evolved as we did (and will continue to evolve, in ways that no philosopher is competent to prognosticate, as we evolve). That language is embedded in our lives, our interests and our needs and in the kinds of beings we are with the capacities we have. If a word in that language has a meaning, it is because, as our lives are, we have a use for it (although that use might not be the one we report when asked to think about the matter). Our acquisition of language is dependent upon the fact that we respond in various ways to what happens around us, from infancy onwards, in the language communities into which we are born. Thus, as we saw, we can acquire a capacity properly to use the word "pain" only because we respond to painful stimuli in certain ways. The same goes for words like "elegant". We can learn that word only if certain lines and movements move us to a certain sort of delight. In this respect words like "person" (as contrasted with "mere thing") as much rest on a propensity to react in a certain way (what Weil calls the interval of hesitation) as does a word like "pain". And, as we saw, words like "fair", together with kindred words like "just" and a whole battery of related moral terms of praise and censure, may rest on a natural propensity to react spontaneously, as early as the infant playground, to perceived inequities of treatment. If we are puzzled about a term like "mind", "time" or "real" that is because we cannot command a clear view of the way these operate in our lives.

Peter Winch

Problems 1: A wet blanket
I have heard it reported that people think that this sort of account dampens down philosophy. Thus one philosopher has been reported as saying that this account puts a wet blanket over metaphysics (by which I suppose he meant made metaphysics impossible to do) (Wright 1992: p. 205). For two reasons that is not so. First, and the state of the philosophy of mind as influenced by scientific and quasi-scientific models confirms this, people are always going to be misled into metaphysical error. Second, as Winch's *The idea of a social science* shows, there is nothing to stop someone talking about what reality is. Nor need it be thought that this is simply a matter of looking a word up in the dictionary or conducting a bit of collective armchair reflection on use. The forms of our lives, the distinctions that we can make, the activities that express themselves, are highly varied and highly complex and extraordinarily subtle. (And not just at the level of higher education, as those who talk to the aficianados of jazz or rock music or clothes will quickly find). Any enquiry worth undertaking will be immensely laborious as it traces the ramifications of what we say, when and why. (Here we might think of the painstaking investigation of the temptations to talk of inner processes that we find attempted by Wittgenstein and of the way in which he compared such a task to repairing torn spider's webs with our fingers). Winch's presidential address, to which I referred above (Winch 1996), shows, in discussing belief, for example, how subtle the work of philosophy is required to be.

Problems 2: Explanations
Wittgenstein says that, confronted with a use of language that is woven into a life and is operative in the practice of that life (the use of evaluative terms in discussing clothes as it might be overheard in a shop for example) all we can do is say "This game is played". Doesn't that foreclose on change?

To begin with, we might reflectively come to think that we should not speak in a certain way that is embedded in a speech community. Thus in English "man" is used when both men and women are being referred to. One could reflectively decide that this is not right. So, too, doubt has arisen over the use of such terms as "negro", "handicapped", and "retarded".

Nothing Wittgenstein says denies these possibilities of conscious linguistic change. "Reforms are always possible" he tells us "for particular purposes" (Wittgenstein 1953: ss. 23, 132). But the deliberations we engage in when we discuss these changes are conducted in a language, and not from some Archimedean point outside language. It is because other terms, like "fair" and "just" and "equality" remain stable that we can discuss these changes at all. Moreover, we cannot simply stipulate a change to people who do not see the point of the changes, and hope to get them to speak meaningfully in new ways, as opposed to blindly conforming under compulsion.

More interesting, perhaps, is the case where we come to feel that a term is dead for us. We learn "ugly" with respect to certain things, including certain human things. Toads would be a common reference class. But we might, on reflection, cease to see the point in using that word; cease to see the difference between a toad and a cat with respect to ugliness. That, too, is something that may happen, often through dialectic with others. But if it does happen, the term ceases to have a use in our lives and thereby ceases to have a meaning for us. Nothing in Wittgenstein's account suggests that this sort of change is impossible.

When Wittgenstein said "this language game is played", I suspect that he did not mean that a word like "ugly" might go out of use or that an individual word like "man" might change its use. He was concerned with the way in which a whole region of our language might be founded on a direction our lives take, so that aesthetics involves a whole vocabulary reflective of a whole set of inclinations and responses. I think his view was that it does not make any clear sense to object to that whole activity. On what grounds would the objection be made? One could object to someone engaging in aesthetic activities at inappropriate times, as we might castigate one whose enjoyment of the mellifluous quality of fire alarms caused too many false callouts. But it is not clear what it would be to object to the fact that human beings respond aesthetically. It is this that, I think, Winch is after when he says that we might well object to punishment as a social practice, but that this became harder to do when one realized that the kinds of reactions that give rise to the institution of punishment also underpin morality in a wider sense, so that the reasons for abandoning punishment might entail a massive rethinking of the institutions of morality.

Peter Winch

Problems 3: Explaining language games
But I suspect that there is another more troublesome worry, one that underlies the feeling that the slogan "language game is played", which is meant to "do away with explanation" of those language games, dispenses too quickly with a certain kind of illuminating explanation.

Suppose I am told that there is an "interval of hesitation" in my encounter with another that signals my recognition that I am encountering a person and not a lamp-post. I am supposed to think that this is primitive, a spontaneous reaction, not undertaken for a reason, and so not one that could be taught. For if someone did not react in that way it would be because he or she did not see that certain things were persons, and I no more think that I can reason someone into seeing that than Wordsworth thought that he could reason someone into an approbation of his poetry.

However, if someone does not respond to another as a person, it does seem possible to ask why someone might not so respond and, in finding that out, one finds out also why some others do. My guess is that the kinds of explanation appropriate for my culture will be of the kind, although not necessarily the one, that is sometimes offered of formative infant psychology. It will be an account of the ways in which a child in infancy encounters various kinds of resistances to its will, and forms certain sorts of relationships with its parents. Why then, in giving such an explanation, have I not explained the roots of a language game? In precisely the same way, as I remarked in an earlier chapter, David Bloor has argued that Wittgenstein's characterization of the notion of a language game, if language games are intended to be used as tools for the understanding of social life, leaves too much unexplained, including, notably, and in a way kindred to what I have just said about infant psychology, the social institutions within which different language games are generated (Bloor 1983).

That touches on something that I have sometimes felt to be missing from Winch's account of ethics, and that is notably missing from most treatments of ethics *simpliciter*, Richard Wollheim being a notable exception. This is what might be called moral psychology. (Sad, then, that so acute a thinker as Richard Norman should delete this subject from the second edition of his book, even though it calls into question "the very idea of 'morality' as traditionally conceived" (Norman 1998: Preface to the second edition).) For our ethical lives are generated, at least in part, from kinds of things that happen to us from our very earliest infancy. And our moral happiness and unhappiness can, as Wollheim has notably argued (Wollheim 1993), at least in part be explained and characterized in those terms. This would simply be to illuminate our ethical understanding.

In my *Aesthetics* I argued that one of the things we have to do in a philosophy of art is explain the *power* of art. This, I claimed, had something to do with art as *expression*. I could have left it there, but that would have left the power of art unexplained because it left the power of expression unexplained. So I suggested that light might dawn, if we could see artistic expression as continuous with expression as one of the devices by which an individual achieves, restores or imposes internal order. But that would have to invoke psychological considerations in the search for a philosophical question about the power of art.

The same seems to me true of ethics. We want to know why ethical matters are so important to us, and are not treated merely as prudential rules we have devised for keeping the peace. That he has so clear an understanding of how deep the ethical goes is a reason for cherishing the work of Peter Winch. But I cannot see that this understanding can finally be achieved if we simply accept that the ethical language game is played and do not try to tell a story of its roots in our most formative experiences.

Here I find some remarks by Winch relevant. Malcolm had said:

> Philosophy can observe a complicated linguistic practice and describe how one movement in it is related to another. But philosophy cannot explain why the practice exists: nor can the "hard" sciences of physics, chemistry, biology; nor the "soft" sciences of psychology, sociology, anthropology.
> (Malcolm 1995: p. 85)

Winch remarks, "But this seems to me neither true in itself, nor implied by anything Wittgenstein wrote. He was concerned with the peculiar pseudo-sense in which *philosophers* seek 'explanations'" (Winch 1997b: p. 105).

He adds:

> Malcolm begins to write as though there are no intelligible questions to be raised at all concerning the nature or causal conditions of the ability of a child to learn to speak.... [Compare] ... two children, one of whom does learn the language of his or her community while the other does not. Why the

Peter Winch

> difference? The answer might be in terms, for example, of the development of one child's brain as contrasted with that of the other; it might be answered in terms of differences in the social or psychological circumstances in the two cases.
>
> (Winch 1997b: p. 107)

He concludes:

> Furthermore as far as the "human" and "social" sciences (as distinct from philosophy) are concerned, Wittgenstein's point was not ... that language games are intrinsically beyond the power of those sciences to provide explanations, but rather that any explanation they might offer would turn out to be quite useless as far as the philosopher's characteristic puzzlements are concerned. ... But this does nothing to show that explanations may not be found by such sciences which provide perfectly good answers to other kinds of questions. For instance, there are many cases in which historians, anthropologists or linguists give well founded explanations of the existence of this or that practice. Why ever not? The important question for us is: what relevance would such explanations have to the resolution of philosophical difficulties.
>
> (Winch 1997b: p. 105)

In Winch's account, then, there is nothing in Wittgenstein's philosophy to prevent someone seeking explanations of language games. But Winch seems to deny these explanations are philosophical or that they answer any philosophical questions. Why?

I suspect the answer would have to be that Winch takes Wittgenstein to be interested in questions of the meaning of terms, where an account of how a way of using language in a whole region of life, religion, perhaps, or aesthetics, came about is irrelevant to the question of what meaning terms have within that practice, granted that it has come about. It is worth noting in that connection that as far as Wittgenstein was concerned we might just as well have woken up speaking a language: "It is all one to us whether someone ... has learned the language, or was perhaps constituted from birth to react ... as a normal person" (Wittgenstein 1953: ss. 495).

The question might then, however, transpose itself into the question of whether understanding the story of the genesis of an activity might cause it to *lose* its sense for someone. For then a genetic account would have an impact on the meaning of terms within a practice. Thus, accepting Freud's account, in *The future of an illusion,* of the way in which the concept of an omniscient God arises out of certain facts of human psychology, might shake someone's confidence so much that religious practices ceased to have a point. More pertinently, an account of the formative process of moral character might simply undermine an inclination to blame those who endured certain forms of deprivation of love. To which, I repeat, it does seem that sometimes we need these kinds of explanations if we are to account for something like the power of art or ethics or, even, of religion.

Problems 4: Idealism
Bernard Williams has argued that the kind of philosophy I have attributed to Wittgenstein and Winch commits those philosophers to an untenable idealism (Williams 1974).

Williams's argument runs thus:

1 "*S*" has the meaning we give it.
2 A necessary condition of our giving "*S*" a meaning is *Q*.
3 Unless *Q*, "*S*" would not have a meaning.
4 If "*S*" did not have a meaning, "*S*" would not be true.
5 Unless *Q*, "*S*" would not be true.

Statement 1 is, I hope, clear enough, and seems to capture the notion that the meaning of our terms depends on us and our practices. Let us, though, for clarity of exposition, replace "*S*" by "The sun is hot". Statement 2 is best understood if for "*Q*" we put, as Williams does, a reference to human practices, human existence etc. Thus statement 2 might read "It is a necessary condition of our giving 'The sun is hot' a meaning, that we exist". That seems fair enough. From that statement 3 follows: "Unless we existed 'The sun is hot' would not have a meaning". That, too, seems fair enough. Similarly statement 4 becomes "If 'The sun is hot' did not have a meaning, 'The sun is hot' would not be true". And that seems fair enough. So it follows that if we did not exist, "The sun is hot" would not be true. And that makes it look as if the heat of the sun (and anything else we want to substitute for "*S*") depends on us. Truly, as Williams says, an amazing consequence.

In his reply Winch observes that in his *Philosophical grammar* (Wittgenstein 1974: s. 6, para. 79), Wittgenstein asks whether we should write "'*p*' is true" or "*p* is true" (Winch 1987b: pp. 36–7). The question invites us to think what we are doing when we put, as Williams does, quotation marks round an expression. As the word "quotation" suggests, the marks indicate that *someone is saying something*, so that all the "*S*"s in Williams's argument are reports of assertions by someone. But, then, even if the argument is valid, statement 5 is quite innocuous, For all it says is, "unless people existed, there could be no true assertions". That is true. But from that it does not follow that what makes an assertion true, for example, the sun's being hot, depends on our existence. In order to say that Williams would have to write the *S* in statement 5 without quotation marks, so that it said not, "If we did not exist the assertion 'The sun is hot' could not be true", but, rather, "If we did not exist then the sun is hot could not be true". But then the quotation marks have to be removed throughout. If we do that, then we get gibberish. Statement 1, for example, comes out as "that the sun is hot has the meaning that we give it".

Apart from any discussion of Williams, we need, when discussing the view that the meaning of terms depends upon their use in our language, to distinguish two claims. On the one hand, there is the claim that the meaning of the term "real", and the meaning of such cognate notions as "existing", "fact", "objective" and "true" is determined when we have determined the uses of these terms by human beings as they go about their various businesses (including reflecting on what they say). The other claim is that this first claim commits us to the belief that there is nothing independent of us. But that first claim does not entail the second. For when I reflect on the way in which the term "real" is used I may see that, in one use or in some cluster of its uses, when I say that something is real, I can only do so if I am prepared to say that the something to which I am referring exists independently of me. Our practices commit us to the independent existence of things.

In the *Philosophical investigations*, Wittgenstein wrote, the words in quotations being the words of an imaginary interlocutor: "So you are saying that human agreement decides what is true and false?" – It is what human beings say that is true and false; and they agree in the *language* they use. This is not agreements in opinions but in forms of life" (1953: ss. 241).

What is true and false is not the sun coming up, rain falling or the dance of the atoms, although these may make *something I say* true or false. What are true and false are human assertions, and without us, or language-using creatures like us, there would be no true or false assertions. And there can only be assertions if there are languages and languages only if there are agreements in the projections of language that we make. But to say that truth in a sense depends on us, since we alone make the assertions that are true, is not to say that we make those assertions true.

A last word on philosophy

It is worth anyone's efforts to read Winch simply as a wide-ranging philosopher, working, unusually, across the *whole* of that discipline, with insights to offer on such parts of our lives as are to do with such things as religion, sociology and ethics. But above all, I think, he should be read for the questions he raises about philosophy itself. Whether his views on that matter are right or wrong, they are a corrective to views that are currently fashionable and too little challenged. I would like to conclude by saying of him what Peter Hacker says so eloquently of Wittgenstein

> Wittgenstein's legacy was a new vision and new methods. . . . His legacy is a vision of philosophy as the pursuit not of knowledge but of understanding. The task of philosophy is not to add to the sum of human knowledge, but to enable us to attain a clear understanding of what is already known. . . . His bequest is an array of methods for disentangling conceptual confusions that are the business of philosophy, for curing us of the diseases of the intellect to which we are all prone. Practised with skill they can lead us to a correct logical point of view . . . from which to see the world aright. The resultant understanding is the only prize that philosophy can offer. To achieve it in the ever changing stream of human history is a goal towards which each generation must strive afresh. Whether and when philosophy will turn back to Wittgenstein's methods, and properly assimilate his great insights, I cannot venture to guess. But I should like to believe that what he wrote of others can be applied to him too: "The works of great masters are suns which rise and set around us. The time will some for every great work that is in the descendent to rise again" (Hacker 1996: p. 273).

Peter Winch

Further reading

Only two small notes are given, although, such is the complexity of the issues discussed in this chapter that a multitude would be possible. First, the most comprehensive work in the realism–anti-realism debate is, of course, Crispin Wright's *Realism, meaning and truth* (Wright 1993). To that I add a reference to his *Truth and objectivity* (Cambridge, Mass.: Harvard University Press, 1992), if only because it would be a nice task, which I leave for the reader, to compare and contrast what Wright says in that work with many things that Winch has said about realism, truth and objectivity. Of very recent writing that might help the reader to get into these matters I was struck by a judicious article by W. Stirton, "Anti-realism, truth-conditions and verificationism", *Mind* **106**, pp. 697–716, 1997, which discusses *inter alia* anti-realism and empiricism. Second, for more on assertibility and truth conditions from a Wittgensteinian perspective, see Cora Diamond, "Rules: looking in the right place", in *Attention to particulars*, D. Z. Phillips & P. Winch (eds) (London: Macmillan, 1989).

Envoi

Henry Fielding provided the motto for this work and he shall provide its epitaph.

> We are now, reader, arrived at the last stage of our long journey. As we have therefore travelled together through so many pages, let us behave to one another like fellow travellers, who have passed several days in the company of each other; and who, notwithstanding any bickerings or little animosities which may have occurred on the road, generally all make up at the last and mount, for the last time, into their vehicle with chearfulness and good humour.
>
> (*Tom Jones,* Book 18, Preface)

Thoughts of journeys have a particular relevance to my project. Home, as a poet once platitudinously remarked, is where all journeys start from. But having started, journeys can take one of two forms (although mixtures of them are possible). There are journeys, of the kind made by the starship *Enterprise*, journeys that seek new worlds and, in the glorious split infinitive of the Star Trek manifesto, seek to boldly go where no one has gone before. Home, then, is left behind. But there is also the journey of self-discovery, undertaken not to find out new things about *other* things but in the hope of coming to *self*-knowledge. Those modes of journeying correspond to two conceptions of philosophy. The first corresponds to Russell's influential view of philosophy as the most general empirical science, a view according to which our philosophical problems are to be solved by finding out new things about other things. That is now a dominant view. The second, which originates in Socrates's injunction "know thyself", believes the solution to our philosophical problems to be a matter of coming to understand what we already are. The former, as I have argued, treats philosophy as an empirical enquiry, the latter as a conceptual enquiry (but see Hunter 1995). At the beginning of his philosophical life, Peter Winch, following Wittgenstein, firmly nailed his colours to the mast of the latter conception. That being so, I can think of no fitter way to sum up his work than the lines with which Eliot ends the *Four quartets,* with which, by way of *envoi,* I say my farewell:

> We shall not cease from exploration
> And the end of all our exploring
> Will be to arrive where we started
> And know the place for the first time.
> Through the unknown, remembered gate
> When the last of earth left to discover
> Is that which was the beginning;
> At the source of the longest river
> The voice of the hidden waterfall
> And the children in the apple-tree
> Not known, because not looked for
> But heard, half-heard, in the stillness
> Between two waves of the sea.
> Quick now, here, now, always –
> A condition of complete simplicity
> (Costing not less than everything)
> And all shall be well and
> All manner of thing shall be well . . .
>
> ("Little Gidding", *Four quartets* from *Collected Poems, 1909–1962* by T. S. Eliot (Faber and Faber Ltd))

References

Amis, K., E. Cleary, R. Holland, D. Sims & P. Winch. The threat of the practical. *Observer*, 26 February 1961.
Anselm. *Monolgium* (trans. S. Deane) (La Salle, Ill.: Open Court, 1962 [1076]).
Apel, K. Universal principles and particular decisions and forms of life. In *Value and understanding*, R. Gaita (ed.) (London: Routledge, 1990), pp. 72–101.
Austin, J. *Philosophical papers* (Oxford: Oxford University Press, 1961).
Ayer, A. *Language, truth and logic* (London: Gollancz, 1936).
Bloor, D. *Wittgenstein, rules and institutions* (London: Routledge, 1997).
Bloor, D. *Wittgenstein: A social theory of knowledge* (London: Macmillan, 1983).
Brown, S. *Philosophical disputes in the social sciences* (Brighton: Harvester, 1979).
Camus, A. *The myth of Sisyphus* (Harmondsworth: Penguin, 1975 [1942]).
Cavell, S. The availability of Wittgenstein's later philosophy. In *Wittgenstein*, G. Pitcher (ed.) (London: Macmillan, 1968), pp. 151–85.
Cioffi, F. Wittgenstein on making homeopathic magic clear. In *Value and understanding*, R. Gaita (ed.) (London: Routledge, 1990), pp. 42–71.
Croce, B. *The Aesthetic as the science of expression*, (trans. C. Lyas) (Cambridge: Cambridge University Press, 1992).
Davidson, D. Actions, reasons and causes. *Journal of Philosophy* **40**, 1963, pp. 685–99.
Flew, A. & A. MacIntyre (eds). *New essays in philosophical theology* (London: SCM Press, 1955).
Fodor, J. & J. J. Katz. The availability of what we say. *Philosophical Review* **LXXXII**, 1963: pp. 57–71.
Gaita, R. *Value and understanding* (London: Routledge, 1990).
Gaskin, D. *The quest for eternity* (Harmondsworth: Penguin, 1972).
Gellner, E. *Words and things* (Harmondsworth: Penguin, 1968).
Gellner, E. *Cause and meaning in the social sciences* (London: Routledge and Kegan Paul, 1973).
Gellner, E. Relativism and universals. In *Rationality and relativism*, M. Hollis & S. Lukes (eds) (Oxford: Blackwell, 1982), pp. 181–200.

Giddens, A. *New rules of sociological method* (London: Hutchinson, 1976).
Giddens, A. *The constitution of society* (Cambridge: Polity, 1984).
Hacker, P. *Wittgenstein's place in twentieth century analytic philosophy* (Oxford: Blackwell, 1996).
Hollis, M. & S. Lukes. *Rationality and relativism* (Oxford: Blackwell, 1974).
Horton, R. Material-object language and theoretical language. In *Philosophical disputes in the social sciences*, S. Brown (ed.) (Brighton: Harvester, 1979), pp. 197–224.
Hume, D. *A treatise on human nature* (London: Dent, 1911).
Hunter, G. Quine's "Two dogmas of empiricism" or the power of bad logic. *Philosophical Investigations* **18**, 1995: pp. 305–28.
Jackson, F. *From metaphysics to ethics* (Oxford: Oxford University Press, 1998).
Kant, I. *Prolegomena* (trans. P. Lucas) (Manchester: Manchester University Press, 1953).
Keat, R. & J. Urry. *Social theory as a science* (London: Routledge and Kegan Paul, 1975).
Kripke, S. *Wittgenstein on rules and private language* (Oxford: Blackwell, 1982).
Lash, S. *The sociology of post-modernism* (London: Routledge, 1990).
Leech, G. *Towards a semantic description of English* (London: Longman, 1969).
Leech, G. *Semantics* (Harmondsworth: Penguin, 1974).
Lundberg, G. *Foundations of sociology* (New York: Mackay, 1964).
Lyas, C. On not interfering with the words with which we talk of personal identity (or anything else). In *Wittgenstein and the philosophy of culture*, K. Johannessen & T. Nordenstam (eds) (Vienna: Verlag-Hölder-Pilcher-Tempsky, 1996), pp. 183–200.
Lyas, C. *Aesthetics* (London: UCL Press, 1997).
MacIntyre, A. *A short history of ethics* (London: Macmillan, 1966).
MacIntyre, A. *After virtue* (London: Duckworth, 1982).
Mackie, J. *Inventing right and wrong* (Harmondsworth: Penguin, 1977).
Mackie, J. *The miracle of theism* (Oxford: Clarendon, 1982).
Malcolm, N. *Ludwig Wittgenstein: A memoir* (Oxford: Oxford University Press, 1958).
Malcolm, N. *Wittgenstein: A religious point of view?* (London: Routledge, 1993).
Marcuse, H. *One dimensional man* (London: Abacus, 1972).
Marcuse, H. *Negations* (Harmondsworth: Penguin, 1968).
Marshall, G. Intelligibility and the imagination. In *Value and understanding*, R. Gaita (ed.) (London: Routledge, 1990), pp. 32–41.
Mates, B. On the verification of statements about ordinary language. *Inquiry* **1**, 1958, pp. 161–75.
McLellan, D. *Simone Weil: Utopian pessimist* (London: Macmillan, 1989).
McNaughton, D. *Moral vision* (Oxford: Oxford University Press, 1988).
Merleau-Ponty, M. *Signes* (Paris: Gallimard, 1960).
Mill, J. An examination of Sir William Hamilton's philosophy. In *Theism*, R. Taylor (ed.) (New York: Bobbs Merrill, 1957).
Milligan, D. The idea of a social science. *Proceedings of the Aristotelian Society* **49**, 1968–9, pp. 51–72.
Monk, R. *Ludwig Wittgenstein: the duty of genius* (London: Cape, 1990).
Mundle, C. *A critique of linguistic philosophy* (Oxford: Oxford University Press,

References

1970).
New, C. G. A plea for linguistics. *Mind* **66**, 1971, pp. 368–84.
Neilsen, K. Sociological knowledge. *Philosophy and Phenomenological Research* **42**, 1981–2, pp. 465–91.
Norman, R. Making sense of realism *Philosophical Investigations* **20**, 1997, pp. 117–35.
Norman, R. *The moral philosophers*, 2nd edn (Oxford: Oxford University Press, 1998).
O'Neill, O. The power of example. *Philosophy* **61**, 1986, pp. 5–29.
Palmer, A. Review of Gaita "Value and understanding". *Philosophical Investigations* **15**, 1992, pp. 276–84.
Pears, D. *Wittgenstein* (London: Fontana, 1971).
Phillips, D. Z. The presumption of theory. In *Value and understanding*, R. Gaita (ed.) (London: Routledge, 1990), pp. 216–41.
Pike, N. Hume on evil. *Philosophical Review* **72**, 1963, pp. 180–97.
Rashid, D. Winch on the unity of Wittgenstein's philosophy. In *Value and understanding*, R. Gaita (ed.) (London: Routledge, 1990), pp. 263–73.
Rhees, R. *Rush Rhees on religion and philosophy*, D. Z. Phillips (ed.) (Cambridge: Cambridge University Press, 1997).
Säätela, S. *Aesthetics as grammar* (Uppsala: Department of Aesthetics Uppsala, 1998).
Schleiermacher, F. *On religion* (trans. T. Tice) (Richmond, Virginia: John Knox Press, 1969).
Sharpe, R. Moral tales. *Philosophy* **67**, 1992, pp. 155–68.
Sharpe, R. Two cheers for simulation theory. *Inquiry* **40**, 1997, pp. 1–17.
Smith, M. *The moral problem* (Oxford: Blackwell, 1994).
Sosa, E. & M. Tooley (eds). *Causation* (Oxford: Oxford University Press, 1993).
Swinburne, R. *The existence of God* (Oxford: Oxford University Press, 1979).
Tessin, T. & M. von de Ruhr (eds). *The philosophy and grammar of religious belief* (London: Macmillan, 1995).
Weil, S. *Oppression et liberté* (Paris: Gallimard, 1955).
Wiggins, D. Substance. In *Philosophy*, A. Grayling (ed.) (Oxford: Oxford University Press, 1995), pp. 214–45.
Williams, B. Wittgenstein and idealism. In *Understanding Wittgenstein*, G. Vesey (ed.) (London: Macmillan, 1974), pp. 76–95.
Williams, B. *Ethics and the limits of philosophy* (Cambridge Mass.: Harvard University Press, 1985).
Wilson, B. *Rationality* (London: Routledge and Kegan Paul, 1970).
Winch, P. The notion of "suggestion" in Thomas Reid's theory of perception. *Philosophical Quarterly*, 1953, pp.327–41.
Winch, P. Contemporary British philosophy and its critics. *Universities Quarterly* **X**, 1955–6, pp. 24–37.
Winch, P. Social science. *British Journal of Sociology* **7**, 1956, pp. 18–33.
Winch, P. The universities and the state. *Universities Quarterly* **XII**, 1957–8, pp. 14–23.
Winch, P. *The idea of a social science* (London: Routledge and Kegan Paul, 1958).
Winch, P. Authority. *Proceedings of the Aristotelian Society* **32**, 1958–9, pp. 225–40.
Winch, P. Review of "The logic of social enquiry". *History and Theory* **2**, 1961–2,

pp. 74–8.
Winch, P. Mr. Louch's idea of a social science. *Inquiry*, **8**, 1964, pp. 202–8.
Winch, P. (ed.) *Studies in the philosophy of Wittgenstein* (London: Routledge and Kegan Paul, 1969).
Winch, P. Reply to Jarvie. In *Understanding and explanation in the behavioural sciences*, R. Borg & F. Cioffi (eds) (Cambridge: Cambridge University Press, 1970).
Winch, P. *Ethics and action* (London: Routledge and Kegan Paul, 1972).
Winch, P. Causation and action. In *Essays on explanation and understanding*, J.Manninen & R. Tuomela (eds) (Dordrecht: Reidel, 1976) pp. 123–33.
Winch, P. Wittgenstein: picture and representation. *Tijdskrift Filofisk* **49**, 1987a, pp. 3–20.
Winch, P. *Trying to make sense* (Oxford: Blackwell, 1987b).
Winch, P. He's to blame. In *Attention to particulars*, D. Z. Phillips & P. Winch (eds) (London: Macmillan, 1989a), pp. 151–64.
Winch, P. *The just balance* (Cambridge: Cambridge University Press, 1989b).
Winch, P. Certainty and authority. *Philosophy* (supplement), 1990, pp. 223–37.
Winch, P. Certainty and authority. In *Wittgenstein centenary essays*, A. Phillips Griffiths (ed.) (Cambridge: Cambridge University Press, 1991), pp. 223–8.
Winch, P. Review of Norman Malcolm. *Philosophical investigations* **15**, 1992a, p. 223.
Winch, P. Review of MacIntyre "Whose justice, whose rationality?" *Philosophical Investigations* **15** 1992b, pp. 223–6.
Winch, P. Discussion of Malcom's essay. In *Wittgenstein: A religious point of view?* N. Malcolm (London: Routledge, 1993) pp. 95–136.
Winch, P. Mind, body and ethics in Spinoza. *Philosophical Investigations* **18**, 1995, pp. 216–34.
Winch, P. *The expression of belief*. Presidential address to the American Philosophical Association, central division, 1996.
Winch, P. Can we understand ourselves? *Philosophical Investigations* **20**, 1997a, pp. 193–204.
Winch, P. Review of Malcolm "Wittgensteinian themes". *Philosophical Investigations* **20**, 1997b, pp. 51–64.
Wisdom, J. *Philosophy and psychoanalysis* (Oxford: Blackwell, 1953).
Wittgenstein, L. *Philosophical investigations* (Oxford: Blackwell, 1953).
Wittgenstein, L. *On certainty* (Oxford: Blackwell, 1969).
Wittgenstein, L. *Philosophical grammar* (Oxford: Blackwell, 1974).
Wittgenstein, L. Cause and effect (trans. P. Winch). *Philosophia* **6**, 1976, pp. 391–445.
Wittgenstein, L. *Notebooks 1914–16* (Oxford: Blackwell, 1979).
Wittgenstein, L. *Culture and value* (trans. P. Winch), 2nd edn (Oxford: Blackwell, 1984).
Wollheim, R. *Art and its objects*, 2nd edn (Cambridge: Cambridge University Press, 1980).
Wollheim, R. *The mind and its depths* (Cambridge, Mass.: Harvard University Press, 1993).
Woolf, V. *To the lighthouse* (Harmondsworth: Penguin, 1992 [1927]).
Wright, C. *Truth and objectivity* (Cambridge, Mass.: Harvard University Press, 1982).
Wright, C. *Realism, meaning and truth* (Oxford: Blackwell, 1993).

Index

academic senates 39–40
acquisition argument 188
action 170–71
  logic 77–8
  moral 111–12
  reasons 43–5, 64–5
aesthetics 158
  objectivity 185
agents, reasons 65
American Philosophical Association 6, 194, 196
Amis, Kinglsey 2
analogy 95–6
  religious experience 142–4
Analysis 6
Anselm 139–40
anti-realism 188–9
Apel, K. 4, 71, 81, 90–92, 113
assertability conditions 190, 203
attitudes 164
Austin, J. L. 19, 22
authority 162
Ayer, A. J. 81, 102, 146

Beardsmore, Dick 6
beauty 179
behaviour
  logical 77
  reasons 77
  social 32, 42–7
belief, religious 129, 138, 149

Billy Budd 112–13, 118
Birkbeck College, London 6
blame 102, 125
Bloor, David 47, 63, 124, 198
Bradbury, Malcolm 40
brain 50, 183–4

Camus, Albert 168, 183
causes
  Humean 43–5, 50–51
  reasons 43
Cavell, Stanley 31
censorship 3
certainty, morality 122
Chariots of the gods 140
charity, principle of 136–8
child sacrifice 115
Cioffi, F. 81
communication 31
concepts, analysis of 15
conceptual enquiry 21, 23–4, 62
confirmation procedures 18–19
consciousness, false 64–5
consensus 113
conservatism 26–28, 33–4
convention 107–8
Croce, Benedetto 33, 47
cultural relativism 25, 72, 97
culture, homogenization of 89–90
culture independent rationality 87–9

211

Davidson, Donald 43
Dawn 3
decision 108
Derrida, Jacques 55
Descartes, René 170
determinism 55
dialectic 18–19, 76, 115–16, 157
disapproval 116
distinctions 22
Douglas, Mary 63
drives 56
Durkheim, Émile 77
duty 112, 162

e. e. cummings 141
effect 44
Eliot, T. S. 118, 206
empirical enquiry 14, 23–4, 62
empirical informant testing 17
empirical linguistics 15–20
enigmas 32–3, 74
enquiry 59, 174
   conceptual/empirical 21, 23–4, 62
equilibrium 175–7
errors 36
ethical life 101–27, 198–9
ethical properties 120–21
ethical vocabulary 105
ethics 156
   good examples 101–2
   opposed judgements 113–14
   realism 185–6
   religion 142
Evans-Prichard, E. 83–4
evidence 130–32
examples 125
   good 101–2
   moral philosophy 117–18
existence 150–51, 191–2
experiences, primitive 143
explanation 56–8, 61–2, 198–201
expression 22, 31, 143–5, 199

facticity 108
facts 23
false consciousness 64–5
feeling safe 165–6
fiction 101, 118
Flew, Antony 147–8

Fodor, Jerry A. 16
Foot, Philippa 104
forms of life 31, 169
   language 72–5, 79–80
freedom 65

Gaita, Rai 192
Gaskin, D. 132
Gellner, Ernest 4–5, 16, 26, 64, 81, 87–90, 115
generalization 50
gestures, meaning 42
Giddens, Anthony 64
God, existence of 133–4, 139–40, 150
"good examples" 101–102

Habermas, Jürgen 4
Hacker, Peter 181, 203–4
happiness 27
Hare, R. M. 110
harm 125
Harré, Rom 53
hermeneutics 4, 61, 90
hesitation 108, 164–5, 179, 194
   interval of 177, 198
Hobbes, Thomas 161–2
Holland, Roy 3, 4, 111, 192
Hollis, Martin 52, 92, 97
Horton, Robin 81
human life 96
human nature
   limiting conditions 107
   morality 105–6
Hume, David 44, 52–3, 121
Humean causation 43–5, 50–51

Idea of a social science 5, 12, 30, 37, 39, 50, 52, 54, 56, 66, 80, 82, 97, 142, 146, 176, 206
idealism 187, 201–3
ideology 64–5
illumination 63–4
imperatives 110
incommensurability 178–9
influence 59
informant tests 19–20
intelligibility 14, 81–3, 169, 187–8
the intelligible 29–30

Index

intention 171
interactions 72–3
interpretation 35
interval of hesitation 177, 198
intuition 17
irrationality, religion 132–4

judgements, opposed 113–14
justice 161–2, 176

Kant, Immanuel 24–5, 109–10, 111–12
Katz, 16
Keat, Russell 52–5
King's College, London 4, 6
Kripke, Saul 23, 34–6
Kung, Hans 130

language
 acquisition 30–31, 195
 analyses 15–20
 meaningfulness 80, 82
 realism 186–7
 reality 29–30
 religious 137, 140, 146–9
 sense 84
 sharing a form of life 72–5, 79–80
 social foundation 36
 understanding 93–5
 usage 21–5
language games 196–200
Lash, Scott 64
Leech, Geoffrey 17, 19
legality 161–2
Leslie, Hild 86
Levi, Primo 6
life
 ethical 101–27, 198–9
 forms of 31, 72–5, 79–80, 169
 human 96
 limiting conditions 95–6, 107
 social 170
 Winch's 1–7
limiting conditions 95–6, 107
linguistic communities 21
"linguistic" philosophy 2
linguistics, empirical 15–20
Locke, John 11

logic 78–9, 138–9
 action 77–8
Lukes, Steven 92
Lundberg, G. 54
Lyas, Colin 55, 172, 182

McGhee, Michael 172
MacIntyre, Alasdair 64–5, 80, 81–82, 104–6, 147–8, 193
Mackie, John 119, 120, 121, 132, 146
McLellan, David 156
McNaughton, David 114, 158
Malcolm, Norman 1, 4, 5, 129, 199
manifestation argument 189
Marcuse, Herbert 26–8
Marshall, G. 192
Marx, Karl 53–4, 55
Mates, Benson 16, 18
meaning 30–31
 gestures 42
 language 80–82
 rules 34–6
 social behaviour 42–7
 speech practices 172
meaning questions, religion 130–31
Melville, Herman 112
Merleau-Ponty, Maurice 55
military service 1
Mill, John Stuart 41, 110, 147
 criticism of 50–51
Milligan, D. 64
mind 176, 195, 196
mind-brain interaction 50, 183–4
models 182–3
modernism 70
Monk, Ray 1
moral act 111–12
moral life 115–16
moral vision 114
morality 156
 certainty 122
 decision 108
 human nature 105–6
 ontogeny 119–20
 primitive bases 108–9
motives 56
Mundle, C. K. 16
Murdoch, Iris 102

213

"*Nachlass*" 5
natural geometry 174–5
Neilsen, K. 62
neutrality of philosophy 26, 160
New, C. G. 16, 18
Newcomb, 56–7
non-communication 73–6
Norman, Richard 111, 119, 123, 185, 199

objective correlation 19
objectivity, aesthetics 185
O'Neill, O. 101
ontological vocabulary 185
ontology 6, 11, 119–20
opposed judgements 113–14
oppression 160–61, 170
others 177–8
Oxford, University of 1

pain, primitive experiences 143
Palmer, Tony 4
Pareto, Vilfredo 29, 76, 77
Pears, David 16
Phillips, D. Z. 7, 102
philosophy
  as conceptual enquiry 23
  good examples 101–2
  "linguistic" 2
  methods 16–20
  neutrality of 26, 160
  political 161–2
  underlabourer account 11–12
  view of 10, 48–9, 195
physical science 59
pictures, religious use of 141–2
Plato 104
pointing 30, 30–31
political philosophy 161–2
positivism 54
practices, religious 138–9
prediction 55–6
prescriptions 110
primitive experiences 143
Principle of Universal Consensus 90
projectibility 31, 35, 73, 75–6
proof, religion 131–2
properties, ethical 120–21

punishment 109, 163

questionnaire sampling 19–20
quotation marks 202

Rashid, D. 5
rationality 70–71
  culture independent 87–9
Rawls, John 176
reactions 173–5
real, meaning of 15–18, 24
realism
  ethics 185–6
  language 186–7
  moral philosophy 118–25
  syndrome of 187–8
realist science 52–3, 54
reality 83–5, 151, 196
  claims 134–6
  concept of 12, 24, 29–30, 84
  observational evidence 13–14
  as "systematically ambiguous" 25
reasons
  for acting 43–5, 64–5
  behaviour 77
  causes 43
  regularities 52–4
relativism 71–2, 92–3
religion 129–54
  belief 129, 138, 149
  ethics 142
  irrationality 132–4
  language 137, 140, 146–9, 166–7
  meaning questions 130–131
  pictures 141–2
  reality 152
  strong attitude 131–2
  understanding 139–46, 156–7
Rhees, Rush 4, 134
Rousseau, Jean-Jacques 170
rules 23, 28–9
  ethical vocabulary 105
  meaning 34–6
  social behaviour 45–7
Ryle, Gilbert 1

Säätela, S. 143
safe 165–6

Index

Sartre, Jean-Paul 108, 111
science 59, 181–2
  causation 50–52
  realist 52–3
  reality 12–14
semantic theory 17
sensations 173
sense, reality 84
Sharpe, Bob 58, 94
Singer, Isaac 191
Smith, Michael 119
social behaviour
  as meaningful behaviour 32, 42–7
  rules 45–7
social context 59–62
social institutions
  structure of 63–64
  understanding 59–61
social life 170
social science 4–5, 29, 36, 39–67
  explanation 62
sociality 47
society 27
  ethical life 104–5
  science of 41–42
  understanding 76
sociology 39–40, 60
  central problem of 48–50, 60
  realist science 55
Sosa, E. 44
speech practices, meaning 172
Spinoza, Baruch 169
spiritual values 166–167
subject 10, 48
supernatural 180
Swansea, Wales 1–2
Swinburne, Richard 132

technical terms 61
Tessin, Tim 6
theodicy 133
theology 143
theory-theory 58
thought 29, 172–3
Timasheff, 54
tolerance 69, 115–17
Tooley, M. 44
transcendental self 172

truth 179, 193–4
truth conditions 189–91
trying 45, 171

underlabourer account of philosophy 11–12
understanding 157
  moral 103
"Understanding a primitive society" 5, 25, 72, 73, 76, 92, 98, 102, 118, 120, 142, 143, 164
Universal Consensus, Principle of 90
universal reason 70–71, 76
universalization 109–14
universities, no purpose 2–3
Universities Quarterly 2
University of Bergen 5
University College, Swansea 1
University of Illinois 6
Urry, John 52–5
utilitarianism 110–11

Vico, Giambattista 96
virtue ethics 103–109
vocabulary
  ethical 105
  ontological 185
Von Danniken, Eric 140

Weber, M. 47
Weil, Simone 57, 108, 112, 147
  influence of 155–80
Weltanschauung 26
Wiggins, David 185
will 171
Williams, Bernard 101, 201–2
Wisdom, John 167
witchcraft 85–7
Wittgenstein, Ludwig
  influence of 4, 5, 9–38, 195
  language 21, 22, 28
  language games 196–200
  mind–brain interaction 183–4
  reality 24, 151
  reasons 65
  rules 23, 28, 34–6
  truth conditions 189–91
  willing 171

Peter Winch

Wollheim, Richard 167, 198–9
Woolf, Virginia 144–5
words, usage of 15–16

Wright, Crispin 188, 196

Zeigarnik, 57